The Common Law and the Environment

Rethinking the Statutory Basis for Modern Environmental Law

Edited by Roger E. Meiners
and Andrew P. Morriss

ROWMAN & LITTLEFIELD PUBLISHERS, INC.
Lanham • Boulder • New York • Oxford

ROWMAN & LITTLEFIELD PUBLISHERS, INC.

Published in the United States of America
by Rowman & Littlefield Publishers, Inc.
4720 Boston Way, Lanham, Maryland 20706
http://www.rowmanlittlefield.com

12 Hid's Copse Road
Cumnor Hill, Oxford OX2 9JJ, England

British Library Cataloguing in Publication Information Available

Library of Congress Cataloging-in-Publication Data
The common law and the environment : rethinking the statutory basis for modern environmental law / edited by Roger E. Meiners and Andrew P. Morriss.
    p. cm. — (The political economy forum series)
    Includes bibliographical references and index.
    ISBN 0-8476-9708-8 (cloth : alk. paper) — ISBN 0-8476-9709-6 (paper : alk. paper)
    1. Environmental law—United States.   2. Common law—United States.   I. Meiners,
Roger E.   II. Morriss, Andrew P. 1960–
    KF3775.C66   2000
    344.73'046 21—dc 21   99-045508

Printed in the United States of America

(∞)™ The paper used in this publication meets the minimum requirements of American National Standard for Information Sciences—Permanence of Paper for Printed Library Materials, ANSI/NISO Z39.48—1992.

Contents

Part III: The Institutions of the Common Law

Part IV: Perspectives on the Shift away from the Common Law

    Todd J. Zywicki

9   On the Commons and the Common Law   211
    Jason Scott Johnston

10 On Being Regulated in Foresight versus Being
    Judged in Hindsight   242
    Jeffrey J. Rachlinski

    Index   265

    About the Political Economy Forum and the Authors   275

Tables and Figures

TABLES

FIGURES

Acknowledgments

For a decade, the Political Economy Research Center (PERC) has been hosting an annual Political Economy Forum. Unlike many PERC research projects, which have particular expected outcomes, the forum is more "purely academic," that is to say, it is a more risky venture. The senior associates at PERC pick a topic of interest, come up with a list of scholars they would like to see invited to address the topic (some of whom have not been to PERC before), and tell the forum directors (who vary from year to year) to get busy. Terry Anderson, PERC's executive director, also has to work to secure funding for the forum. His success in that regard is much appreciated.

This volume is the result of the 1998 Political Economy Forum. It was made possible by the generous support of Dunn's Foundation for Understanding Capitalist Knowledge and Unregulated Markets. William Dunn's willingness to support the forum's academic work indicates that PERC has earned the trust of donors who realize that even speculative ventures such as this one can produce interesting and worthwhile products that make a difference in the world of ideas.

Besides thanking the contributors to the volume and the others who attended the Political Economy Forum and made substantive comments on earlier drafts of these chapters, we want to thank those who take chapters written in various formats and create from them a readable collection. Dianna Rienhart has, with at least the appearance of good humor, pressed the editors to press the authors to get corrections made and turned in so the book could be produced. Thank you, Dianna, and the other staff members at PERC who make our work look a lot better than it would otherwise—and get to print a lot quicker.

Good ideas are lost if not shared. Thanks to Rowman & Littlefield for publishing the Political Economy Forum Series. In this age of highly competitive commercial publishing, we are grateful that our publisher finds this series worthwhile, as, we believe, will many people interested in serious thinking about environmental issues.

Introduction

Reclaiming the Common Law's Role in Environmental Law

Andrew P. Morriss and Roger E. Meiners

Anglo-American legal systems rely mostly on two quite different legal institutions for solving problems: common law and statute law. Most problems between individuals have traditionally been dealt with through the common law. Until comparatively recent decades, statute law was reserved largely for the details of the relationship between state and citizen and for "correcting" particular rules of the common law. Since 1970, however, the dominant means of addressing environmental problems in the United States has been through comprehensive federal statutes.

In place of the case-by-case determination of the rights of the litigants, modern environmental statutes substituted sweeping administrative reallocation of the rights of broad sections of society. In place of generalist judges drawn from the affected, the statutes substituted technically trained (and not so trained) agency officials in Washington, D.C., operating under the direction of Congress. In place of gradual evolution of rules, the statutes substituted sharp discontinuities in legal obligations. The rather sudden introduction of these major changes may have reflected a consensus at the time that the common law had failed and that a new, radical approach was needed to address a growing crisis.

PERC brought together a diverse group of lawyers, economists, and other social scientists at a conference held near Emigrant, Montana, October 1–4, 1998. Participants discussed the essays presented here, which concern the causes and consequences of the fundamental change in American environmental law that occurred over the past three decades.

Addressing environmental problems through the law requires a choice among various legal institutions. For almost thirty years, environmental law in the United States has been constructed on the basis of the choices made in the early 1970s. The resulting almost exclusive emphasis on national statutes has shaped almost every aspect of the way Americans relate to their environment. The authors, coming from varying perspectives, found they shared at least a degree of skepticism about whether we have made the right choices.

David Schoenbrod's chapter opens the volume with a "nonfundamentalist" approach to the choice of legal institutions. Schoenbrod, a participant in the creation of the modern environmental administrative state, looks back critically at the choice of a statutory framework. He urges that we seek institutions that provide an alternative to both the administrative state and the common law to capture the benefits of the common law while avoiding its flaws. In essence, he suggests protecting the environment according to "the spirit of the common law."

The next three chapters address some of the facts needed to choose among competing institutions. Although the debate over environmental law has largely been premised on the failure of common law institutions to save the environment, these authors provide compelling evidence that not only are common law institutions capable of protecting the environment but also in some instances do so better than statutory law institutions.

Indur M. Goklany provides a comprehensive survey of the scientific evidence regarding air quality in the United States. He provides data that show how the combination of common law and state and local regulation had already brought air pollution under control before the Clean Air Act Amendments of 1970 "nationalized" air pollution control. Goklany's data provide striking evidence of the effectiveness of pre–Clean Air Act institutions. Beyond the facts, the chapter offers a theoretical framework that takes into account the long-term trends in air pollution, suggesting that far from the much feared "race to the bottom" among state governments to "sell out" to industrial polluters, what is more frequently experienced is a "race to the top." Goklany's results suggest that if national, statutory-based regulation were reduced, excessive "not-in-my-backyard" (NIMBY) regulations would more likely be a problem than excessive pollution.

Roger E. Meiners, Stacie Thomas, and Bruce Yandle investigate common law remedies for water pollution centered on a revisionist account of the infamous 1969 burning of the Cuyahoga River in Cleveland, Ohio. Politicians seized on the specter of a river on fire to help press the case for national regulation. The authors trace the way that statutes produced the flammable river by classifying the Cuyahoga as an industrial sewer, thereby preventing common law actions against polluters. They also offer a framework for analysis of the institutional choice among potential suppliers of law. Custom and tradition, the common law, statutory law, and even international institutions can all provide the legal rules necessary to govern disputes over environmental quality. The rise of local watershed groups offers a hint of the rich mix of institutions that will govern water quality in the future—a mix that combines elements of each of the earlier institutions.

Roger Bate offers a different set of examples of the success of the common law. Over the past fifty years the British Anglers' Conservation Association (ACA) has quietly brought hundreds of common law suits to preserve and to improve water quality. With a small staff and only part-time lawyers, the ACA managed to maintain more than forty cases per year and to win millions of pounds in settlements. Its success at overcoming the free-rider problem is impressive and suggests that the conventional view of the common law overemphasizes its deficiencies. Individual anglers, each desiring quality fishing opportunities, have cooperated to enforce the right to water quality.

The third part of the book presents three chapters that address issues surrounding the definition of the common law approach. Understanding environmental statutes is challenging, given their breadth and complexity, but at least the statutes and regulations can be physically gathered into one place. Delineating the common law has always been more of a challenge because it involves rules, institutions, and a particular type of process that is often mysterious to nonlawyers (and even many lawyers) when compared to seemingly straightforward statutes.

However common law is defined, property rights are central to the common law, and the right to exclude is central to property rights. Although scholars associated with PERC and other scholars have made enormous strides in exploring how property rights protect the environment, allowing private property rights in environmentally sensitive areas remains anathema to many concerned with the environment. David Schmidtz examines historical examples of initial appropriation and the Lockean justification for property rights to explore the justification of any institution that recognizes a right to exclude. Schmidtz concludes that not only is private property compatible with preserving the environment and the Lockean proviso to leave "enough and as good for others," but also the right to exclude others is crucial for the preservation of resources. The combination of the compatibility of property rights with environmental protection and the destruction of the environment made possible by the absence of the right to exclude make a powerful argument for environmental solutions built on private property rights.

Modern environmental law is hardly the first attempt to displace the common law in America. Andrew Morriss's chapter looks at nineteenth-century attempts to replace the entire common law system with a comprehensive civil code and compares that episode to modern environmental law. The decisive rejection of those earlier efforts to eliminate the common law suggests a number of reasons why citizens should care about the common law's survival in environmental law. Most important, the common law is more than a set of rules; it is also an adaptive, evolutionary institution for developing rules.

Jonathan R. Macey and Henry N. Butler address another critical part of the common law: the importance of competition among jurisdictions. From its earliest development in England among the competing, polycentric court systems through its modern incarnation in the various state legal systems of the United States, the common law has evolved from institutions faced with competitive pressures. Macey and Butler offer a "Matching Principle" for determining the best fit between environmental problems and the problem-solving jurisdiction.

The final part of the book addresses explanations for the shift from common law to statutory institutions. Todd J. Zywicki's chapter applies public choice theory to environmental legislation. Rather than being seen as a zero-sum conflict between polluters and environmentalists, Zywicki argues that the current regulatory regime is best seen as the outcome of cooperation among interest groups seeking rents at the expense of the dispersed public interest.

Jason S. Johnston's chapter offers a different perspective. Considering the choice of institutions from the perspective of individuals seeking allocations of property rights, Johnston asks about the conditions that will lead individuals to choose particularistic balancing through litigation over general rights entitlements through legislation, and vice versa. He finds that the establishment of general entitlements through legislation will be of greatest value to the groups least likely to prevail in particularistic balancing tests, those with the lowest valuations on their particular use. Johnston then tests his analysis on case studies involving particularly serious nineteenth-century environmental externalities: the hydraulic mining controversy in California and nineteenth-century nuisance-law disputes between coal mine owners and surrounding landowners in Pennsylvania.

In the last chapter, Jeffrey J. Rachlinski uses psychology theory and evidence of the existence of a hindsight bias to explain why polluters might prefer a regulatory regime to a common law system of liability. Because people, and hence jurors, have a tendency to view events that occur as more predictable ex post than the events actually were ex ante, "even defendants who took reasonable precautions against harm are apt to be found liable." As a result, polluters have a powerful incentive to seek regulatory safe harbors. Rachlinski argues for a mixed system in which regulations serve as standards rather than mandates.

The authors in this volume raise a series of important questions about the modern American approach to environmental problems. We hope that the steps presented here toward answering those questions will prompt a reconsideration of the national regulatory approach to control of the environment. The logic and evidence in practice of the common law gives reason to consider reinvigorating its spirit to allow ordinary people to play key roles in protecting their own environment. No human institution is perfect. The challenge of reform is always to identify how to capture the good without also incorporating the flaws. These chapters represent steps in that direction.

Part I

Reviving the Common Law

1

Protecting the Environment in the Spirit of the Common Law

David Schoenbrod

America's modern administrative state has done a terrible job with pollution control. Yes, the environment is much cleaner than it was, but, as Indur Goklany (1997, 2000) suggests, pollution was being reduced at least as quickly before the early 1970s as afterward, when the administrative state took over. The prior progress was made through a combination of private actions, common law suits, and diverse state and local regulations. The administrative state added comprehensive, command-and-control regulation by the national Environmental Protection Agency (EPA). The administrative state is many times more expensive, in terms of both direct cost and the drag on the economy (Schoenbrod 1997, 12). Yet, despite the cost and the obsessively complicated systems to guard against risk, the public, according to polls, is more worried about the environment than ever.

This volume—*The Common Law and the Environment: Rethinking the Statutory Basis for Modern Environmental Law*—asks the question: Should the common law replace the administrative state as the means to protect the environment? This question has received two diametrically opposed answers. Supporters of the administrative state respond with a litany of reasons why the common law is not up to solving modern pollution-control problems. Some of their points are telling, and they are reviewed in the next section of this chapter. But the key thing to see now is that the wholesale rejection of the common law approach is fundamentalist: It displays little if any interest in finding ways to make the common law more useful today. Rather, it seeks to buttress the administrative state.

The diametrically opposed fundamentalist point of view urges that the common law, taken literally, be *the* way to protect the environment. Sometimes, the flaws in the common law are ignored. Sometimes, they are acknowledged not by showing that the common law could provide adequate protection despite them

3

but, rather, by arguing that the administrative state also has flaws. That it does, and they might well be worse than those of the common law. As Roger Bate (2000) argues, the chief problem that the common law encountered in protecting streams in Britain was interference from legislators and administrators. But pointing out the wastefulness of the administrative state will not work politically to justify the gaps that the common law would leave in protecting public health. To voters, society's loss in efficiency counts for nothing when the issue perceived is someone else's profit versus my children's health (Zywicki 2000).

This chapter urges us to look for an alternative to the administrative state and the common law, an alternative that gives us the benefits of the common law while avoiding its flaws. Such an alternative should protect the environment according to the spirit of the common law but not necessarily according to its letter. In other words, this chapter is a plea for a nonfundamentalist approach to the common law of the environment.

The next section of this chapter explains my doubts about the common law, taken literally, as the sole law of the environment. The section is brief because my purpose is constructive. The next major section identifies what makes the modern administrative state such an ugly way to deal with environmental problems. The following section points out the virtues of the common law. The next section suggests how we can protect the environment in a way that replicates the spirit of the common law but that does not always follow it to the letter. The last section considers whether such reform is feasible in the real world.

WHY THE COMMON LAW CANNOT DO THE WHOLE JOB

When it comes to the common law of the environment, there are believers, non-believers, and wanna-be-believers. I am a wanna-be-believer because there is so much wrong with the administrative state, yet I doubt whether a literal application of the common law would suffice for some categories of environmental protection, particularly pollution control.

In trying to solve modern pollution problems, the common law would encounter problems in judging liability, providing remedies, and securing sufficient enforcement.

Liability

Liability for air pollution cannot be based on the kind of absolute liability found in the law of trespass. If we are not allowed to let particles of air pollution escape the boundaries of our land, not only industrial society but all human activity would have to come to a halt. We can't grow beans without kicking up dust, and we can't cook them without emitting fumes, even if only from the beans themselves. So, liability must be founded on some standard that considers the consequences of the pollution.

According to an old maxim defining liability under the common law of nuisance, one must not use one's property in a way that injures that of another. But, such maxims do not, by themselves, settle cases. A case applied the maxim to hold that operating a pigsty near a neighbor's parlor was a nuisance (*William Aldred's Case* 1611). But, as Ronald Coase (1960, 42–43) would be quick to ask, who was injuring whose property? Was the pig defendant injuring the parlor plaintiff by introducing pungent odors, or was the parlor plaintiff injuring the pig defendant by preventing the operation of the sty? The maxim begs the question because the conclusion it reaches depends on an underlying understanding of how things ought to be. In the early English cases, that understanding was based on custom. Apparently, the pigsty was put in a neighborhood in which parlors were customary. Case closed. The outcome would have been entirely different if the parlor were in an area otherwise devoted to converting piglets into porkpies.

Custom is a less satisfactory basis for establishing liability in the modern world. Science has progressed so that we think about pollution as a matter of degree as well as of kind. It is much easier to discern a custom against the existence of pigsties in a certain neighborhood than a custom about how many pigsties there should be. A few refineries in a large metropolitan area may be fine, but not dozens. Custom does not tell us where to draw the line. Custom also does not tell us how to discern whether new technologies are acceptable, nor does it provide any help when people come to want less pollution than was customary.

Courts have, of course, tried to overcome the limits of custom by balancing the benefits of the plaintiffs' activity against the benefits of the defendants' activity. Under the test set out in the *Restatement (Second) Torts* (American Law Institute 1977, § 691 cmt.1a), the balancing is supposed to reflect considerations of both efficiency and fairness, which partially reflect custom. Here, however, the judge is not mirroring the customs of the people but rather engaging in a kind of policy making that is akin to the work that legislators are supposed to do and that the EPA often does. Such balancing has judges making the trade-offs that advocates of common law environmentalism want to leave to private ordering.

Remedy

Even if the court can adjudicate liability, it will have trouble providing satisfactory remedies for many kinds of modern pollution problems. The common law (in which in this context I include the doings of the courts of equity) gears its remedies to harms that can be proven. Damages are available only for harms that the plaintiff can show are caused by the defendant's wrongdoing. Injunctions are available only against harms that the plaintiff can show are imminent and substantial. Overcoming these barriers to relief would be easy enough in the pigsty case. But consider, in contrast, the many kinds of modern pollution that cause nontrivial risks of great harm, the ultimate harmfulness of which cannot be proved by a preponderance of the evidence, or anything like it. The common law is unable to ward off such risks or, in most cases, compensate for harms possibly caused by them afterward.

Even if the plaintiff can show that the harm is sufficiently certain to warrant relief, the court will often hear a plea from the defendant to deny injunctive relief because it would impose an undue hardship. We all know *Boomer v. Atlantic Cement* (1970), the case in which the court balanced the costs and the benefits of abating pollution in deciding whether to grant an injunction. Here again, the court was making a social policy decision of the sort that common law environmentalists would prefer to leave to private ordering.

Enforcement

Where there is one person hurt by a defendant's pollution, as in the case of the pigsty, it is obvious who should do the enforcing, if it is worth doing at all. But where there are thousands or millions of victims, as there often are with modern industrial pollution, enforcement may well be worthwhile but worth no one's while.

WHY THE MODERN ADMINISTRATIVE STATE IS UGLY

What, to me, makes the common law so attractive in comparison to the administrative state is that the administrative state is "idealistic" in a phony, intellectualized sort of way. Consider the ideals that became the foundations of modern environmental law—protection of health without regard to cost by a deadline, zero discharge of water pollution by 1985, and other such lovely concepts loved only by the unthinking. Such ideals are a far cry from a common law built on custom. Such ideals seek to "improve" or to "reform" society through the coercive power of the state in contrast to the common law, which seeks to vindicate the values of society.

The regulatory system that came to the fore in the first half of the twentieth century was a big departure from the common law, but it was closer to the common law than to the modern administrative state. Helping society better achieve its values was what those early elitists, the Progressives, meant by governing in "the public interest." But starting somewhere around 1970, government began to try to force society to achieve not societal values, but rather ideals that were intellectually generated and imposed from on high. This "idealism" justified the state in intruding itself on society far more aggressively than it had previously. The elite enlarged its conception of government's role because the elite itself had changed. In the words of David Gelernter, a Yale computer science professor whose splendid writing got more of the attention that it deserved after he was wounded by the Unabomber:

> Today's elite is intellectualized, the old elite was not. . . .
> The old elite got on fairly well with the nation it set over. But the enmity be-tween Intellectual and Bourgeois is sheepman against cattleman, farm against city, Army versus Navy: a cliché but real. Ever since there *was* a middle class, intellec-tuals have despised it. When intellectuals were outsiders, their loves and hates never mattered much. But, today they are running things, and their tastes matter greatly.
> Members of the old social upper-crust elite were richer and better educated than the public at large, but they approached life on basically the same terms. The public went to church and so did they. The public went into the army and so did they. . . They agreed (this being America) that art was a waste, scientists were questionable, en-gineering and machines and progress and nature were good—some of the old-time attitudes made sense and some didn't, but the staff and the bosses were basically in accord. . . .
> Today's elite loathes the public. Nothing personal, just a fundamental difference in world view, but the hatred is unmistakable. (Gelernter 1997, 128)

The seed of the new elite was in the old elite's rationale that intellect justifies the exercise of power without accountability. Having taught that creed from the beginning of the twentieth century, the top universities began to take it to heart in the late 1940s by changing their admissions and hiring policies to emphasize intellect. They had always had some intellectuals on board, but previously wealth was the main way into the student body and social connections were helpful in getting on the faculty. The Ivy League was known for producing gentlemen, not eggheads. As part of the new trend, Jews such as myself were welcomed in larger numbers. Gelernter concluded that intellectuals came to dominate the faculties by the early 1960s, so the first wave of students fully indoctrinated as intellectuals emerged from graduate school in the late 1960s.

As a graduate of Yale Law School in 1968, my contemporaries and I who were so instrumental in helping to launch the Environmental Protection Agency and the Natural Resources Defense Council as well as other "public interest" environmen-tal groups were charter members of the new wave. We felt fully entitled to remake society according to our ideals. In retrospect, our hubris is hard to excuse. We thought we knew everything because we could reason. But what passed for rea-soning was often little more than "society should be as we think it should be." Besides, there is more to wisdom than reasoning. Here, again, Gelernter is helpful.

There is a crucial distinction between propositions you arrive at by reason . . . and ones that are based on emotion or experience or horse sense. The Talmud calls this elusive stuff *derekh eretz*, literally "way of the world"—a phrase that also means "deference" or "humility." One of the Talmud's deepest assertions is also one of its simplest: *yafeh talmud Torah im derekh eretz*, Torah study *together with* worldly experience is beautiful. Ideas against a background of humility and common sense. (Some of the greatest Talmud thinkers didn't earn their living as rabbis; they were shoemakers, merchants, or carpenters.) (Gelernter 1997, 12)

But according to the generation of elite students graduating from the late 1960s on, only those who earn their living by thinking are thinkers. By this calculus, my Grandfather Marschak, with his scant education, would not count as a thinker despite his wide reading and deep cogitation. He understood that one's own direct experience should count for as much as the doctrines of professors, pundits, and politicians in how one thinks about one's government.

Having dismissed the great bulk of humanity as lacking in thoughtfulness, we considered ourselves entitled to far more power than the result of one vote at the polling place. We looked down on government as it then operated because society seemed to us to be moving too slowly toward the ideals we admired. As the chant went:

What do we want?

[insert the ideal of the day]

When do we want it?

Now.

We wanted new kinds of statutes that would force agencies to bend society to our ideals on a timetable. One of the first of the kind of statutes we wanted was the Clean Air Amendments of 1970 (the 1970 Clean Air Act). It became the prototype for many statutes regulating the environment and other fields. Under the Clean Air Act, the EPA is not left to regulate in "the public interest" but, rather, is mandated to achieve an ideal—to protect the health of all Americans from all harmful pollutants by the end of the 1970s without regard to cost. As a young attorney at the Natural Resources Defense Council, I saw my role as forcing the EPA to live up to this ideal. A quarter-century of experience has taught me that legislation by ideal is unkind to people and their society.

The ideals—clean air, no asbestos in the schools, special education, or the security offered by the various kinds of entitlements and government insurance— become real only in the concrete. Protect-health-from-pollution-without-regard-to-cost is only an ideal until there are laws requiring someone to reduce pollution to the required extent. In enacting ideals instead of rules of private conduct (such as emission limits on specific kinds of industrial plants), Congress does only half the job of making law; it creates rights without imposing corresponding duties (Schoenbrod 1993, 58–59). It does the popular and shuns the unpopular part of lawmaking. The same is true of all its other idealistic tricks to evade democratic accountability.

It is strange to think that Congress could do a better job by legislating ideals instead of rules of conduct because, in so doing, it would disengage itself from the interests that must give way if the ideals are to be realized. Consider what happened after New York State adopted a plan to implement the ideal of the Clean Air Act in New York City. The plan relied on many strategies, including tolls on the bridges over the Harlem and the East rivers to produce the money needed to improve mass transit and thereby to encourage commuters to leave their cars at home. When a new governor and a new mayor refused to implement the plan, my colleagues and I at the Natural Resources Defense Council got a court order requiring implementation. To protest the tolls, which were unpopular with their constituents, all the members of the Brooklyn congressional delegation marched across the Brooklyn Bridge and vowed to amend the act to get rid of the tolls. I rushed down to Washington to defend the Clean Air Act, but I discovered that only two members of the New York City delegation might oppose the amendment. One member represented a district in which most of the voters already rode transit rather than drove cars. The other said that he supported tolls on the bridges—except on those bridges leading to his district. The legislators from Brooklyn said they still supported the ideal of clean air, but they were not prepared to say what concrete steps should be taken to achieve it. The lawmakers were for a right to clean air and against imposing duties to deliver the right, as if there can be rights without duties. A private person who behaved that way would be diagnosed as schizophrenic.

Legislators and agency officials cannot know whether they really believe in achieving their loudly proclaimed ideals until they face up to the interests that must give way in order to achieve them. It turned out that achieving the ideal of the 1970 Clean Air Act would have required taking most of the cars off the roads in Los Angeles and halting construction of new factories in many areas with high unemployment. No one in public office was willing to defend such results.

It is no good trying to excuse the idealism on the basis that there is time enough for Congress to face the hard choices after the ideal is enacted. Statutes that launch regulatory agencies, impose unfunded mandates, and create entitlements are not trial balloons. People come to depend on the entitlements; they save less for retirement in reliance on Social Security, or they build a house on a flood plain in reliance on government flood insurance. Once people get something from government, they will fight to keep what they feel is their right, even if they would not have missed getting it in the first place. Besides, repealing an enacted ideal requires going through the Constitution's legislative process. The House, the Senate, and the president all were given a say in enacting statutes so that government would not act rashly. By legislating ideals, Congress evades the procedural checks on acting rashly, but those checks come fully into play in stopping new legislation to temper rash promises. Besides, once Congress legislates a new ideal, subgovernments grow up around it and defend their thing. No, a legislated ideal is almost as hard to take back as a slap in the face.

As my generation of petulant young elitists came to understand the ways of power, it learned how the magic wand of idealism could be used to get power. The trick was to put off the hard choices to another time or place. Thus, the 1970 Clean Air Act could be enacted because neither clean air nor the laws needed to clean the air would have to be produced now—the deadline was 1977. Present ideals were sacrificed for present power. When 1977 arrived with the ideal unachieved, the EPA held the whip hand over society because it theoretically had the power to shut down factories and to close gas stations on the massive scale needed to produce what it had defined as clean air. But the EPA was not about to exercise that power for then it would lose all its power. Instead it deigned to allow society more time if the agency's power was increased. In the jockeying over the legislation, the EPA had two other critical advantages—(1) any softening of the regulatory timetable would have to get through the legislative process, and (2) the EPA was now itself the center of a subgovernment with some considerable political clout.

In the 1977 Clean Air Act, the EPA and its allies allowed the 1977 deadline to be eased to 1982 for some pollutants and to 1987 for others in exchange for vast increases in the EPA's power to impose procedural and substantive requirements on society. After the 1982 and 1987 deadlines proved impossible, the EPA allowed the deadlines to be eased out as far as 2010 in exchange for still greater increases in its power. The sequel to the futuristic movie *2001*, originally released in 1968, is set in 2010. Now, it seems that the present health goals may be largely met by 2010. If that would happen, EPA would lose power. But the EPA has promulgated new, tougher goals that project its power into the ever-distant future. Many mayors and governors, including many Democrats, think the standards are wasteful, unnecessary to protect health, and impossible to achieve. The agency replies that it will decide on a case-by-case basis whether to give state and local officials more time to meet the goal. With the EPA making those decisions, the EPA and the president will have tremendous leverage on governors and mayors.

The growth in EPA's power can be gauged roughly by the growth in the length of the Clean Air Act—from 8 double-spaced, typed pages in 1965, to 76 pages in 1970, to 272 pages in 1977, to 718 pages in 1990.

The vast increases in federal government power typified by the Clean Air Act can't be justified by good results. The air people breathe is much cleaner today not because of the ideal handed down from Washington, but because society wanted it so. State and local governments had responded to the demands of voters for cleaner air long before the federal government got involved (Goklany 1997, 2000). At the federal level, the most important step that Congress took in 1970 was to enact a rule of conduct, not some abstract ideal, to cut emissions from new vehicles. Public support for cleaner air would have brought many further steps at all levels of government. But, instead of enacting other concrete laws in response to popular demand, Congress enacted its grand ideal.

One might hope that legislation by ideal would make people worry less about pollution because a national EPA is standing guard. After all, they want to feel safe as well as be safe. But, the idealistic approach has left people feeling unsafe. According to opinion polls, the public is more worried about the environment now than it was in the 1970s.[1] Yet, the public should have less reason to worry about pollution after spending $1,850 per household annually throughout most of the 1990s (Schoenbrod 1998, 12). The public worries more despite the facts because the idealistic approach puts the EPA in the business of getting the public to worry about the "failure" to attain unattainable ideals. The agency and others who get power and money from pollution control are far more ready to identify problems and to propose increases in their power than to say that things are reasonably safe. With the drumbeat of missed deadlines and with all the money the EPA spends— and gives to its supporters to spend—to generate popular demand for its increasing power, it is no wonder that the public worries more (Melnick 1984, 123).

Perhaps the most telling evidence of the EPA's success at worrymongering is that 68 percent of the public tell pollsters that most other people don't worry enough about the environment (Darnay 1992, 844). Here is the ultimate irony. The voters who succeeded in getting government to do something substantial about pollution have been convinced by that government that people like themselves are too dumb to care about their own health. Government by ideal creates a state—literally a state of mind—in which people feel they must be put in the hands of nurses. By sowing self-doubt, the state increases its power.

My complaint is not that the EPA moved too fast to clean the air. Indeed, it was woefully slow in some instances, such as lead in gasoline and interstate pollution. In other instances, it has imposed pollution-control costs for no discernible benefit. Rather, my complaint is that without legislation by ideal, we would have achieved comparable improvements in public health with far less harm to society.

The Clean Air Act and the many other statutes modeled on it allow a federal agency to run major segments of civil society on quasi-military lines through a chain of command that runs from Congress down through the EPA to states and ultimately to the regulated entities. Operating this chain of command entails compiling a great mountain of statutes, regulations, guidance documents, plans, permits, and reports. Producing all these documents is in itself a vast waste of time, but the waste of time is chiefly important as a marker of something more subtle— the loss of flexibility that comes from trying to run society from on high. Not only is everything controlled directly or indirectly from Washington, but it is controlled in excruciating detail.

Before considering the astonishing detail of that control, it is worth recalling how the legal system used to discourage antisocial activity. As a rough generality, if you acted wrongly, but caused no harm, you paid token damages or nothing at all. No harm, no foul. If you did cause damage, you paid for it, but you were not punished unless you did something society judged awful. It was because only awful conduct was made a crime that ignorance of the law was no defense, the reason being that you should have known better. So long as you avoided awful conduct, you were free to act as you wished, but you were responsible for the consequences.

Such an approach would not work for many modern environmental concerns because it is hard for judges to place a dollar value on the harm done by many pollutants. But, for these pollutants, legislatures have many fairly nonintrusive ways to limit total emissions from all sources or total emissions from any one plant. Our modern environmental statutes control conduct in far more detail than that. Instead of limiting total emissions from each plant, the regulatory system frequently slaps a separate emissions limit on every one of the many smokestacks, pipes, and vents coming out of the typical plant. The agency regulates not only emissions but sometimes also the techniques used to control them, monitor them, and report them. All this must be pinned down in a permit to be secured before going into operation. And to get the permit, you must pay a tax sufficient to keep the regulators in business. Another thing: if the source needs to change what it is producing or how it operates, which can happen every few weeks in this computer age, it will need an amended permit. Beyond all this, a source that violates a requirement can be punished heavily even if no harm was done and even if the violation was neither intentional nor negligent.

No major facility can hope to avoid violating such an exacting system of legally binding requirements. A recently published environmental-law treatise acknowledges that "it is virtually impossible for a major company (or government facility) to be in complete compliance with all regulatory requirements. [And yet] virtually every instance of noncompliance can be readily translated into a [criminal] violation" (Campbell-Mohn, Been, and Futrell 1993, 55). More than a few former colleagues of mine at the Natural Resources Defense Council, who now work for corporations trying to comply with environmental law, tell me the same thing: their clients can't help but violate the law, no matter how hard they try, because the legal requirements are just too complex and confusing. Government now uses the criminal law, "civil" penalties, and other forms of punishment to punish much conduct that ordinary people would not think reprehensible.

The point of this compulsive system is power, not environmental quality. This became clear when state environmental commissioners seized upon President Clinton's and Vice President Gore's promises during the 1996 election campaign to let states and businesses find smarter, cheaper ways of protecting the environment. Prior to the election, the commissioners got the blessings of EPA Administrator Carol Browner to negotiate with agency staff to "reinvent government." Four months of hard bargaining produced a sixteen-page agreement allowing the states to deviate from rigid federal requirements when the EPA agrees that such innovations would save money and not harm environmental quality.

Once the election was over, the EPA official in charge of the talks killed the deal. In a "Dear Reinvention Ombudspersons" letter, Deputy Administrator Fred Hansen wrote that the states would be allowed to try only "minor, and I stress minor, changes." Moreover, the EPA would get to decide how the state-generated savings would be spent. The EPA was seeking to maintain its share of power rather than enforce environmental standards.

The philosophy of "reinventing government," if taken seriously, is that those closer to a problem can solve it better. Given the opportunity, state and local governments could reduce environmental costs without sacrificing environmental quality. That is why the EPA won't loosen its grip on state and local governments. Environmental policy might go the way of welfare—successful, federally sanctioned state experiments could lead to a wholesale devolution of power. States are more open to real experimentation; and it makes more sense to experiment one state or one city at a time. State and local environmental agencies continue to develop innovative approaches to every type of pollution problem, despite federal mandates consuming such a large proportion of their energy and resources. The drive is there at the state and the local levels for the same reason that states and localities spearheaded environmental improvement before 1970—officials who are closest to the citizens who experience the pollution and to the facilities that are regulated are most aware of the need to find sensible solutions. The Framers of the Constitution wanted to let the states serve as laboratories for different policies. The federal chain of command kills state-by-state experiment. But experiment is what we need.

It would be wrong to think of this compulsive style of regulation as a problem only for large national corporations. Indeed, it is far less of a problem for them than for ordinary people. National corporations are more concerned about how they are treated relative to their competitors than they are about the absolute level of regulation. If their competitors are similarly regulated, they can pass the costs of compliance on to consumers. Moreover, national corporations can live with the complications of federally mandated regulation. They have in-house staffs and outside lawyers, often hired away from national environmental groups and the EPA, who specialize in decoding the regulatory requirements and negotiating with regulators.

The ones who suffer most directly are not large corporations, but state and local governments, farmers, and small businesses. Also harmed are homeowners or other property owners with, for example, wetlands, asbestos, lead paint, or radon problems. They are not well equipped to lobby for changes and still less well equipped to deal with highly complex regulatory requirements. Quickly growing small businesses also find themselves prevented from building new plants to compete with established firms because the regulations give a large preference to existing plants. Big businesses love this protection from competition, whereas the small businesses lack the power to lobby effectively to get rid of the disadvantage. Because big businesses have many ways for using federal regulation to protect themselves from competition, major new EPA regulations frequently increase the stock price of large established companies because they are being protected from competition. Big businesses also use federal regulation to shield themselves from liability for damage (Rachlinski 2000).

Legislation by ideal harms the public in ways that most of us never see because we don't connect the ideals to higher prices and taxes or to lower salaries or to pensions. The best estimates are that we could have achieved the present level of environmental quality at a quarter of the direct cost. Saving three-quarters of pollution control bucks to get the same pollution control "bang" would make a huge difference when we are spending $1,850 per household annually (Schoenbrod 1998, 12). This figure represents only the *direct* costs of pollution control in terms of capital equipment and operating costs.

The current regime of pollution control also creates immense *indirect* costs by imposing paperwork requirements and by discouraging new plants and innovations. One study estimated that the Clean Air and the Clean Water acts alone reduced national income 2 percent by 1981 and 6 percent by 1990 (Hazilla and Kopp 1990, 853). This loss in income grows cumulatively and, moreover, takes account of only two of the many environmental statutes.

Such numbers do not prove that government is too big and centralized. We would pay gladly to avoid invasion, unmitigated pollution, or starvation of the poor. We must have certain public services. The question is not whether the total cost of government outweighs the total benefit, but whether, in [the] words of Thomas Paine (1995, 7), government provides security to society "with the least expense and greatest benefit." Our idealistic government imposes vastly inflated expenses, yet leaves us feeling insecure.

We are hurt not just in our pocketbooks but in our ability to live our lives in ways that are most fulfilling to us. When I talk to friends and neighbors about what they would really like to do, they often mention developing some talent into a little business that they could operate on their own or in conjunction with a few friends. What often stops their hopes before they stir too far is feeling daunted by the various regulatory and record-keeping requirements, of which the environmental laws are but one of many examples. Some people decide to proceed anyway, but illegally. They become new recruits to the underground economy. Others do not go underground but cut corners and are left worrying about getting caught. Most, however, stay where they are, cogs in large organizations. The large organizations provide the capacity to deal with the government-imposed complication, but at the price of doing things the organizations' way. Small businesses are right to see the state as their enemy.

I don't want to exaggerate. Plainly, small business continues to exist. But consider the drag of an officialdom that cares first and foremost about protecting its turf. The drag is not just on small business but also on those who work in large corporations and governments. My sister, Nancy, who runs a day care program for children with AIDS in a city hospital, complains bitterly about how bureaucratic requirements divert her attention from the children. Her complaints are typical of those of managers in government-run health care and education. When innovators from the private or the public sectors explain their success in finding new or better ways to provide people with what they want, the stories they tell often show that it was tougher jumping through the regulatory hoops than coming up with the idea or implementing it. The stories they don't tell are those of the innovations that died because getting the permits was just too expensive, too time consuming, or too discouraging. It is a sign of the times that the artists Christo and Jeanne-Claude, whose projects include wrapping public monuments in gossamer fabrics, make their years-long efforts to get the necessary permits part of the work of art. In art, as it imitates life, government is a drag on individual creativity.

When the state throttles individual initiative, we lose something even more precious than money and what it can buy. We lose the enjoyment of life. Marvin Devino, our nearest neighbor in upstate New York, fixes the tractors and the trucks of local farmers and loggers not just for money, but also for society. When he complained of being too busy, I told him, as I had learned as a good intellectual, that he could work less and earn more by raising his prices. His reply: "But, then I wouldn't get to see my friends." Take, for another example, my uncle Bruce Marschak whose business also runs on personal satisfaction. As a certified public accountant, he felt squelched in someone else's organization. So, he pursued what interested him, metal working, despite his utter lack of training in it. Now he has a large factory of room-sized machines most of which he designed and built himself. Not the least of the good that comes from his business is that a man in his seventies who doesn't need the money and could easily retire finds joy in working with the hundred or so people from around the world who are on his payroll.

Legislation by ideal is puritanical. It upholds virtue in the sense of pious adherence to notions of purity but destroys virtue in the sense of using our personal powers to express ourselves to the fullest. And, it does so relentlessly. As the philosopher C. S. Lewis wrote,

Of all tyrannies a tyranny sincerely exercised for the good of its victims may be the most oppressive. It may be better to live under robber barons than under omnipotent moral busybodies. The robber baron's cruelty may sometime sleep, his cupidity may at some point be satiated; but those who torment us for our own good will torment us without end for they do so with the approval of their own conscience. They may be more likely to go to Heaven yet at the same time likelier to make a Hell of earth. Their very kindness stings with intolerable insult. To be "cured" against one's will and cured of a state we may not regard as disease is to be put on a level with those who have not yet reached the age of reason or those who never will; to be classed with infants, imbeciles, and domestic animals. (Lewis [1949] 1970, 292)

Like many of the others graduating from top schools in the late 1960s, I thought of myself as an idealist intellectual, as committed to peace, freedom, and the love of humanity. Despite our talk of peace and freedom, we launched regulatory systems that work on quasi-military lines and that unnecessarily curb freedom. Despite our talk of love, our idealism has taken a form that is contrary to love. To love another human is to see that being as a whole and to hope for the full realization of that wholeness. To impose idealism on society is to focus on one aspect of other people—their desire for clean air, for instance—and to insist that that aspect should trump all others. Such conduct between individuals would in the days of the counterculture have been called "laying a guilt trip." Today, guilt is the state's ticket to power.

Government by idealism is premised on the notion we can't trust ourselves to support laws sufficient to protect society and so must instead commit ourselves in advance to ideals regardless of the consequences. My Marxist father and my libertarian grandfather Marschak had a long-running debate about whether a Marxist state could improve human nature. Grandfather Marschak's ultimate rejoinder to my father was that the state would fail because human nature can't be changed. To support his case, grandfather copied out a quotation from Arnold Toynbee, which I found in a box of old family photographs:

Now human nature can be subjugated by main force . . . [but] has shown itself as refractory, and as recalcitrant to human control, as a goat or a camel or a mule. When man tries to coerce human nature, he defeats his own purpose; for so far from cowing it, coercion merely stimulates its obstinacy, rebelliousness, and animosity. It was human nature that Horace had in mind when he wrote that nature will always keep coming back at you, even if you drive it with a pitchfork.

Grandfather had it right. As Alan Watts argued in *Psychotherapy, East and West,* intellect provides humans with no protection against the parts of their natures that they distrust:

There is really no alternative to trusting man's nature. This is not wishful thinking or sentimentality; it is the most practical of practical politics. For every system of mistrust and authoritarian control is *also* human. The will of the would-be saint can be as corrupt as his passions, and the intellect can be as misguided as the instincts. . . . The alternative [to faith in our own nature], as Freud saw, is the swelling of guilt "to a magnitude that individuals can hardly support." (Watts 1975, 121)

Distrusting our own natures, we modern Americans have produced a state that literally writes the book for us. The book not only bars us from doing wrong, but also tells us to how to behave right. The fly in the ointment is that we won't live by the book. We are, most of us, guilty on multiple counts. This fact, usually swept under the rug, came inconveniently into public attention when President Clinton nominated Zoe Baird for attorney general. She had violated several laws, including one requiring employers of household help to file various withholding taxes and forms. Such violations were rampant. Zoe Baird, nominated for the highest law enforcement position in the land, came to personify the arrogance of an officialdom that imposed requirements with which good citizens find it hard to comply. The public reacted to Baird as they did to Leona Helmsley when she allegedly said "[W]e don't pay taxes. Only the little people pay taxes."[2] The government's embarrassment deepened as it came out that candidate after candidate for attorney general, Supreme Court justice, and other top jobs were guilty of the same offense. So many were guilty that it was finally deemed acceptable for violators to get appointed if they went through a ritual in which guilt was acknowledged, back taxes paid, forms filed, and some routine fine levied.

By changing the embarrassing law, Congress, for its part, attempted to show that it was not in the habit of enacting laws that millions of good citizens would care to violate. But the problem is not isolated, as the impossibility of complying fully with environmental laws shows. The government itself routinely violates the environmental laws by fudging figures to close the gap between the ideals that it has promised to live up to and the actions that the citizens will tolerate (Schoenbrod 1983, 766–77). We commit to paying entitlements faster than we are willing to set aside the money needed to meet the commitments. The upshot is massive government debt, which is to say massive collective guilt.

I am not complaining of any material want. I have what I need and much more. What I lack is living in a society not oppressed by the state. In society, a rising tide does raise all ships. The other guy's success is good for me because he has more joy to spread in every way. But when government regulates or spends, the other guy's gain is usually my loss. Such government sits athwart the routes of social intercourse exacting a toll whenever it can. It gains power by sowing jealousy, self-doubt, guilt, and fear.

THE VIRTUES OF THE COMMON LAW

After describing how the modern administrative state handles pollution control, it is easy to identify the virtues of the common law. *First*, the common law enforces the norms of society, whereas the administrative state tries to impose intellectually generated norms on society. Common law rules tend to limit liability to conduct that society deems unjust, whereas the administrative state imposes liability where the state deems it useful to achieve its objectives.

Second, the common law decision makers—judges—do not gain in power or prestige should the environmental protection rules that they administer be made more protective; whereas the decision makers of the administrative state—Congress and the EPA—do gain in power and prestige should the rules they administer be made more protective. Common law rules are, metaphorically speaking, boundaries between holders of rights. Cases arise in which the boundaries are uncertain. Moving the boundaries will not necessarily give judges more power. But Congress gains in power by granting the EPA broader jurisdiction, and the EPA gains in power by using that jurisdiction aggressively, as when it ratchets up the stringency of its ambient standards. When it comes to growing its own power, the EPA is no umpire blandly calling balls and strikes, but rather an empire builder.

Third, the common law took an evolutionary approach to lawmaking, whereas the administrative state works through great spasms of legislative authorization, as shown by Andrew Morriss's chapter in this volume. Morriss (2000) demonstrates as a corollary that the common law works in light of the very real facts of real cases, whereas the cataclysmic statutory authorizations of the administrative state are premised perforce on imagined facts. It was imagined facts that gave rise to such goofy notions as "technology forcing," which was supposed to let the country achieve the ambient air quality standards by the mid-1970s and to end all water pollution by 1985. As a further corollary, the common law issues orders only to those before the lawmaker. In contrast, statutes are meant to apply to the whole world; and because their authorizations are framed so abstractly, those potentially affected may well not even know that they will be affected (Schoenbrod 1993, 89–90). Even when the EPA makes industry-specific regulations, small regulated businesses may well not know of the consequences for them until they are brought up on charges, by which time it is too late to question the EPA's rule (see *Adamo Wrecking*).

Fourth, common law rules tend to be cost sensitive, whereas those of the administrative state are often not supposed to take cost into account, as shown by Meiners, Thomas, and Yandle (2000) in this volume.

Fifth and finally, the common law relies principally on private ordering, whereas the administrative state, with its command-and-control mindset, seeks to order vast swaths of human activity through public power. The common law provides rules for dealing with externalities but otherwise leaves decisions about whether to control pollution, and how, up to private persons. So, for example, as discussed earlier in this chapter, the common law prefers compensating or preventing harm rather than requiring adherence to the law as an abstract duty. For another example, those with duties and rights under the common law are usually free to trade them among and between themselves. In contrast, with the administrative state, all rights are inalienable, and duties may be traded, as with emissions trading, only if the administrative state approves. The arrogant way in which the EPA treated the state environmental commissioners shows the EPA's reluctance to give up control in this or any other way.

HOW TO PROTECT THE ENVIRONMENT IN THE SPIRIT OF THE COMMON LAW

We can imagine a system of pollution control law that is more like the common law and less like the modern administrative state. The system would start, of course, with the common law. We need to remember that, at least between rural neighbors, the common law is the chief regulator of pollution. But, for the reasons identified earlier, the common law of pollution needs supplementation through legislation.

This need for supplementation should come as no affront to those who understand the spirit of the common law. Frederich A. Hayek (1973, 88–89) argued convincingly that common law needs legislation to rescue it from lines of cases that went down blind alleys. We also sometimes need legislation to identify bright lines, to take account of changes in society, and to construct remedies for pollution that is not certain to cause harm but does present significant risk.

For Hayek, the key difference between the law and the fiats of the administrative state was *not* that one was made by judges and the other was made by politicians. No, for him, the difference was that law prescribes only unjust conduct (Hayek 1973, 87, 88).

There is, of course, no way to guarantee that legislated law will prescribe only unjust conduct. But, we could change the modern legislative practices in two ways that would go a long way in that direction. First, the federal government should deal with only those environmental issues that the states are institutionally incompetent to handle. As I argued in a previous PERC volume, this would leave most pollution regulation at the state and the local levels (Schoenbrod 1997, 268, 269). Second, legislation, whether at the federal, the state, or the local level, should be restricted to enacting rules of conduct, not ideals such as "to protect health" and "the public interest." What I am talking about here is no delegation of legislative power to administrative agencies.

The consequence of these two changes would be that legislated rules of conduct would tend to have many of the virtues of the common law. With lawmakers close to home having to take responsibility for the rules of conduct, the rules that they would enact would tend to be in accord with the values of society. With legislators having to take responsibility for the hard choices and deprived of the political profit that comes from unfunded mandates, from blame shifting through delegation, and from case work, legislators would lose their stake in growing the power of the state. To the contrary, they would be inclined to intervene only where

David Schoenbrod

existing law was clearly deficient. Their intervention would be likely to take the form of limited fixes rather than the imposition of whole new systems. For example, when Congress found itself forced to enact a rule of conduct to limit emissions of new cars in 1970, it enacted an emission limit only for new cars. The rest of the 1970 Clean Air Act delegated broad-ranging lawmaking power to the EPA. But, were delegation foreclosed, any further intervention by Congress would be limited to specific categories of plants or even to specific categories of plants in a specific region. Or Congress would enact common law–like rules of the sort that Merrill (1997) suggested for controlling interstate pollution.

Such lawmaking would replicate additional virtues of the common law: it would be evolutionary rather than cataclysmic, based on real rather than imagined facts, and cost sensitive rather than pretending to be cost ignorant. Because particular industries would be targeted, they will press to defend themselves. As a result, the proponents of legislation would bear the burden of showing why the legislation is really needed to prevent harm and why it is a proportionate response to the harm. Moreover, because the elected legislators would be responsible for the consequences, they would find it to their advantage to allow scope for private ordering. We see evidence of that in the acid rain program under the 1990 Clean Air Act. With Congress on the hook for the costs, the statute allowed emissions trading.

To complete my wish list for remaking statutory environmental law in the spirit of the common law, real injury would be required for standing; permit requirements would be eliminated (emissions limits plus permits is like belts and suspenders); remedies would emphasize, to the extent possible, damages and injunctions tailored to prevent harm, rather than emphasizing criminal and civil penalties; and such penalties would be barred when there is neither harm nor fault.

IS REAL REFORM FEASIBLE?

Would the result of my wish list be perfect? Here is how I addressed the same question when I made a similar proposal to the board of trustees of the Natural Resources Defense Council (NRDC) in 1997:

> Environmental protection has taken a wrong turn against which the grandfather of modern environmentalism, Aldo Leopold, warned when he wrote of the kind of conservationist more taken with his own prowess than with nature. Among many others, he included the poets who write bad verse on birchbark and
>
>> "the professional, striving through countless conservation organizations, to give the nature seeking public what it wants, or to make it want what he has to give. Why, it may be asked, should such a diversity of folk be bracketed in a single category? Because each, in his own way, is a hunter. And why does each call himself a conservationist? Because the wild things he hunts for have eluded his

grasp, and he hopes by some necromancy of laws, appropriations, regional plans, reorganizations of departments, or other form of mass wishing, to make them stay put." (Leopold 1970, 282)

It is Congress that has turned environmental law into mass wishing—perfectly healthy air by 1977, zero discharges to the water by 1985, and other absurdities. It has been the only game that Congress has seen fit to set up in this town. NRDC has played that game with maximum advantage to the environmental side. But, now is the time to see that it is the wrong game.

The mass wishing has not only failed. It also endangers the environment. A public otherwise sympathetic to environmental protection is angry about overly fussy regulation and politicians who evade personal responsibility. Environmental law suggests the anger is reasonable. The consequences so far are the Unfunded Mandates Reform Act of 1995 and majorities in support of term limits and a balanced budget amendment. While these initiatives may fail, the anger and its causes will remain. Congress may respond in a way that does real harm to the environment, especially if hard times return.

The mass wishing also departs from the roots of environmentalism. Aldo Leopold set out to teach ordinary people about the environment because he believed that those who don't understand nature will make bad decisions about it. No understanding is needed for voters to wish or Congress to promise. Rather, the laws come down from the agency experts on high. Leopold, in contrast, wanted to save the environment from the bottom up. His vision was not unlike that of the Framers of the Constitution, many of whom were thoughtful naturalists. They sought to root the laws in popular support by requiring that they be made by elected legislators. Such laws will reflect human nature and so therefore will not be perfect. But, the quarter-century since [the first] Earth Day has demonstrated a corollary to Leopold's teaching: Those who can't accept human nature will make bad decisions about how government should protect nature. I urge the Natural Resources Defense Council to include democracy among the natural resources it defends. In other words, it should continue to educate the public, fight for the necessary laws, and enforce them in court, but also, in addition, insist that the laws be made by legislators, and to the extent practicable by the legislators closest to the people. (Schoenbrod 1999, 771)

It will not shock you to hear that NRDC did not leap to support my proposals. What did shock me was that there was very little defense of the present system as right and just. Rather, the essence of the reply was, it works for us.

I also made the same proposals to the state presidents of the American Farm Bureau Federation. Their response, if I gauge it correctly, was, the present system is unjust and that it doesn't work for us.

But can any force bring reform? There are three possibilities: the courts, Congress, and the people. It is hard to imagine the Supreme Court doing the job all on its own. The Court let lapse the constitutional doctrines limiting the powers of the national government and the delegation of legislative powers at a time when the public wanted a centralized, parental government. These doctrines were deemed dead by legal pundits. But the Court has tentatively begun to talk of them as if they have real force (*United States v. Lopez* 1995; *Printz v. United States* 1996; *Loving v. United States* 1996; *Clinton v. City of New York* 1998). What has changed, I think, is that popular opinion has begun to sense that limits on the national government and accountability are essential to good government.

It is also hard to imagine Congress doing the job on its own. Members of Congress have so far gained great political advantage from unfunded federal mandates and from the delegation of legislative power. But, they, too, are sensing a change in public opinion. They enacted the largely toothless Unfunded Mandates Reform Act of 1995[3] and the completely toothless Congressional Review Act. Senators Orrin Hatch and Don Nickles presented the latter as a way to deal with lawmaking by unaccountable bureaucrats. The act provides a procedure under which Congress can vote to reject newly issued agency regulations. But it does not require Congress to take responsibility for such regulations. Congress can avoid responsibility by not voting on new regulations, and, in fact, only one vote has been taken in the two years since the act was signed into law.

Congressman J. D. Hayworth and Senator Sam Brownback introduced alternative legislation that would require Congress to take responsibility for all new federal regulations by preventing agency regulations from going into effect unless enacted by Congress. Their bills have seventy plus sponsors in the House and thirteen in the Senate, but the Republican leadership has prevented the bills from coming to the floor.

The third possible source of change is the people themselves. Opinion polls show majorities concerned about the lack of accountability in government and the growth of government power. But the public also wants its health to be protected. The people have yet to have explained to them how public health can be protected through a government that is accountable and closer to home. When that vision is provided, there will be stronger support for environmental protection in the spirit of the common law and, so, support for further action by the courts and Congress. To provide that vision is the job ahead.

NOTES

The participants at the PERC conference at which this essay was originally presented provided me with many excellent suggestions. I thank them as well as Ross Sandler and Jerry Taylor for their always helpful comments on an earlier draft of this essay and Phillip Caal and Floyd Englehardt, New York Law School class of 1998, for their always able research assistance.

1. A poll by the Roper Organization revealed that from 1972 to 1990 there was a marked increase in the percentage of the population who thought that environmental protection laws and regulations had "not [gone] far enough"; likewise there was a marked

increase in the percentage of the population who believed that preserving and protecting the environment was more important than economic growth. See Kempton, Baster, and Hartley (1995, 4).

2. From an article in the *Chicago Tribune*, 13 June 1995, 2(N).

3. Unfunded Mandates Reform Act of 1995, P.L. 104-4, 109 Stat. 48 (1995).

REFERENCES

American Law Institute. 1997. *Restatement (Second) Torts.* St. Paul: West.

Bate, Roger. 2000. Protecting English and Welsh Rivers: The Role of the Anglers' Conservation Association, this volume.

Campbell-Mohn, Celia, Barry Been, and William J. Futrell. 1993. *Sustainable Environmental Law.* St. Paul: West.

Coase, Ronald. 1960. The Problem of Social Cost. *Journal of Law and Economics* 3(1): 1–44.

Darnay, Arsen. 1992. *Statistical Record of the Environment.* Detroit: Gale Research.

Gelernter, David. 1997. *Drawing Life: Surviving the Unabomber.* New York: Free Press.

Goklany, Indur M. 1997. The Federal Role in Improving Air Quality in the United States: Evidence from Long-Term Trends in Air Pollution. Paper presented at the American Society for Environmental History Conference on Government, Science, and the Environment, Baltimore, MD, March 6–9.

———. 2000. Empirical Evidence Regarding the Role of Nationalization in Improving U.S. Air Quality, this volume.

Hayek, Friedrich A. 1973. *Law Legislation and Liberty.* Vol. 1, *Rules and Order.* Chicago: University of Chicago Press.

Hazilla, Michael, and Raymond Kopp. 1990. Social Cost of Environmental Quality: A General Equilibrium. *Journal of Political Economy* 98(4): 853–73.

Kempton, Willet, James S. Baster, and Jennifer A. Hartley. 1995. *Environmental Values in American Culture.* Cambridge, MA: MIT Press.

Leopold, Aldo. 1970. *A Sand County Almanac.* New York: Ballantine Books.

Lewis, C. S. [1949] 1970. The Humanitarian Theory of Punishment. In *God in the Dock: Essays on Theology and Ethics*, ed. Walter Hooper. Grand Rapids, MI: Eerdmans, 287–300.

Meiners, Roger E., Stacie Thomas, and Bruce Yandle. 2000. Burning Rivers, Common Law, and Institutional Choice for Water Quality, this volume.

Melnick, R. Shep. 1984. Pollution Deadlines and the Coalition for Failure. *Public Interest* 75: 123–34.

Merrill, Thomas W. 1997. Golden Rules for Transboundary Pollution. *Duke Law Journal* 46(April): 931–1019.

Morriss, Andrew P. 2000. Lessons for Environmental Law from the American Codification Debate, this volume.

Paine, Thomas. 1995. Common Sense. In *Collected Writings*, ed. Eric Foner. New York: Library of America, 1–59.

Rachlinski, Jeffrey J. 2000. On Being Regulated in Foresight versus Being Judged in Hindsight, this volume.

Schoenbrod, David. 1983. Goals Statutes or Rules Statutes: The Case of the Clean Air Act. *UCLA Law Review* 30: 766–77.

———. 1993. *Power without Responsibility: How Congress Abuses the People through Delegation.* New Haven, CT: Yale University Press.

———. 1997. Why States, Not EPA, Should Set Pollution Standards. In *Environmental Federalism*, ed. Terry L. Anderson and Peter J. Hill. Lanham, MD: Rowman & Littlefield, 259–70.

———. 1998. *Time for the Federal Environmental Aristocracy to Give up Power.* St. Louis: Center for the Study of American Business, Washington University.

———. 1999. Remarks to NRDC Board of Trustees, Washington, DC, March 12, 1997. *Cardozo Law Review*, 767–73.

Stewart, Richard B. 1998. Controlling Environmental Risks through Economic Incentives. *Columbia Journal of Environmental Law* 13: 153–62.

Watts, Alan. 1975. *Psychotherapy, East and West.* New York: Vintage Books.

Yandle, Bruce. 1989. *The Political Limits of Environmental Regulation.* New York: Quorum Books.

Zywicki, Todd J. 2000. Industry and Environmental Lobbyists: Enemies or Allies? This volume.

CASES CITED

Adamo Wrecking v. United States, 434 U.S. 275, 98 S.Ct. 566, 54 L.Ed. 2d 538 (1978).

Boomer v. Atlantic Cement Co., 26 N.Y. 2d 219, 257 N.E. 2d 870, 309 N.Y.S. 2d 312 (Ct. App. N.Y. 1970).

Clinton v. City of New York, 524 U.S. 417, 118 S.Ct. 2091, 141 L.Ed. 2d 393 (1998).

Loving v. United States, 517 U.S. 748, 116 S.Ct. 1737, 135 L.Ed. 2d 36 (1996).

Printz v. United States, 518 U.S. 1003, 116 S.Ct. 2521, 135 L.Ed. 2d 1046 (1996).

United States v. Lopez, 514 U.S. 549, 115 S.Ct. 1624, 131 L.Ed. 2d 626 (1995)

William Aldred's Case, 9 C.Rep. 57, 77 Eng. Rep. 816 (K.B. 1611).

Part II

The Environment under the Common Law

2

Empirical Evidence Regarding the Role of Nationalization in Improving U.S. Air Quality

Indur M. Goklany

Had the Ancients known about air pollution, Zeus, to make mankind pay for the theft of fire, would not have presented Pandora, with her box, to Prometheus's brother, Epimetheus. Air pollution would have been vengeance enough.

By and large, general ignorance of air pollution and its effects persisted into the twentieth century despite the occasional voice raised against it. To make matters worse, a distinct school of thought was that smoke had antiseptic and curative powers. A 1914 survey of health effects of air pollution undertaken by Pittsburgh's Mellon Institute of Industrial Research noted that it "has been for years a common custom for those affected with [tuberculosis] to resort to coal mines, or to build fires and inhale the smoke" (Cohoe 1914, 12).

Such attitudes combined with ignorance, the lack of real alternatives to coal, the existence of more visible and immediate causes of death and disease that rendered life "nasty, brutish, and short," and—once the industrial revolution got going—the association of smoke with industrialization and, therefore, jobs and prosperity ensured that there would be little progress in controlling air pollution for most of human history.

However, matters began to change in today's developed countries toward the end of the nineteenth century. And today, air quality in the developed countries is the best it has been for the past several decades (Goklany 1995b and 1996).

Conventional wisdom—one of the cornerstones for the justification of the nationalization of air pollution control legislated in the Clean Air Amendments of 1970—is that there was little, if any, progress in cleaning the air prior to nationalization because states had been engaged in an inevitable "race to the bottom" driven by the relentless competition for jobs and economic growth (Dwyer 1995;

Percival 1995; Stewart 1977; Revesz 1992). In this chapter, I verify whether empirically derived information on various air quality indicators does indeed support conventional wisdom and examine the federal government's contribution to the twentieth century's improvement in U.S. air quality.[1]

LONG-TERM TRENDS IN AMBIENT (OUTDOOR) AIR QUALITY IN THE UNITED STATES

It is possible to construct "national" trends for ambient air quality by stringing together data from various annual reports on air quality trends from the Environmental Protection Agency (or its forebears), annual *Environmental Quality* reports from the Council on Environmental Quality (CEQ), and the *Statistical Abstracts of the United States*. Each of these publications provides data for a few (ten to twelve, but more recently twenty) years at a time from national monitoring networks. These data can be combined to construct a much longer time series, but it should be recognized that these trends are qualitative, rather than quantitative (Goklany 1995b, 360 and associated endnotes).

Particulate Matter

It is not until the mid-1950s, when the federal government commenced a program to monitor total suspended particulates (TSP) nationwide, that there are sufficient data to formulate a "national" composite for TSP air quality. Prior to that, some data are available from some of the polluted urban areas. Such data show that dustfall in Pittsburgh has probably been declining since the early 1920s (figure 2.1). There may have been a slight upturn in the late 1930s and during World War II, after which it continued to drop more or less continuously (Davidson 1979). Dustfall data for Chicago and Cincinnati from the 1930s, for New York from the 1940s, and for Detroit and Philadelphia from the 1950s are consistent with the general pattern seen in figure 2.1 (Ludwig, Morgan, and McMullen 1970). These data, although suggestive of a broad pattern and consistent with emission estimates, must still be considered anecdotal.

   Figure 2.2A gives an overview of national composite trends for particulate ambient air quality from 1957 to 1996. It shows that the "national" TSP levels, based on the mean of the annual average concentrations for several monitors, declined between 40 and 50 percent between the late 1950s and 1990. The national "average," which used to be above the old primary (public health-related) National Ambient Air Quality Standards (NAAQS) of 75 micrograms per cubic meter ($\mu g/m^3$), is now 35 percent below that level.

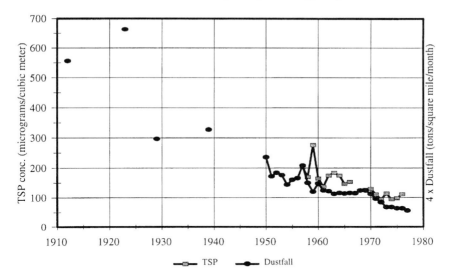

Fig. 2.1   Pittsburgh Dustfall and TSP, 1912–1977

Source: Davidson (1979).

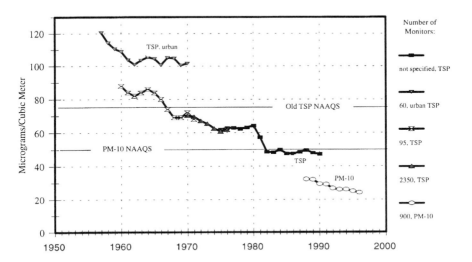

Fig. 2.2A   TSP and PM-10

Mean Annual Average, 1957–1996

Sources: CEQ (1971, 1979, 1981, and 1991); OAQPS (1998).

The ambient air quality data (figure 2.2A) indicate that urban air quality for particulate matter, as measured by TSP, has been improving at least for as long as the data are available (i.e., since 1957). The mean of annual average readings for an ensemble of monitors in sixty urban areas shows declines from 121 to 102 $\mu g/m^3$ from 1957 to 1970. The story with respect to nonurban areas is mixed. CEQ's 1971 report indicated that the average of twenty rural monitors rose from 23 to 37 $\mu g/m^3$ between 1958 and 1970. But subsequent trend analysis done by the EPA for 1960 through 1971 using eighteen nonurban monitors showed that annual TSP levels went up at two monitors, declined at five, and stayed constant for eleven. Aggregating these monitors resulted in no overall trend because a decline in the 1960–68 period was offset by an increase in the 1968–71 period—the latter possibly due to decreased rainfall (OAQPS 1973b, 4-4 to 4-13).

Regardless of which set of trend data one employs, the average levels for nonurban areas were, at all times, far below urban average levels and comfortably below either the primary (health-related) or the "secondary" (welfare-related) NAAQS promulgated in 1971. Most important, the worst areas (major cities) were getting better long before the 1970 Clean Air Act was passed or became effective, whereas rural areas may or may not have been getting worse.

Overall, these trends imply that adverse public health effects of TSP should have been declining. The "national" average based on eighty monitors indicated an improvement from 96 to 89 $\mu g/m^3$ between 1958 and 1970 (CEQ 1971, 242). Average levels for a second ensemble of 95 monitors showed a more rapid improvement nationally, from 84 to 72 $\mu g/m^3$ between 1960 and 1970 with a further decline to 68 $\mu g/m^3$ the following year (CEQ 1981, 243). These improvements apparently continued until 1975, about the time the federally enforceable state implementation plans were becoming more fully effective.

After a period of little change, TSP levels dropped sharply in 1981 and 1982, only to stabilize once again. One reason for the declines in 1980 and 1981 was the steep reduction in economic activity—the recession (OAQPS 1985, 3-5 to 3-10). The rate of the decline, however, may be exaggerated because in 1979 the EPA changed its supplier of the filters used in the monitors to trap TSP and then reverted to the original supplier in 1982. The filters used in the interim were found to be more alkaline, which may have inflated TSP readings—gases in the incoming air were more likely to form sulfates, nitrates, and other secondary particulates on the filter.

In 1987, the TSP NAAQS were replaced by the PM-10 standards, which include only "particulate matter" less than 10 micrometers (microns) in diameter. This change was made because PM-10 is a better indicator of health impacts than TSP—smaller particles are more likely to be inhaled deeper into the lungs. The national composite annual average for PM-10 declined 25 percent from 33.2 to 24.2 $\mu g/m^3$ between 1988 and 1996 (OAQPS 1998). For comparison, the primary annual NAAQS for PM-10 is 50 $\mu g/m^3$.

Sulfur Dioxide

Some data on sulfur dioxide (SO_2) levels are available from 1962 to 1969 and from 1974 onward (figure 2.2B). SO_2 concentrations declined quite dramatically in the 1960s. Between 1962 and 1969, based on twenty-one urban monitors, the mean annual average dropped about 40 percent, from 69.4 to 42.5 $\mu g/m^3$ (CEQ 1981, 243). The corresponding primary NAAQS is 80 $\mu g/m^3$. Between 1974 and 1996, the national average dropped more than 60 percent, from about 38.4, to about 14.6 $\mu g/m^3$.

Carbon Monoxide

Data on ambient carbon monoxide (CO) air quality are sparse until the early 1970s. What little data there are suggest that CO air quality may have begun improving, at least in urban areas, in the mid-1960s as indicated by the short segment of data from 1963 to 1968 (figure 2.2C). That segment was obtained from the federally operated six-city (Chicago, Cincinnati, Denver, Philadelphia, St. Louis, and Washington, D.C.) network that began collecting data in 1962 (CEQ 1971, 242; Office of Air Programs 1972, 1–3). The fact that declines apparently commenced prior to the Federal Motor Vehicle Control Program going into effect indicates that stationary source reductions may have played a key role in the initial turnaround.

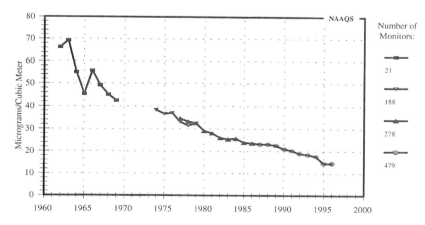

Fig. 2.2B   Ambient SO$_2$ Concentrations
Mean Annual Average, 1962–1996
Sources: CEQ (1971); USBOC (1981); OAQPS (1998).

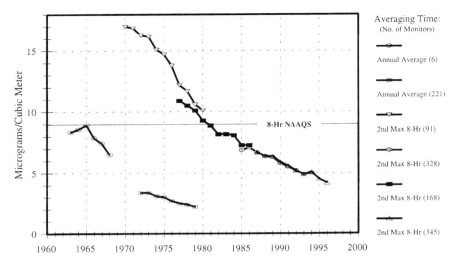

Fig. 2.2C   Ambient CO Concentrations, 1963–1996

Sources: CEQ (1971 and 1981); USBOC (1981); OAQPS (1995a and 1998).

These improvements then gathered momentum as an increasing number of vehicles became subject to federal tailpipe controls starting with model year 1968 (CEQ 1971, 214, 242).

Data from California also indicate that CO air quality, by and large, began to improve in the period 1965–67 (OAQPS 1973a, 4-14 to 4-23). The frequency of days with exceedences of the future (1971) 8-hour CO NAAQS in, for instance, Lennox, in the Los Angeles basin, peaked at 99 to 100 percent in 1965 and declined to 42 percent in 1971. In Burbank, the peak frequency with which the future CO NAAQS would have been exceeded dropped from 93 to 100 percent in 1966 to 34 percent in 1971 (OAQPS 1973a, 4-23).

Figure 2.2C shows that between 1970 and 1996, the national mean CO concentration (based on the mean of the second-highest 8-hour concentration at each location) decreased about 75 percent.

Ozone

Figure 2.2D indicates a roughly 30 percent improvement between 1974 and 1996 in outdoor ozone (O_3) air quality (CEQ 1981; OAQPS 1995b; OAQPS 1998). These data commence after 1974 because prior to that there were not enough monitors outside of California to allow a reasonable "national" trend to be constructed (OAQPS 1973a, 1-11 to 1-12). This poor national coverage only con-

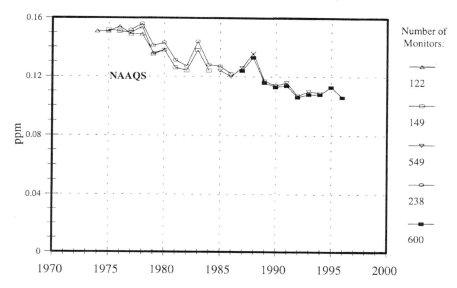

Fig. 2.2D   Ambient Ozone, 1974–1996
Average of Second High Daily Max Value
Sources: CEQ (1981); OAQPS (1995a and 1998).

firms that photochemical smog was not perceived by many to be a major air pollution problem nationally until the late 1960s, or even the 1970s.

California data suggest that oxidant concentrations commenced declining there at least by the period 1966–67. For instance, Azusa, in the Los Angeles basin, registered 1,636 hours of exceedences of the future (1971) oxidant NAAQS in 1966; by 1972, the number of hours had declined to 1,082. Similarly, the number of would-be exceedences in downtown Los Angeles also peaked in 1966 at 1,163, dropping to 516 in 1972. Also an EPA analysis of oxidant trends at three sites on the East Coast (Bayonne, Newark, and Camden, New Jersey) also showed improvements in oxidant air quality between 1966 and 1969 and once again between 1969 and 1972 (OAQPS 1973a, 4-23 to 4-28).

Nitrogen Dioxide

Reliable nitrogen dioxide (NO_2) monitoring data are available only after the early 1970s. Figure 2.2E indicates that NO_2 peaked around the period 1978–79 and has declined by about 30 percent since then. It also indicates that improvements came to NO_2 much more slowly than for other pollutants. There are several reasons for

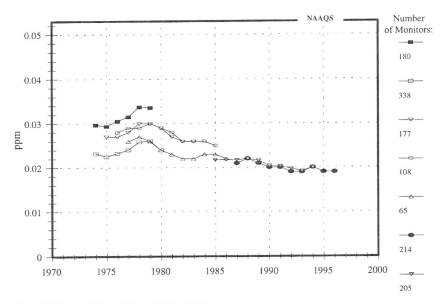

Fig. 2.2E   Ambient NO$_2$, 1974–1996
Annual Average Concentrations
Sources: CEQ (1981 and 1984); USBOC (1981 and 1988); OAQPS (1995a and 1998).

this. First, NO$_2$ health effects are relatively minor. Second, very few areas were ever designated nonattainment for NO$_2$, so it was never perceived to be a widespread problem (Goklany 1998d). Third, many measures to increase fuel efficiency and to reduce CO and volatile organic compound (VOC) emissions increased combustion temperature and, thus, increased NO$_2$ emissions. Finally, although NO$_x$ (nitrogen oxides) were also implicated in O$_3$ formation, the national emphasis for attaining O$_3$ NAAQS was on controlling VOC, partly because of the control costs (Goklany 1995b, 1998b).

WHEN CLEANUP COMMENCED—TRENDS IN EMISSIONS PER GROSS NATIONAL PRODUCT

In a society that has an expanding economy, for any pollutant, the measure of national emissions per gross national product (E/GNP) serves as a leading environmental indicator for that pollutant. Unless there is a sustained decline in that leading indicator, there will be no eventual downturn in emissions (though air quality may well improve). E/GNP measures the aggregate effect of technological change on all of society's activities responsible for that pollutant's emissions (Goklany 1996, 1997). E/GNP may increase if, for instance, coal replaces natural gas; or it may decrease if old processes are replaced by new, more efficient technologies due to either economic factors or regulatory requirements. Alternatively, E/GNP may change with the structure of the economy.

A peak in E/GNP indicates the most recent year by which cleanup efforts had started, either consciously or unconsciously due to economic and technological progress. E/GNP peaked in the 1920s for SO_2 (figure 2.3A), in the 1930s for VOC and NO_x (figures 2.3B and 2.3C, respectively), and in the 1940s (or earlier) for PM-10 and CO (figure 2.3D), after which E/GNP for those pollutants have been declining, more or less, steadily.[2] Eventually, these declines in E/GNP were followed by reductions in total emissions—in 1950 for PM-10 (figure 2.3D), 1967 for VOC (figure 2.3B), early 1970s for CO (figure 2.3D), 1973 for SO_2 (figure 2.3A), and 1978 for NO_x (figure 2.3C).

Figures 2.3A, 2.3B, and 2.3C also indicate the general (approximate) periods during which the body politic came to realize—or, more important, to perceive—that the pollutants in question needed to be controlled because of their effects, real or otherwise, on the public's health and welfare. These periods are denoted in the figures by p(P), or the period of perception. Each of these figures also shows the year when federal regulations first went into effect for the relevant pollutants, which is denoted by t(N), or time of national control.

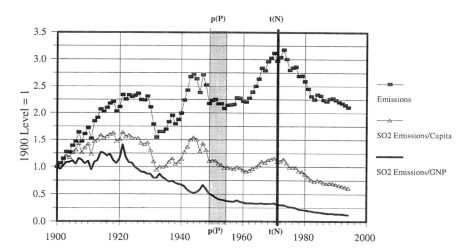

Fig 2.3A   Sulfur Dioxide, 1900–1994
Emissions, Emissions/Capita, and Emissions/GNP

Note: p(P) = period of perception; t(N) = time of national control.
Source: Goklany (1998d).

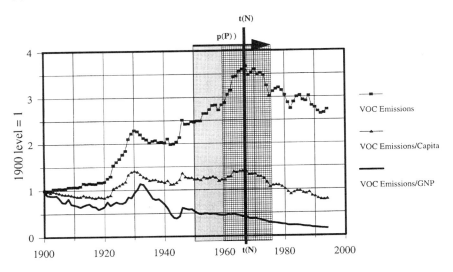

Fig. 2.3B   Volatile Organic Compounds, 1900–1994
Emissions, Emissions/Capita, and Emissions/GNP

Note: p(P) = period of perception (California underwent its p(P) earlier than elsewhere; in fact, many areas were not aware they had a problem until the 1970s, see text); t(N) = time of national control.
Source: Goklany (1998d).

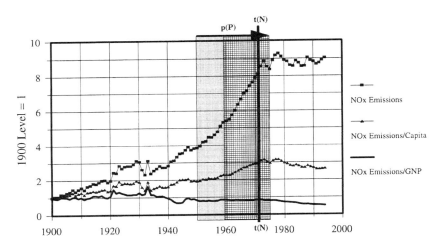

Fig. 2.3C   Nitrogen Oxides, 1900–1994

Note: p(P) = period of perception (California underwent its p(P) earlier than elsewhere; in fact, many areas were not aware they had a problem until the 1970s, see text); t(N) = time of national control.
Sources: OAQPS (1995a); USBOC (1975, 1995, 1996).

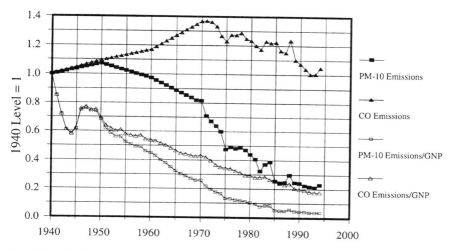

Fig. 2.3D   PM-10 and CO, 1940–1994
Emissions and Emissions/GNP
Sources: OAQPS (1995a); USBOC (1975, 1995, 1996); Goklany (1998d).

Prior to p(P), one should not expect state or local jurisdictions to have required, or private entities to have undertaken, any measures to specifically control the specific substance. Thus, pre-p(P) trends tell little about state or local jurisdictions' or private entities' desire or ability to control pollution. However, as the peaks for E/GNP in figures 2.3A, 2.3B, and 2.3C indicate, cleanup for SO_2, VOC, and NO_x had commenced not only before nationalization, but also before the public perceived or recognized these substances to be public health threats.

TRENDS IN INDOOR AIR QUALITY, 1940 TO 1990

Even though the federal government defines *healthful air* in terms of the air quality at a fixed point outdoors, indoor air quality, particularly in the home, is a far better indicator of the impact of air pollution on public health.[3]

Empirical studies of human exposure to pollutants show that the concentration of a pollutant in outdoor air contributes only a small amount to the total dose of that pollutant received by human beings. For example, a U.S. study showed virtually no correlation between CO levels in the blood—the physiological route by which CO affects people—and outdoor monitored levels. Ambient concentrations explained less than 3 percent of variation of CO levels in the blood. Similarly, outdoor concentrations of nitrogen dioxide (NO_2) are relatively poor predictors of total population exposure, whereas average indoor concentration explains 50 to 60 percent of total exposure.

Among the reasons for the poor correlation between ambient air quality and public health impacts are that, first, virtually no one spends an entire day, let alone an entire year, rooted at the same spot outdoors. In fact, most people spend the vast majority of their time indoors, generally at home. Studies of human activity patterns in the United States indicate that the average person spends about 93 percent of his or her time indoors, 5 percent in transit, and the remaining 2 percent outdoors. About 70 percent of the average person's time is spent indoors at home. The average homemaker spends an even greater amount of time indoors at home (nearly 89 percent) (Office of Air and Radiation 1989). Second, traditional air pollutants often have their own indoor sources and sinks. Thus, air quality is often worse indoors than outdoors. Indoor sources include heating and cooking equipment that use fossil fuels and biofuels (e.g., wood and, in developing countries, dung), smoking, solvents, and various cleaning solutions used or stored in the home. Thus, CO, NO_x, and TSP are generally higher in homes employing natural gas than they are outdoors, whereas SO_2 and O_3 are higher outdoors by a factor of two to five.

Although air quality in the average home is the single most important indicator of air quality with respect to public health, no long-term indoor-air-quality measurements are available for the home or elsewhere. A crude proxy for long-term trends for in-home concentrations, particularly applicable to nonsmoking households, can be constructed for some pollutants by dividing EPA estimates of residential fuel combustion emissions by the corresponding number of occupied housing units.[4] Fuel combustion is the major source of residential emissions for the traditional pollutants.

Using this approach, I estimate that the average "nonsmoking" household's in-home concentrations between 1940 and 1990 declined (i.e., improved) 91 percent for particulates (PM-10), 90 percent for CO, 97 percent for SO_2, and 51 percent for NO_x (see figure 2.4).

For PM-10, over 99 percent of improvements occurred before 1970—before nationalization. Similarly, 97, 92, and 27 percent of the improvements for CO, SO_2, and NO_x respectively, occurred prior to 1970. The relatively smaller effect on NO_x was due to the fact that switching from wood and coal to oil and gas decreases NO_x less than it does SO_2 or PM-10 and that many methods to burn fuel efficiently result in higher temperatures during combustion, which increases NO_x formation.

Using the preceding methodology, I also estimate VOC concentrations in a "nonsmoking" home due to combustion to have declined 85 percent from 1940 to 1990. But this improvement may have been offset by increases in indoor emissions of solvents and other volatile substances stored or used in the home. Also, increased energy conservation measures instituted in response to the 1970s' oil

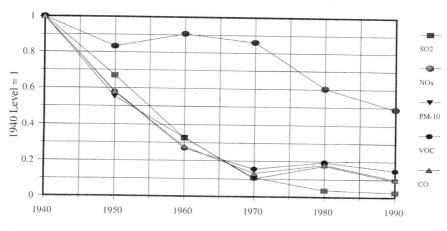

Fig. 2.4   Indoor Air Quality, 1940–1990

Note: Residential emissions per occupied housing unit were used as a proxy for indoor air quality.
Sources: USBOC (1975, 1992); OAQPS (1995a).

shocks, by reducing air exchange rates between indoors and outdoors, may have aggravated indoor air pollution and contributed to the relatively large increase in the prevalence of deaths due to asthma since the mid-to-late 1970s (Goklany 1999).

CRITICAL MILESTONES AND TRANSITIONS IN THE EVOLUTION OF AIR QUALITY TRENDS

Table 2.1 summarizes various milestones for the various indicators for each traditional pollutant. It identifies the period of perception [p(P)] and when national control [t(N)] was imposed for each major air pollutant. Based on figures 2.2A through 2.4, table 2.1 lists for each pollutant the year when each national indicator—indoor air quality, outdoor (ambient) air quality, emissions, and emissions/GNP—peaked (or went through its period of transition).

Several features emerge from table 2.1. First, for each pollutant, the period of transition depends on the precise indicator or leading indicator, for example, whether it is indoor or outdoor air quality, emissions, or E/GNP.

Second, air quality had begun to improve substantially before federal government control, particularly for the pollutants associated with excess mortality during the air pollution episodes of the 1940s, 1950s, and 1960s (i.e., TSP and SO$_2$) and in the areas where the levels of these pollutants were the highest. In addition, oxidant air quality had begun to improve in the Los Angeles area, the

Indur M. Goklany

Table 2.1 National Milestones and Transitions for Various Pollutants and Indicators

Substance	Perceived to Be a Pollutant [p(P)]	First Federally Regulated [t(N)]	Worst Year(s) or Period of Transition[a]		
			Outdoor Air Quality	Emissions	Emissions/GNP[b]
PM	Before 1900	1971[c]	Before 1957	1950[d]	1940s or earlier
SO_2	Around 1950	1971[c]	Early to mid-1960s	1973	1920s
CO	Around late 1950s	1967[e]	Mid- to late 1960s	1970–71	1940s or earlier
VOC/O_3	1950s to early 1970s[f]	1967[e]	Mid- to late 1970s	1967	1930s
NO_x	1950s to early 1970s[f]	1971[c]	1978–79	1978	1930s

[a]The worst years of indoor air quality were before 1940.

[b]The peak in this leading indicator shows the latest time by which "cleanup" had begun.

[c]The Clean Air Act of 1970 was signed on the last day of 1970, but most federal regulations went into effect later.

[d]For PM-10.

[e]Model year 1968 for automobiles.

[f]Early 1950s for California. Many areas elsewhere were unaware of their oxidant problem, which is caused by reactions of VOC and NO_x in sunlight, until the early 1970s.

Sources: Goklany (1997, 1998b, 1999).

area with the nation's worst smog problem, before nationalization had any effect in California.

Third, based on peaks in E/GNP, "cleanup" for each pollutant had started decades before nationalization. In fact, as noted, for some pollutants, "cleanup" commenced prior to the general perception of a substance as a pollutant [p(P)]: PM-10 was perceived as a pollutant nationally before 1900, SO_2 around 1950, and CO in the late 1950s. However, although VOC/O_3 and NO_x were first perceived as pollutants in California in the 1950s and the 1960s, they were not recognized as major pollutants nationally until the 1970s (Goklany 1998d, 1999).

Finally, for some pollutants, air quality improved despite emission increases, for example, SO_2 and CO in the late 1960s. On the other hand, improvements in O_3 air quality preceded VOC emission reductions.

In summary, improvements in the indicators of air quality for pollutants known (or perceived) to cause the largest public health impact came before those for the "lesser" pollutants; in indoor air quality before outdoor air quality; in outdoor air quality before total emissions (for primary pollutants); and for primary pollutants before secondary pollutants.

DECIPHERING THE TRENDS—THE ENVIRONMENTAL TRANSITION

An inexorable logic underlies table 2.1 and the order in which the various peaks occurred for each pollutant and indicator (Goklany 1995b, 1997, 1998a, 1998b, 1998d). This can be explained by a framework represented as a stylized graph in figure 2.5. This framework is based on the hypothesis that society is on a continual quest to improve its quality of life, which is determined by numerous social, economic, and environmental factors. The weight given to each determinant is constantly varying, depending on society's precise circumstances and perceptions (Goklany 1998c). In the early stages of economic and technological developments, which go hand in hand, a society attempts to improve its overall quality of life by placing a higher priority on increasing affluence than on other determinants, even if that means tolerating some environmental degradation, because greater affluence provides the means for obtaining basic needs and amenities (e.g., food, shelter, water, and electricity) and for reducing the most significant risks to public health and safety (e.g., malnutrition, infectious and parasitic diseases, and child and maternal mortality) (Goklany 1995a). As society gets wealthier, progress is made on these priorities, but environmental degradation increases. Eventually, environmental problems move up to a higher priority on society's list of unmet needs; that is, environmental quality becomes a more important determinant of the quality of life. Generally, a society will enshrine its priorities into laws and regulations unless a priority is self-executing (or perhaps even then, for the sake

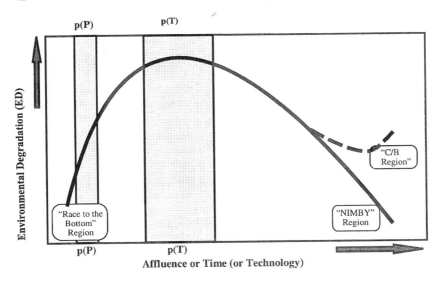

Fig. 2.5 The Environmental Transition

Notes: p(P) = period of perception; p(T) = period of transition; in the NIMBY (not-in-my-backyard) Region, benefits far exceed costs borne by beneficiaries; in the C/B Region, costs and benefits have to be more carefully balanced.
Source: Goklany (1998d).

of symbolism—and which politician can resist taking credit for fortunate outcomes, even if they are inevitable?).

Moreover, the wealthier the society, the more it can afford to research and to develop new and improved technologies. Perhaps more important, greater wealth increases the ability to purchase and to operate such technologies, particularly if their initial costs are high, as they almost invariably are for add-on, or "end-of-pipe," controls and many process changes. In turn, cleaner technologies become more affordable, and that leads to greater compliance and, it can be argued, to more stringent regulation. Thus, not only do technological change and affluence reinforce each other, they also bolster a more stringent regulatory regime. Consequently, society goes through a period of transition [p(T)] during which it undergoes an environmental transition. Environmental degradation peaks, and, following that, additional economic and technological development, instead of worsening environmental quality, actually improves it.

Because society became progressively wealthier and technologically more advanced during the twentieth century, an environmental transition manifests itself as a peak in a post-p(P) temporal trend line for environmental degradation.

Figure 2.5 shows a simplified representation of each of the figures 2.2A through 2.4 subsequent to p(P). In some instances, for example indoor air quality (figure 2.4) and ambient air quality (figure 2.2A) for TSP, there are no apparent peaks corresponding to any environmental transitions, but this is because for these cases the national trend data are available only for posttransition periods. Once past the environmental transition, depending on the precise set of circumstances surrounding the costs of action and inaction environmental degradation may continue to reduce, may stay more or less constant, or, if degradation has been sufficiently reduced, may even turn up slightly.

Each environmental transition is strengthened by the path taken by society in its economic development. Economic development and technological change co-evolve to transform the structure of the economy. First, technological change is essential for the transformation of an agrarian society to an industrial society. Without such change, labor would not be freed up from the farm, nor would there be factories to absorb the surplus labor. During this phase, E/GNP increases. Then, technological change aids the creation of a postindustrial knowledge- and service-based economy. In this phase, E/GNP decreases because economic growth is driven by relatively low-polluting enterprises. The rise and fall of E/GNP is further amplified because, as the polluting sectors' contribution to national employment and GNP waxes and wanes, so does its economic and demographic influence—and its political power. In a democratic society, the decline of such power eventually results in increasingly tougher environmental policies in a postindustrial era. Thus, it is hardly surprising that we see today—and will continue to see in the future—increasingly more stringent regulations for industries and sectors such as mining, timber, and agriculture, as their economic and demographic power diminishes (Goklany 1997).

Because of the combination of all the preceding factors, the timing of an environmental transition for any pollutant should depend on the general level of affluence, on the state of the technology, on pollutant effects relative to other societal risks, and on affordability of control or mitigation measures. But these factors are not independent: affluence helps create technology, and vice versa; knowledge of a pollutant's effects is itself a product of technology; and affordability depends on affluence and technology. In short, an environmental transition should ultimately be determined by affluence and technology.

Table 2.1 is, indeed, consistent with the environmental transition hypothesis. With greater prosperity and the advent of new technologies in the early decades of the twentieth century, the worst problems—and the easiest to address—were dealt with first. Households voluntarily cleaned up their personal environment, the indoors, of the most obvious problems—smoke and, to some extent, CO— before anything else. They started switching away from wood and coal to gas, oil, and, occasionally, electricity for cooking and home heating. These changes also led to reduced outdoor pollution in their immediate neighborhoods. In addition, industries and commercial establishments invested in new technologies and practices to improve efficiencies of boilers and other fuel-burning equipment to reduce smoke, partly because smoke was a symptom of poor efficiency and a sign of needlessly higher fuel bills and partly because their investment testified to their civic conscience. Moreover, because SO_2 and VOC are associated with solid fuel combustion, the investment also reduced SO_2 and VOC indoors and helped initiate the long-term declines in their E/GNP (figures 2.3A, 2.3B, and 2.4), although neither SO_2 nor VOC was generally perceived as being particularly harmful at that time (table 2.1).

Next, attention turned to outdoor air. Once again, the first target was smoke because it was the most obvious and an acknowledged pollutant. New technologies and prosperity helped move the industrial and commercial fuel mix from coal and wood toward oil and gas and generally helped increase fuel efficiencies across all economic sectors. As a result, soon after World War II, if not earlier, most urban areas had gone through their environmental transitions for smoke and PM (table 2.1).

With greater prosperity, better health, and reduced mortality, the risks of other outdoor air pollutants became easier to infer or to detect. In the years following World War II, deadly air pollution episodes occurred on both sides of the Atlantic, which were ascribed to PM, to SO_2, or to both. Thus, transitions for outdoor PM and SO_2 air quality came next, followed in time by CO and O_3. That the transition for NO_x came last is fitting for a pollutant that was never ranked very high in terms of adverse effects at measured ambient levels and that was also the most expensive to control—in large part because many technologies for improving fuel efficiency and for reducing smoke, unburnt carbon in ash (both constituents of particulate matter), and CO inadvertently increased NO_x emissions.

WAS NATIONALIZATION NECESSARY TO IMPROVE AIR QUALITY?

One of the justifications for nationalization is that it was necessary to improve the nation's air quality because "states had failed to act" and they "could not be trusted to adopt adequate environmental controls" because of interstate competition for business (Dwyer 1995, 1191, 1193 n32, n37; see also, Stewart 1977, 1197); hence, "Congress imposed national regulations to control pollution only after its efforts to prod states to act had failed" (Percival 1995, 1160–61).

In fact, whether or not states may have acted, the empirical data in table 2.1 and figures 2.2A through 2.2E show there was remarkable progress in improving air quality prior to nationalization becoming effective. This is true for those pollutants that were generally known or perceived at that time to be the sources of public health problems, and it was particularly true in those areas where the pollutants were most regarded as problems by policy makers and the general public. Moreover, the slopes of the trends for the various indicators do not show more rapid declines in emissions or in improvements in air quality once nationalization became effective (figures 2.2A through 2.4), except for motor vehicle emissions outside California. And, in fact, the federal motor vehicle emission control program was, itself, derived from a state (California) program, and it was enacted not because states were doing too little, but because auto companies and Congress feared some might do too much by enacting separate and inconsistent laws.

An alternative explanation for the empirical data is that the improvements in air quality came despite state inaction and badly written and poorly enforced laws. Although this is a legitimate point of view, it, too, does not provide a rationale for nationalization.

Ironically, although nationalization was ostensibly imposed because in the three years between the 1967 Air Quality Act and the 1970 Clean Air Act Amendments, state and local agencies had not moved fast enough to solve their air quality problems, today, over three decades later, numerous areas are still not meeting federal air quality standards. As of June 1998, despite an overall relaxation of the original 1971 oxidant standard (which today targets only one of several species of oxidants addressed originally, namely, O_3), fifty-seven areas in the nation were designated "nonattainment areas" for O_3. In addition, twenty-eight areas were nonattainment for the CO NAAQS; thirty-four for SO_2; and one for NO_2. Furthermore, seventy-seven areas were designated nonattainment for PM-10, which "replaced" the TSP standard (EPA 1998). However, the two standards are not strictly comparable.

If the success of the 1970 nationalization is judged by the same criterion that many of its proponents applied to state and local controls and to the Air Quality Act of 1967, then nationalization must also be judged to be a failure. And although meeting unrealistic timetables for attainment was, and remains, a flawed criterion for judging success (or failure), it does undercut one of the major arguments advanced for nationalization.

A RACE TO THE BOTTOM, OR TO THE TOP?

The notion that states participate in a race to the bottom, relaxing air pollution requirements and reducing net state welfare, is critical to any rationale for federalizing environmental control. A corollary to the race-to-the-bottom hypothesis is that before nationalization, there should have been no improvements in air quality anywhere (except by accident or happy economic circumstance). But, in fact, as discussed earlier, there were broad improvements in air quality for several pollutants prior to nationalization, and the race, if any, seems to be in the other direction.

The data presented in this chapter are inconsistent with a race to the bottom on several counts. *First*, TSP and SO$_2$ ambient air quality had gone through environmental transitions nationally, and CO had either gone through or was on the verge of its own transition by the time the federal government began regulating those specific pollutants (table 2.1; figures 2.2A, 2.2B, and 2.2C). Moreover, oxidants/O$_3$ had gone through a transition in California, an area where they were widely recognized to be a problem, before nationalization had any real impact in that state. Outside California, few areas made any effort to reduce oxidants, not because they were racing to the bottom, but because they were in no rush to solve problems they did not know they had. The inability to construct a national composite for ozone or oxidant air quality prior to the early 1970s because of insufficient monitor coverage is perhaps the best proof of that.

Second, in a trend that is inconsistent with any race to relax, county and state air programs grew significantly during the 1960s. Between 1960 and 1970, the number of county programs increased from seventeen to eighty-one, and state programs increased from eight to fifty (Stern 1982). Even if these programs were established as sops to the public—and figures 2.2 (A–E) and 2.3 (A–D) suggest they were not—their very presence would, at the very least, send the wrong signal to industry about the desire to attract industry and would be at odds with the rationale for a race to the bottom.

Third, opacity and process weight emission standards were progressively tightened in numerous jurisdictions nationwide prior to the 1970 Clean Air Amendments, in effect, bidding standards up, rather than down, the very antithesis of either a race to the bottom or a race to relax. In fact, a 1970 report provided to Congress by the EPA's forerunner, the National Air Pollution Control Administration, suggested that one reason for the limited acceptance of the American Society of Mechanical Engineers' 1966 model air pollution control regulations for fuel-burning equipment may have been because its "control requirements . . . are generally lenient compared to other modern regulations"; the report also suggested that "[m]any new industrial plants install equipment for purposes of eliminating all visible plumes, even if not required to do so" because that constituted good public relations and reduced complaints (Stumph and Duprey 1970).

Fourth, the federal preemption of motor vehicle emission standards outside of California indicates that the automobile industry and Congress were concerned not about a race to the bottom or a race to relax but about a movement toward greater control. And partly to contain such movement, uniform standards were imposed to avoid a hodgepodge of requirements among the non-California states.

During the industrial era, when jobs and prosperity were better correlated with air pollution, the quest for a better quality of life may have seemed like a race to the bottom of environmental quality; but in today's postindustrial era, prosperity is often inversely correlated with pollution. Nowadays, the service sectors account for three out of every four nonfarm jobs. Accordingly, many jurisdictions maximize jobs by catering to the needs of the service sectors (and their employees) while actively discouraging polluting industries altogether. For instance, Florida has banned oil drilling off its Gulf coast to protect tourism and commercial fishing (*Greenwire* 1995, 1997). In effect, Florida is maximizing its quality of life by adopting a "not-in-my-backyard" (NIMBY) stance.

THE TRANSITION FROM A RACE TO THE BOTTOM TO NIMBY

The apparent existence of both the race to the bottom and the NIMBY phenomena can be explained by an affluence- and technology-driven environmental transition caused by a "race to the top of the quality of life" (figure 2.5). During the early phases of economic and technological development (or when the net costs of controlling that pollutant are perceived to be excessive), the "race to the top of the quality of life" may superficially resemble a "race to relax" or a race to the bottom of environmental standards. But once a society (or group) gets past the transition and matters improve, the race to the top of the quality of life may drive the environmental degradation trajectory in one of several different directions.

If the benefits of control for the society (or the group) are substantially less than its costs, or if the costs are shifted to others while benefits are retained, environmental degradation (ED) will be driven down; that is, society will move toward greater cleanup (as indicated by the solid posttransition curve in figure 2.5). In effect, the race to the top of the quality of life would look like a race to the top of environmental quality, and it would masquerade as a NIMBY situation. Thus, the apparent race to the bottom and the NIMBY effect are, in fact, two aspects of the same phenomenon, but the former occurs prior to, whereas the latter occurs after, an affluence- and technology-driven environmental transition, and only if perceived benefits far exceed perceived costs.

However, if the perceived social and economic costs are in the same ballpark as the perceived benefits (which may occur if costs cannot be shifted to someone else), then the precise trajectory—whether it continues downward but not as steeply as in the NIMBY case, goes up, or stays more or less constant—will depend on a more careful balancing of the costs and the benefits. The dashed line in figure 2.5 depicts a case in which perceived benefits no longer exceed perceived costs, and, therefore, ED swings upward. I denote this region on the ED versus affluence space as the "CB region." ("CB" is a handy mnemonic for "careful balancing of costs and benefits.") Such an upswing in ED could occur if, for example, based on new information or changes in societal values and attitudes, society concludes that past control efforts, for whatever reason, went too far or were unnecessary; if limits of clean technologies have been reached for the affected activity, there are no substitutes for the activity, and additional activity would necessarily end up in greater impacts; or, for whatever reason, if society perceives that scarce financial and human resources should be allocated to other problems (Goklany 1995b, 371 n4).

Finally, the timing of a transition depends on the specific pollutant (or indicator) and the relative social, economic, and environmental costs and benefits of addressing that pollutant (or indicator). Accordingly, it is possible for a society, a group, or an individual to be simultaneously to the left of the environmental transition for one pollutant but to the right for another. Hence, it is quite rational to oppose, say, carbon dioxide controls on one hand while supporting stricter controls on carbon monoxide on the other. Also it would not be unusual to support VOC controls at refineries but to oppose mandatory inspection and maintenance of one's own vehicle.

CONCLUSION: THE ROLE OF NATIONALIZATION IN IMPROVING AMERICA'S AIR QUALITY

Figures 2.2A through 2.4 show that the nation's air is far cleaner today than it has been in several decades, despite the fact that population, consumption, and economic output—according to many environmentalists, the culprits fundamentally responsible for environmental degradation—have never been higher. The air is cleaner because, with the various environmental transitions, prosperity and technology were transformed from being problems responsible for air pollution to being solutions responsible for its cleanup.

Empirical data showing that the nation had, in the aggregate, gone through its environmental transitions for smoke, TSP, SO_2 air quality, and stationary source CO emissions before nationalization directly contradicts any race-to-the-bottom rationale for nationalization, as does the fact that oxidant air quality had begun to improve in California. In fact, that rationale is intrinsically flawed: if there is any race, it is not to the bottom of environmental quality but to the top of the quality of life. Environmental transitions are logical outcomes of a race to the top of the quality of life. During the early phases of economic development, such a race may superficially resemble a race to the bottom for environmental quality; but in the later phases, the race to the top of the quality of life will increasingly favor environmental quality and, if benefits substantially outweigh costs, could lead to a NIMBY phenomenon.

By the time air pollution control was nationalized in 1970, air quality had improved substantially, particularly in the areas with the worst problems and for the pollutants perceived to be responsible for most of the public health risk. Without nationalization, air quality would probably have continued to improve, but perhaps not as rapidly in some areas. Given these underlying trends, the absence of any real race to the bottom, and the fact that democratic societies—no less than private individuals—hope to maximize the quality of life, one should expect that there would have been continued improvements in air quality even in the absence of nationalization.

Probably the most positive feature of nationalization was the establishment of the NAAQS, which provided a yardstick for people to gauge whether their air quality is "healthful." Just as the mere existence of the Toxics Release Inventory (OAQPS 1995c, ch. 8) has helped reduce the amounts of those emissions (yet another refutation of the race-to-the-bottom rationale), the very existence of NAAQS created pressures to improve air quality.

On the whole, federal intervention also was effective in reducing motor vehicle emissions outside California. Uniform requirements enabled manufacturers to lower the costs of emissions controls by enabling them to design to one rather than forty-nine (non-California) standards and to spread their fixed costs over larger numbers of vehicles. And these mobile source emissions were important to control in order to reduce ozone and carbon monoxide levels. In addition, motor vehicle emission controls were instrumental in bringing about dramatic improvements in lead air quality, albeit as much by chance as by design. Nationalization of new source requirements (including New Source Performance Standards and PSD requirements) also helped ensure that gains from existing source controls would not be lost. However, the downside of these technology-forcing programs was that they were applied whether or not automobile owners and sources were in nonattainment areas—costs were borne by individuals and firms whether or not it was (and is) necessary. Moreover, as experience with emissions trading schemes have shown, the command-and-control regulations that drove these additional improvements exacted a higher price than necessary (McLean 1997), and the total current risk to public health would have been lower had there been a conscious effort to maximize risk reduction for the total costs incurred by society. In fact, some of the recent high-cost, low-benefit expenditures on air pollution control could well have purchased greater improvements in public health and welfare if they had been diverted elsewhere. This is true even within the realm of air pollution control itself (Goklany 1992). Studies suggest, for example, that the cost-benefit ratio for controlling ozone is relatively low, whereas that of controlling fine PM is much higher (Krupnick and Portney 1991). Thus, society would be better off if the former was deemphasized, with at least some of the resulting savings applied to the latter.

In light of the progress made in the air and the fact that the easy as well as several tough reductions have already been made, further improvements in air quality may not be sustainable if they compromise the broader quality of life. To help ensure that the two go hand in hand, emissions trading should be expanded to allow trades between old and new sources, and the pollutant-by-pollutant approach should be replaced by one that focuses on reducing overall risks to public health and welfare at local and regional levels.

Control of interstate pollution should be negotiated between affected states, with the downwind states being free to accept, in lieu of additional control of specific air pollutants, other reductions in risk to public health and welfare funded by the upwind (polluting) states if the downwind states deem that would provide greater benefits to their populations. Such risk reduction should not be limited to efforts to reduce risks just from air pollution or, for that matter, other pollution. They could include, for instance, sponsorship and funding of wider screening for cancer, heart disease or high blood pressure, vaccinations, or other routine-but-underutilized health care procedures. For intrastate pollution, the federal government should step back from its role as the micromanager of air pollution control and, instead, should enter into a more equal partnership with the states, as suggested by Macey and Butler (2000) in chapter 7 of this volume.

Under the federalist approach outlined in this chapter, the federal government would establish NAAQS as a set of idealized goals, and states would determine their own attainment schedules and control measures for pollutants produced within and affecting their own jurisdictions.

Given where the nation and states currently are in their environmental transitions for the traditional air pollutants (i.e., to the right of their peaks), devolution is unlikely to lead to a rollback of the past gains in air quality. If states compromise the quality of their citizens' lives by indulging in a race-to-the-bottom today, the powers that be, as is likely in a democracy, will hear from them.

Decisions regarding attainment schedules, control requirements, and whether (and what) to accept as "risk-risk" trade-offs necessarily depend on numerous location-specific factors, such as the magnitude and the mix of emission sources, meteorology, topography, population density, income, education, access to health care, and other socioeconomic factors. The geographical variation in these factors, not to mention community values and sensibilities, essentially precludes any one-size-fits-all approach from being close to optimizing the quality of life for society as a whole.

Because many of the determinants of the quality of life are unquantifiable and because states will be the major winners or losers from their own choices and actions (or inaction), such optimization should be left to each state's political process. To echo Winston Churchill, it may, like democracy, be the worst method—until you consider all the others.

NOTES

Dr. Goklany's contribution to this book reflects his personal views rather than those of any organization with which he has associated, past or present.

1. For a more exhaustive review of this topic, see Goklany (1999).

2. Emissions data were obtained from Sharon Nizich (OAQPS 1995a); economic data were obtained from USBOC (1975, 1996).

3. See Goklany (1995b, 1996) for an expanded discussion.

4. Emissions data were obtained from Sharon Nizich (OAQPS 1995a); economic data were obtained from USBOC (1975, 1996).

REFERENCES

Cohoe, B. A. 1914. The Relationship of Atmospheric Pollution to Health. In *Papers on the Influence of Smoke on Health,* ed. Oskar Klotz and William C. White. *Smoke Investigation Bulletin No. 9,* Mellon Institute of Industrial Research and School of Specific Industries. Pittsburgh, PA: University of Pittsburgh, 7–53.

Council on Environmental Quality (CEQ). 1970–1991. *Environmental Quality.* Washington, DC: CEQ.

Davidson, Cliff I. 1979. Air Pollution in Pittsburgh: A Historical Perspective. *Journal of the Air Pollution Control Association* 29: 1035–41.

Dwyer, John P. 1995. The Practice of Federalism under the Clean Air Act. *Maryland Law Review* 54: 1183–225.

Environmental Protection Agency (EPA). 1998. *USA Air Quality Nonattainment Areas.* [cited June 28, 1998]. Available from: http://www.epa.gov/airs/noattn.html.

Goklany, Indur M. 1992. Rationing Health Care While Writing Blank Checks for Environmental Health Hazards. *Regulation* 15(Summer): 14–15.

———. 1995a. Strategies to Enhance Adaptability: Technological Change, Sustainable Growth and Free Trade. *Climatic Change* 30: 427–49.

———. 1995b. Richer Is Cleaner: Long-Term Trends in Global Air Quality. In *The True State of the Planet,* ed. Ronald Bailey. New York: Free Press.

———. 1996. Factors Affecting Environmental Impacts: The Effects of Technology on Long-Term Trends in Cropland, Air Pollution, and Water-Related Diseases. *Ambio* 25: 497–503.

———. 1997. The Federal Role in Improving Environmental Quality in the United States: Evidence from Long-Term Trends in Air Pollution. Paper presented at the American Society of Environmental History Conference on Government, Science, and the Environment, Baltimore, MD, March 6–9.

———. 1998a. Did Federalization Halt a Race to the Bottom for Air Quality? *EM (Environmental Manager)* (June): 12–18.

———. 1998b. Do We Need the Federal Government to Improve Air Quality? *Policy Study* 150 (December). St. Louis, MO: Center for the Study of American Business, Washington University.

———. 1998c. Saving Habitat and Conserving Biodiversity on a Crowded Planet. *BioScience* 48(11): 941–53.

———. 1998d. The Environmental Transition to Air Quality. *Regulation* 21(4): 36–46.

———. 1999. *Clearing the Air: The Real Story of the War on Air Pollution.* Washington, DC: Cato Institute, forthcoming.

Greenwire. 1995. State Reports—Florida: State Seeks Complete Ban on Gulf Drilling. February 3. Available from: http://www.cloakroom.com by subscription.

————. 1997. Across the Nation—Gov Signs Bill to Impede Oil Drilling. May 30. Available from http://www.cloakroom.com by subscription.

Krupnick, Alan J., and Paul R. Portney. 1991. Controlling Urban Air Pollution: A Benefit-Cost Assessment. *Science* 252: 522–28.

Ludwig, John H., George B. Morgan, and Thomas B. McMullen. 1970. Trends in Urban Air Quality. *EOS* 51: 468–75.

Macey, Jonathan R., and Henry N. Butler. 2000. Federalism and the Environment, this volume.

McLean, Brian. 1997. *Fifth Annual SO₂ Allowance Auctions.* [cited March 26 1997]. Available from: http://www.epa.gov/acidrain/auctions/auc97tlk.html.

Office of Air and Radiation. 1989. *Report to Congress on Indoor Air Quality.* Vol. 2, *Assessment and Control of Air Pollution.* EPA-400/1-89/001C. Washington, DC: EPA.

Office of Air Programs. 1972. *Air Quality Data for 1968 from the National Air Surveillance Networks and Contributing State and Local Networks.* Research Triangle Park, NC: EPA.

Office of Air Quality Planning and Standards (OAQPS). 1973a. *Monitoring and Air Quality Trends Report, 1972.* EPA-450/1-73-004. Research Triangle Park, NC: EPA.

————. 1973b. *The National Air Monitoring Program: Air Quality and Emissions Trends Annual Report.* Vol. 1. EPA-450/1-73-001-a. Research Triangle Park, NC: EPA.

————. 1985. *National Air Quality and Emissions Trends Report, 1983.* EPA-450/4-84-029. Research Triangle Park, NC: EPA.

————. 1991. *National Air Quality and Emissions Trends Report, 1990.* EPA-450/4-91-023. Research Triangle Park, NC: EPA.

————. 1995a. Data Underpinning *National Air Pollutant Emission Trends, 1900-1994.* EPA- 450/R-93-032. Research Triangle Park, NC: EPA.

————. 1995b. *National Air Quality and Emissions Trends Report, 1994—Data Appendix.* EPA- 454/R-95-014. Research Triangle Park, NC: EPA.

————. 1995c. *National Air Pollutant Emissions Trends, 1900-1994.* EPA-454/R-95-011. Research Triangle Park, NC: EPA.

————. 1998. *National Air Quality and Emissions Trends Report, 1996.* EPA-454/R-97-013. Research Triangle Park, NC: EPA.

Percival, Robert V. 1995. Environmental Federalism: Historical Roots and Contemporary Models. *Maryland Law Review* 54: 1141–82.

Revesz, Richard L. 1992. Rehabilitating Interstate Competition: Rethinking the "Race to the Bottom" Rationale for Federal Environmental Regulation. *New York University Law Review* 67: 1210–54.

Stern, Arthur C. 1982. History of Air Pollution Legislation in the United States. *Journal of the Air Pollution Control Association* 32: 44–61.

Stewart, Richard B. 1977. Pyramids of Sacrifice? Problems of Federalism in Mandating State Implementation of National Environmental Policy. *Yale Law Journal* 86: 1196–272.

Stumph, Terry L., and Robert L. Duprey. 1970. Trends in Air Pollution Control Regulations. In *Legislative History of the Clean Air Amendments of 1970.* Washington, DC: U.S. Government Printing Office, 1105–25.

U.S. Bureau of the Census (USBOC). 1975. *Historical Statistics of the United States, Colonial Times to 1970.* Washington, DC: Department of Commerce.

———. 1981. *Statistical Abstract.* Washington, DC: Department of Commerce.

———. 1988. *Statistical Abstract.* Washington, DC: Department of Commerce.

———. 1992. *Statistical Abstract.* Washington, DC: Department of Commerce.

———. 1995. *Statistical Abstract.* Washington, DC: Department of Commerce.

———. 1996. *Statistical Abstract.* Washington, DC: Department of Commerce.

3

Burning Rivers, Common Law, and Institutional Choice for Water Quality

Roger E. Meiners, Stacie Thomas, and Bruce Yandle

Visitors to a U.S. Environmental Protection Agency (EPA) web site (www.epa.gov) in 1998 saw an invitation to community groups to "get connected" with their local watershed. Calling attention to the twenty-fifth anniversary of the 1972 Clean Water Act, the invitation told of President Clinton's American Heritage Rivers Initiative, a new federal effort to bring the firepower of federal programs to bear on ten designated rivers. The web site visitor also learned how efforts by local citizens could make a difference in improving water quality.

Probably seen by many as quaint at best and innocuous at worst, the invitation's message that communities are equipped to deal with local water quality problems is as old as recorded history, and certainly as old as common law. But the notion that the EPA would attempt to rebuild community institutions laid waste by the 1972 Clean Water Act is clearly paradoxical.

If community action, supported by property rights and a rule of law, can deal adequately with water pollution problems, one wonders about federal statutes that nullified programs invented by communities for improving water quality and that weakened the enforcement of common law rules and private property rights. With regard to institutions for managing water quality, why have any federal statutes at all? Why not choose common law and property rights and allow effective community action to evolve? Or is it inevitable that evolutionary forces produce the institutions now in existance?

These questions imply an all-or-nothing decision—either federal statutes or community action—but they also suggest that evolutionary forces deliver a rich institutional mixture. People encounter a portfolio of institutional choices when addressing environmental management problems through collective decision making. We believe the choices are rich, but seldom all-or-nothing. Some choices limit and distort the portfolio for future choices, which is to say that some choices are more costly to reverse than others are.

The relevant portfolio, which evolves continuously, contains custom and tradition, common law, local ordinances, regional compacts, and state and federal statutes and regulations. Incremental choices, when made, involve special interest struggles, competition among purveyors of institutions, and consideration of relevant costs. The choices reflect institutional demand and supply. Which costs are deemed relevant depends on who makes choices and how choices are made. Constitutional constraints affect the competitive positions of some institutions. When an all-encompassing government regulates smaller, subsidiary units such as communities and states, the smaller units lose institutional authority. Investments—personal, political, and proprietary—are based on the resulting institutional structure. Decisions to move to the national level when structuring institutional controls are not easily reversed.

Much has been written about the demand for regulation and about efforts by competing interest groups to affect the legislative process, but less attention has been devoted to responses from the supply side of the market for institutions (Stigler 1971; Peltzman 1976; Posner 1974; McChesney 1991). Although not focusing so much on institutional supply, per se, Rubin (1977, 1982) and Priest (1977) examined pertinent questions regarding the efficiency of common law. Along a related line of inquiry, Ellickson (1991), Benson (1990), and Morriss (1998) dealt extensively with the private production of law. This research reminds us that choices are somehow made among competing systems of law. But only Rubin (1982) attended to forces that might explain why one institutional supplier (statute law) might gain market share in competition with another (common law). Indeed, he used pollution control as an example in his discussion. As Rubin implied, if we are to understand the past and the potential roles for common law environmentalism, we must view common law as a part of a rich mix of institutions that evolve to define and to protect environmental rights (Meiners and Yandle 1998).

Focusing on the array of institutions that affect water quality causes one to recognize that the choices seldom involve zero/one decisions. Instead, the decisions have to do with blending institutions to generate particular outcomes. Consider an analogy. The protection of automobile assets involves a combination of activities that includes the private production of property rights protection—locks, burglar alarms, and garages—as well as the purchase of private and public police protection. There is also a bundle of legal institutions that include common law, state and federal statutes, and even agreements among countries for the extradition of alleged thieves (Lipford and Yandle 1997). Surely, economists would argue that the resulting mixture is somehow related to relative costs and that decisions regarding the control of auto theft have to do with marginal adjustments that are made across the various forms of property rights protection. Decisions about auto protection are not made on an all-or-nothing basis. If we could examine a cross section of auto protection institutions at a moment in time we would see multiple layers of different thickness. If private protection is relatively cheap across some range of enforcement, that layer will be thicker than the layer representing private and public police activities. When relative costs change, levels of institutional activity become modified. At the same time, we would expect to observe the effects of statutes that distort or even nullify the use of some institutions for protecting property rights. For example, statutes requiring the purchase of insurance, limiting tort claims, or modifying legal procedures affect the relative cost of and access to alternative institutions.

This chapter explores the blending of evolving institutions that affect environmental quality and focuses on institutional choices for the delivery of water quality. Doing this requires us first to present an institutional framework and to describe more carefully the conceptual model that underlies our work. Then, we address some episodes in the development of U.S. water quality regulation by considering Cleveland's infamous Cuyahoga River, remembered for having been so polluted that it burned. We then describe some larger episodes in the development of the legal institutions that affect U.S. water quality and end our chapter with thoughts on evolving water quality institutions. In all this, we describe special interest struggles and ways in which shifts in the supply curves of competing institutions can explain the modification of institutional arrangements for protecting rights to water quality.

COMPETING INSTITUTIONS AND WATER QUALITY RIGHTS

Both common sense and strong empirical evidence show that people across time and space find ways to provide life-sustaining water quality. In a recent study of forty-one countries and including a wide range of income levels, Yandle and Xiang (1998) estimated the relationship between levels of dissolved oxygen in the most contaminated river for each country and levels of per capita gross domestic product (GDP). The estimate showed a sagging level of water quality as income rose from very low levels until per capita GDP reached approximately $3,000. From that income level forward, water quality improved. Interestingly enough, the sag in water quality was not large, although the differences in this basic measure of water quality across the forty-one-country sample became greater with higher incomes. Somehow, people in the poorest countries found ways to protect the rights to water quality.

A measure of property-rights protection was also included in the estimating procedure; it showed significant improvements in water quality for countries with greater property-rights certainty. Property-rights protection matters, but the blend of institutions that deliver this protection varies significantly across countries.

Institutional Supply Curves

Imagine a family of water-quality-rights supply curves, with each curve offered by a hypothetical institutional provider. Each supply curve represents a different institutional arrangement for providing water quality rights. Applying a casual interpretation of history, we can imagine the first supply curve as representing custom, tradition, and informal community action. In close-knit communities, informal arrangements for managing the use and the abuse of wells, rivers, and streams can deliver low-cost water quality.

The next supply curve might be a more formal body of law, such as common law, that protects individual rightholders from unwanted harm. Relying on custom and tradition can be costly as communities become more diverse and more transient. The more formal body of rules and procedures offered by common law can provide a lower cost means for assuring protection of water quality rights.

A third supply curve could represent institutions and codes offered by local governments and the state. Here are impersonal rules and regulations that emerge from statutes. If extending the reach of common law across political boundaries is costly or if special interest groups determine regulation to be advantageous, then statutes and regulations may be forthcoming.

The fourth, and final, supply curve offers institutions provided by the national government. If dealing with a diverse set of state and local regulations becomes costly and if special interest groups see an advantage in having national rules, this final supply curve may come to dominate.

The four supply curves can be summed horizontally to provide an aggregate supply for the delivery of water quality rights. Then, picking a price (cost) allows us to identify the community market share maintained by each supplier. We can easily picture a community's demand curve for water quality rights, which cuts the aggregate supply curve at a point and then defines the amount of water quality management provided by each institutional supplier.

Continuing with the conceptual model allows us to consider reallocations that may occur across the various vendors for groups within a given population. As the population becomes more heterogeneous, custom and tradition become less effective in managing water quality; its relative attractiveness falls. As particular special interest groups become more dominant, rules provided through the political process can become less costly to the dominant group than those provided by common law. If information concerning the source or the damaging effects of pollution is scarce, common law judges may find it difficult to adjudicate water quality controversies. Command-and-control regulation may become relatively cheap. If monitoring costs fall, common law can recover a larger share of the market for water quality rights. Through time, these and other forces lead to more or less dominance for particular water-quality-rights institutions.

Property Rights and Institutional Supply

Following this model, we can consider stages of property-rights development associated with water quality management. Custom and tradition usually imply community ownership of rights. Members of the tribe, clan, or community are allowed to consume water quality. Outsiders are banned or strictly limited. There are no transferable private rights. Common law implies a system of transferable private rights. In a common law regime, owners and occupiers of land hold the right to customary levels of water quality, which are not to be diminished against their will. Upstream polluters must either purchase the rights or the associated land or face legal action if rights are taken. State and local statutes and regulation imply a system of public property rights in which elected officials and their appointees hold the rights to water quality and its allocation. Finally, national regulation moves a system of public property rights to the level of the nation. Again, the family of supply curves reminds us that at a moment in time we can have a water quality management system operating with custom and tradition, private property rights, and public property rights coexisting. Shifts among the supply curves yield changes in the diverse bundle of rights.

To this point, the analysis has concerned a population of people in a closed system. We have not considered the effects of competing national governments or of global competition that might affect key participants in the political economy that provides water-quality-rights institutions. Obviously, competition matters. In an open system with multiple states and other political units competing to attract taxpayers, the providers of water-quality-rights institutions will feel the spur of competition. State and local governments cannot readily impose monopoly prices and restrictions on mobile consumers and investors. The lower the cost of voting with feet, the lower will be the cost of water-quality-rights institutions. However, if the national government expands its offering of water quality rights and asserts monopoly power over competing legal institutions, then the more flexible supply of water quality rights previously offered by competing suppliers can wither away. Institutional hardening results in outcomes that are costly to modify or to reverse. Special interest groups that seek favors from the national government will be affected by the powers of dominant governments and the extent of global competition they face in product markets. The lower the level of global competition, the more likely it is that national regulation can provide politically determined rents. Rent-seeking behavior at any level of government is conditioned by the level of competition faced outside the domain of particular government. The extent to which economies are open alters the institutional mix.

Keeping this conceptual model of competing water-quality-rights institutions in mind, we now turn to consider the Cuyahoga River and other episodes that illustrate shifts in institutional supply curves and the ways in which such shifts affected the position of common law as a provider of property rights protection.

A BURNING RIVER AND COMPETING INSTITUTIONS

In June of 1969, the Cuyahoga River in Cleveland, Ohio, caught fire. Stories of fire fighters battling five-story flames left little doubt that rivers could actually burn. Obviously, the Cuyahoga was not swimmable or fishable; the river was biologically dead. Although later environmentalists may be disturbed by the image of a burning river, public outrage in Cleveland at the time was minimal.

On June 23, 1969, the *Cleveland Plain Dealer* ran a small six-paragraph story describing the event, using a low-key headline: "Oil Slick Fire Damages Two River Spans." According to the story, the fire, which was reported at 11:56 A.M., was under control at 12:20 P.M., but not before burning debris from logs and other wood products that were caught below a wooden trestle did $50,000 in damages. A few follow-ups were published on succeeding days, reporting on pledges made by various politicians and bureaucrats to find the source of the pollution (Dirk 1989). Other than determining that an oil slick and debris originated somewhere south of the city, the source of the problem was never nailed down precisely. Apparently, the condition of the Cuyahoga was not a matter of much concern. The railroad company that owned the trestle sustained the damages from the fire. Accumulated debris caught by the trestle was the source of the fire. It is possible that sparks from trains ignited the accumulated debris. The railroad had little basis for a cause of action at common law.

The 1969 fire was not the first time the Cuyahoga had burned. It had burned at least twice before—in 1936 and in 1952. Indeed, the earlier fires put the 1969 incident to shame. The 1952 fire damaged over $1.5 million in property (Van Tassel and Grabowski 1996, 339). From all indications, the Cuyahoga had long been used as an industrial sewer.

That Was Then—This Is Now

Before becoming concerned about the callousness or ignorance of people in the 1930s, 1950s, and 1960s, we must remind ourselves of several important differences between then and now. Incomes were much lower in those decades. Employment, basic nutrition, adequate housing, and avoidance of contagious diseases were seen as far more valuable at the margin than clean water in a river lined by productive factories. The environmental movement that would fan passions was not to be seen until the early 1970s. When the Cuyahoga fire occurred, Rachel Carson's (1962) book, *Silent Spring*, the much-celebrated precursor to that movement, was just beginning to penetrate the national consciousness.

We must also recall that there was a legal/political environment that allowed for and even specified conditions that led to burning rivers. Recognizing this, we must remember that in terms of environmental harms, the early Cuyahoga fires were pretty small potatoes when compared to other environmental threats that were being addressed. Cholera and typhoid, pervasive in waterfront communities at the beginning of the twentieth century, had been systematically eliminated. In short, there was an environmental movement at the time of the fires, but it focused on public health, science, and collective efforts to protect human health. Allowing some rivers to burn gave leeway for communities to focus efforts on more pressing environmental problems.

Thirty years later, the burning Cuyahoga is used as a benchmark when journalists explain how far we have come in cleaning up the environment. Instead of showing pictures of oil slicks and flames, the Crooked River Association, organized and funded by private citizens along the Cuyahoga, now tells about fishing, swimming, and recreational areas. Yet even with these improvements, the threat of fire is still present. Trees, limbs, and other flammable debris still accumulate at places in the river, in fact, at the same railroad bridge that was damaged in 1969; and a spark at the right time and place could yield a burning river.

At some point in the distant past, the Cuyahoga, like every other river, was a commons, an unrationed resource available to all. Then, as scarcity dictated and the prospective gains from rule change made change attractive, rules of law and custom that previously provided a framework for protecting water quality were replaced partly by the rule of politics. A significant bundle of private rights became public property rights. Later the river became subject to all- encompassing federal regulation; most water quality rights became national public property. And now, within the rich context of multiple suppliers of law and regulation, we see a river association, a group of private citizens seeking to claim and to manage environmental rights. This private action is taking place in the context of common law, state and local statutes, and federal law.

The Cuyahoga's Institutional Tissue

So why did the Cuyahoga become so impaired that it caught fire not once but several times? How does this fit into our theory of institutional supply? As we examine the Cuyahoga, or any other river, and peel back the layers of regulation, property rights, and community action, we see a blending of institutions that have evolved over time. The blend reflects political and economic struggles, but it also can be interpreted as embodying a search for efficient use of environmental assets.

Our investigation of the Cuyahoga suggests that the river burned because common law rights that might have precluded its conversion to an industrial dump were blunted by the Ohio legislature. Another supplier of rights that served the interests of an industrializing community replaced important rules of common law affecting community access to water quality. The state established a river classification system, defining the Cuyahoga as an *industrial stream*. When the former holders of common law rights went to court to force a reduction of pollution in the river, they encountered the law of politics. Judges' hands were tied by legislative edict. A system of property rights was in place, one that had transferred rights from parties downstream to polluters upstream. Political negotiations between industrialists, politicians, and other interest groups replaced transactions between polluters and the holders of downstream rights. With a state-approved permit, a Cuyahoga discharger was shielded from common law actions. Later, as pressures increased from border states and distant but affected communities, the federal government entered the fray. Institutional supply curves shifted again. Federal statutes erased the state classification system and delivered much-desired federal taxpayer dollars from Washington to improve water quality. All along, incomes were rising; the demand for environmental quality was increasing. As the federal program took hold, industrial and municipal dischargers became subject to a system of command-and-control regulation that once again allowed approved levels of discharge. Even then, common law causes of action could still be used to supplement regulatory complaints; and custom, tradition, and community action still operated to help conserve water quality. Today, with growing dissatisfaction about resulting river conditions, private citizens have taken the initiative to organize an association that blows the whistle on permit violators and that works to improve Cuyahoga water quality beyond the limits set and enforced by politicians.

The Demise of Cuyahoga Common Law Rights

In 1965, Bar Realty Corporation, as citizen and taxpayer of the city of Cleveland, brought suit in the Court of Common Pleas of Cuyahoga County against the mayor, the director of public safety, the commissioner of health, and the chief of police. Relying on common law logic, which protects holders of water rights from harmful pollution, Bar sought to compel enforcement of the city's pollution-control ordinances against some industrial plants that were discharging waste into the Cuyahoga River and its tributaries. The trial court granted the plaintiff's petition and ordered the respondents to "investigate the nature, character, and extent of the activities of such persons and firms as may be in contravention of the duly enacted ordinances . . . and to order such nuisances . . . to be abated, and to do all other things necessary and proper to effectively abate such nuisances" (*Bar Realty Corp. v. Locher* 1972, 164–65). The court saw the wisdom of common law regarding public nuisances; respondents appealed.

The Ohio Supreme Court reversed the lower court's decision, ruling first that the court could not substitute its powers for the discretion and judgment of public officials charged with regulating water quality. Announcing the fact that property rights had been reallocated, the higher court ruled that Cleveland's ordinances were in conflict with state statutes. The Ohio Water Pollution Control Board had granted permission to industrial firms to discharge wastes into the tributaries of Lake Erie. The state water commissioner had the authority to determine when permits had been violated; the commissioner's discretion could not be overturned by the courts. Another institutional supply curve was now relevant. In short, common law's fundamental role in protecting rights was severely weakened. The institutional supply curves had shifted. The Cuyahoga River was destined to burn.

Months after the 1969 fire, the federal government stepped in and Interior Secretary Walter Hickel opened hearings against four polluters charged with discharging wastes into badly contaminated Lake Erie (Hill 1969). One of the four, Republic Steel, was dumping thousands of tons of chemicals into the Cuyahoga daily. Republic challenged the secretary's authority to press charges, claiming that it conformed to a federal/state cleanup program overseen by the Ohio Water Pollution Control Board. But the federal supply curve was not to be suppressed. In 1970, Cleveland Mayor Carl Stokes testified in Washington hearings on water pollution, claiming that state statutes rendered him impotent in enforcing any sort of control over the pollution of his part of the Cuyahoga (U.S. House 1971). State statutes, he explained, had given industry a license to pollute. Being downstream on the 160-kilometer (100-mile) river, Cleveland received the wastes from the entire 2,100-square-kilometer watershed. If interstate pollution were to be controlled, the federal government would have to step in and erase the state-designed classification system and deal with upstream dischargers. In 1972, Congress passed the Federal Water Pollution Control Act that did just that.

The Cuyahoga Becomes a Symbol

The burning of the Cuyahoga became a symbol of a single state's apparent inability to control water pollution. Some observers credit the incident with pushing the Congress to override President Nixon's veto and pass the 1972 law. Given the facts at the time, the proposition that a "race to the bottom" by states allowed to set their own standards for water pollution control seemed viable. Just as now, states competed for industry to locate, operate, and expand in their jurisdictions. The race to the bottom implied a never-ending trade-off of environmental quality for better paying jobs.

Although this logic has appeal, it overlooks several important facets of the problem. First, the race to the bottom could not take place unless holders of environmental rights lost out in a struggle to protect their common law rights or unless such rights were taken by state statute. State statutes that shielded polluters from common law suits did just that. Next, the fact that downstream cities, such as Cleveland, were at the bottom of the discharge cycle from upstream cities challenged the ability of common law courts to go against the tide. Then there was industry, which faced a mixed bag of institutional supply curves, including strict common law liability. If federal rules could be obtained, the playing field for industry would be made more consistent, and, quite possibly, rents would be generated for some firms. Finally, the fact that cities were struggling to improve life at the bottom suggests that if a race had been underway, it was coming to an end.

The 1972 Federal Water Pollution Control Act took a one-size-fits-all approach to the problem, setting technology-based national standards for all point-source dischargers into the nation's rivers and streams. The federal statute addressed the race to the bottom problem but preempted common law nuisance suits in interstate controversies. Instead of basing water-quality control on limiting damages or economic harm, the federal program focused on technical outcomes that had to do with emissions, not outcomes or harms. A new and simpler property rights regime emerged, one that improved things for polluters. There were now four supply curves providing legal protection for water quality rights: custom and tradition, common law, state and local statutes, and a new federal statute.

Each part of this evolutionary process presents opportunities for interest groups to gain special favors, while competitive forces continuously affect the durability of the legal institutions that evolve. Constitutionally dominant and accompanied by payments of tax dollars to lower levels of government, federal regulation can be viewed as competition for state and local regulation. Common law and custom and tradition compete with all forms of formal regulation. In this sense, communities mix and mingle the different means for managing water quality, with no single approach becoming the exclusive controller of outcomes.

In the process that yields a regulatory regime, environmental catastrophes, special interest struggles, and institutional competition confront other forces that affect the relative importance of the institutional competitors. These forces include factors that affect transaction costs, scientific breakthroughs that enable people to understand the environmental consequences of their actions, expanding national and international competition that affects comparative advantage, and technological change that provides a basis for monitoring and measuring environmental use. A careful study of the history of environmental regulation can shed light on these and other forces that yield the institutions that control water quality.

THE EARLY HISTORY OF EVOLVING WATER QUALITY INSTITUTIONS

We begin our story of U.S. water pollution at the beginning—the arrival of European settlers in the New World. The first New England settlers established rules for protecting natural resources by means of "the ancient charters" (Cumbler 1991, 74). The charters incorporated the traditional English common law. These rules repeated age-old standards of behavior to be followed by one and all. Recognizing the importance of water to the survival and maintenance of the colony, the charters forbade "the corrupting of any spring or source of water" or "the destruction of fish by poisoning water" (75). Water resources were viewed as community property to be protected from the abuse of pollution. Common law rights, incorporated into charters and enforced by the citizens, were accepted as the best protection of the common good.

The early settlers were generous in their praise of the New World and wrote of the "fresh bracing air, the vast acres of fertile land, forests full of game, and streams and lakes of pure water" (Duffy 1990, 9). In 1630 John Winthrop reported to his son: "Here is sweet aire faire rivers and plenty of springes and the water better than in Eng[land]. Here can be noe want of any thinge to those who bring meane to raise out of the earth and sea" (Duffy 1990, 9). The settlers no doubt felt fortunate to have arrived at a place less troubled by infectious diseases and other ills experienced in the Old World.

As the colonial population increased, the resources needed for survival became more scarce (Cumbler 1991). Fathers could no longer rely on obtaining adequate land for their sons to cultivate. Fish populations that had once been abundant were disappearing. The resources that had once been common-access, or free for all, became captured in systems of private property rights and markets. Centers of commerce, cities, emerged as places where consumers and sellers could come together and trade. Merchants bought corn, wheat, cattle, and horses from thousands of farms and fish from hundreds of fishermen. As the cities began to flourish, city dwellers had problems not well handled by custom and tradition: thievery and vice, filth from human and animal wastes simply tossed into the streets, and widespread poverty (Blum et al. 1985, 69).

America's emergence as an industrialized society changed the landscape and altered the water-quality-institution supply curves. What had been primarily a rural culture, capable of relying on custom, tradition, and community courts, was replaced with networks of densely populated cities dedicated to entrepreneurial endeavors. The new urban centers fouled America's waters. Raw human and animal wastes, sulfuric acid used to clean iron, acids and caustic alkali from paper mills, and dyes from textile mills were dumped into streams that conveniently washed them away (Cumbler 1995, 151). Streams and rivers that had previously been clean and full of fish were, by the 1870s and 1880s, blackened by industrial discharges, reeking with human wastes, and unfit to sustain aquatic life.

Consider how these social forces affected the Cuyahoga. The business district of the city of Cleveland fronted on the Cuyahoga River, where steamers, schooners, and canal boats exchanged imported goods for the products of local industry. Later, discharge from oil refineries and steel factories coupled with human waste made the Cuyahoga, according to Mayor Rensselaer Herrick in 1881, "an open sewer through the center of the city" (Van Tassel and Grabowski 1996, 339).

Environmentalists to the Rescue

By the late nineteenth century, an environmental movement was emerging. As now, the emphasis was on technical standards, not economic harm or property-rights protection. But unlike current environmentalism, this first movement founded itself on scientific breakthroughs that had much to do with public health and little to do with aesthetics. James Olcott, in a speech before the Agricultural Board of Connecticut in 1886, called on his audience and Connecticut citizens to "agitate, agitate" in order to "cleanse" the state of the "social evil" of the pollution and "sewage from families and factories." He urged them to halt the "raising of a polluted stream upon any body at the will of ignorant or reckless capitalists" (Cumbler 1995, 149). Olcott was not alone in calling for cleaning the waters of New England. Early water pollution reformers, mostly doctors and scientists from New England's leading families, claimed that health was related to the quality of the environment. Their rallying cries included slogans such as "purity" and "anti-stream pollution" as they pushed for the creation of boards of health and associations for public health. They then would become members or commissioners of these boards and associations, calling on the citizens to clean the streams and the rivers of industrial and sewage pollution, which they also believed led to air pollution (Cumbler 1995, 149).

The reformers came from a background of leadership and social involvement. The Civil War experience gave them an increased appreciation of the state as an agent for change, and they believed the state would yield to their concerns because of their knowledge and social position as privileged Yankees (Cumbler 1995, 150). Scientific generalists who believed in the theory of anticontagionism, or the environmental theory of disease causation, claimed that the problem of pollution was an issue that involved public health, economic well-being, and political stability (151). For example, the Connecticut legislature was told that crime decreased when sanitary conditions were provided: "We are thus led to the connection between sanitary science and political economy." The board of health argued that not only did pollution give rise to "deadly miasmas" that "contaminate the air" and cause sickness, but also it claimed that miasmas led to the riots in Pittsburgh in 1877. The reformers did admit "communism does not originate from unsanitary conditions . . . yet it finds its recruits and most reckless supporters where sanitary reform is most needed." Earlier, Connecticut citizens were reminded that "a pernicious environment in effect roots up the nobler and best instincts of our nature. It brutalizes and dwarfs the intellect, corrupts the morals, breeds intemperance and sensuality, and is ever recruiting the ranks of the vile and the dangerous."

Legislatures, pressured by public health advocates, responded by creating state boards of health that were empowered to investigate pollution and public health. Scientific observation demonstrated the negative impact of industrial wastes and human sewage on water systems and the adverse impact of polluted water on human health. Water quality would be tested by walking downstream from a fouling source, tasting the water, and looking for swimming minnows (Cumbler 1995, 152). Statisticians used mortality data to confirm that, indeed, areas near the polluted waters had significantly higher levels of epidemic diseases.

For example, in 1878, the newly created Massachusetts State Board of Health pushed for legislative action to clean up the rivers and streams. Under the proposed law, "no individual or corporation, and no authority of any city or town, or public institution, shall discharge, or cause to be discharged . . . into any stream or public pond . . . any solid refuse . . . or any polluting substance so as either singly or in combination with other similar acts . . . to interfere with its volume or flow or pollute its waters" (Cumbler 1995, 153). The act ostensibly addressed the newly recognized public health problems, but it also extended protection to industrial dischargers. The act granted existing polluters a "reasonable length of time to comply with the provisions of . . . [the] act." Cities and towns with sewers could allow the sewage of factories "to be discharged through public sewers: provided such sewage contains no poisonous chemicals . . . or any matter injurious to the public health." Despite resistance by some manufacturers, the legislature followed the board's recommendations and passed "An Act Relative to the Pollution of Rivers, Streams and Ponds" (154). Three rivers that had the greatest concentration of industrial use, the Merrimack, the Concord, and the Connecticut were exempted from the act. Some corporations already polluting were allowed to continue either by prescription or by legislative grant. A river classification system with old-source/new-source rules emerged, a scheme to be repeated in 1972 when federal water pollution control legislation formed a new institutional supply curve.

Sound Science and the Discovery Period

While American pollution reformers were promoting their data as evidence that foul miasmas caused disease, European scientists began to suggest that invisible germs were to blame for epidemic disease. The late-nineteenth-century work by the Germans Henle and Koch, the Englishman Lister, and the Frenchman Pasteur was gaining attention in the United States. The new germ theory provided an explanation for why disease tended to emerge in certain areas. Scientists discovered that it was not foul-smelling water or poisonous vapors that caused disease. Invisible germs were the culprits that invaded the water system because of sewage dumping. Germs ingested by downstream drinkers caused the spread of disease. The germ theory opened the door for laboratory science and graduate programs with researchers applying the latest technological instruments and chemical analysis for preventing disease. The scientific breakthroughs contributed to new forms of regulation.

In 1887 Massachusetts ordered the Board of Health to conduct a thorough scientific study of the state's waters. This time, doctors and statisticians did not lead the effort. Ellen Swallow, an MIT laboratory-trained biologist, led the project and developed the world's first water purity tables (Cumbler 1995, 157). In the early 1890s, a group of bacteriologists, chemists, and sanitary engineers at the Massachusetts Board of Health's Lawrence Experiment Station clarified the relationship between sewage in waterways and typhoid (Tarr 1985, 1060). This group proved that bacteria and other germs could be eliminated by filtration through sand and exposure to air and sunlight (Cumbler 1995, 157). Connecticut towns were advised to adopt quickly the Lawrence station model for treating water.

Institutional suppliers shuffled market share when citizens armed with scientific evidence linking specific polluters to damages reinvigorated common law suits for protecting environmental rights. Town officials were pressured to move hastily by a number of successful nuisance actions brought by downstream residents against polluters who dumped noxious wastes into the water they used to nourish their animals and to drink (Cumbler 1995, 157).

Balancing the Benefits and Costs of Pollution

Just nine years after the anticontagionism theorists were successful in getting legislation passed limiting discharge into the waterways, the germ theorists came to dominate. They shifted the concern from a focus on a combination of industrial waste and sewage to one entirely focused on sewage believed to be responsible for epidemic diseases. The germ theory, modern science, and new technology had solved the problem of the spread of many water-born diseases. This new knowledge also solved a problem for industrial polluters. Some believed that industrial wastes were helpful additions to waterways because they killed germs. Early reformers pointed to streams full of fish as a sign of health; but for those opposed to clearing wastes, fish-free rivers and streams were a sign of cleaned waters. An 1888 Connecticut report put it this way: "While the impurity of water may in a measure be indicated by its poisonous action on fishes, and while water sufficiently contaminated to prevent the life of fish in it is unquestionably too much polluted for any domestic purposes, it does not necessarily follow that such contaminated streams must be dangerously polluted. Fish will live in concentrated fresh sewage, but will die when the water contains one hundred thousands part of blue vitriol" (Connecticut Board of Health 1887–88, 183). More important, the same report that included that passage also recognized the trade-off involved with cleaning industrial wastes, stating: "Which are of more importance, fish or the factories, there can be but one answer" (Connecticut Board of Health 1887–88, 168).

COMMON LAW ENVIRONMENTALISM ARISES

Hand in hand with the rise in concern about the effects of industrial pollution and city sewage drainage, which was tied to lower-cost scientific evidence about the harm suffered by those exposed to tainted water, common law cases became more frequent. During the last decades of the nineteenth century and carrying on into the twentieth century, numerous common law suits against polluters, interstate and intrastate, generated a refined body of what would now be called environmental law (Meiners and Yandle 1999 develop this more fully). Nuisance was the most widely applied common law action for protecting environmental rights. Remedies included damages that were the consequence of pollution and, in equity, injunctions against polluters who could not reduce emissions to a tolerable level. Because nuisance law is the centerpiece to the protection of well-defined environmental rights, it is important to understand its institutional traits and the common law doctrine that emerged.

Nuisance Law Concepts and Common Law Doctrine

As Justice Sutherland said, in a famous bit of dictum, "Nuisance may be merely a right thing in a wrong place like a pig in the parlor instead of the barnyard" (*Village of Euclid v. Ambler Realty* 1926, 388). Causes of action for nuisance claims can be either public or private, or they can be combined public and private nuisances.

A *public nuisance* is an act or an omission that causes inconvenience or damage to the public health or public order or an act that constitutes an obstruction of public rights. Normally, only public officers (attorney generals or district attorneys) have standing to sue to abate public nuisances. This common law theory addressed a wide range of environmental ills. A *private nuisance* is a substantial and unreasonable interference with the use and the enjoyment of an interest in land. The interference may be intentional or negligent. Most cases involve a defendant operating in a manner alleged to be offensive or harmful to the plaintiff. The issue posed is whether the defendant's act is an intrusion that is "sufficiently noxious" to give rise to a finding of nuisance.

Nuisance claim cases often discuss the weighing of various factors. Generally, the defendant's conduct will be held to be unreasonable if the gravity of the harm outweighs the utility of the conduct (American Law Institute 1972, § 826(a) at 3). In discussing the "gravity of harm," courts have considered various factors, including (1) the extent and the character of the injury alleged; (2) the social value of the use invaded; and (3) the burden of avoiding harm by the harmed party.

A major consideration by some courts in nuisance cases is, "How useful is the activity causing the nuisance?" It is generally the defendant's goal to produce a useful product or service, which involves employing workers and investing substantial dollars. This factor can sorely test the "weighing process" applied by some courts in nuisance law.

A related issue, which posed problems for some courts in nuisance cases, is whether the balancing process should consider broader social questions related to the welfare of individuals not before the court, such as the workers who will lose their jobs if the activity is enjoined by the court. Traditional nuisance law prefers the narrower view, which does not take account of such issues. The following cases, decided by the same court many years apart, illustrate the difference between the consequences of courts engaging in balancing tests and the enforcement of water rights strictly.

In the oft-cited modern pollution case *Boomer v. Atlantic Cement Co.,* property owners sought an injunction to restrain the operator of a cement plant from emitting dust, noise, and vibrations. Discussing "balancing factors," the New York high court ruled that the $45 million investment in the plant, and the fact that it employed three hundred people, justified a remedy less onerous than the injunction of operations sought by plaintiffs. "It seems fair to both sides to grant permanent damages to plaintiffs which will terminate this private litigation" (*Boomer v. Atlantic Cement Co.* 1970, 875). Damage payments would give the plant owner incentives to minimize the nuisance.

This contrasts sharply with a nuisance case decades before. In *Whalen v. Union Bag and Paper Co.,* a farmer downstream from a new paper mill that cost over $1 million to build and that employed five hundred people sued the mill for damaging the water that passed by his farm that he used for agricultural purposes. The New York high court found the damages to be $312 and issued an injunction against further pollution by the mill that significantly lowered the quality of water downstream. The extent of investment and the jobs created were not to be taken into consideration; the mill owner was bound to know the law and the risk it took by ignoring the water rights of downstream neighbors. "Although the damage to the plaintiff may be slight as compared with the defendant's expense of abating the condition, that is not a good reason for refusing an injunction. Neither courts of equity nor law can be guided by such a rule, for if followed to its logical conclusion it would deprive the poor litigant of his little property by giving it to those already rich" (*Whalen v. Union Bag and Paper Co.* 1913, 5). Under the traditional view, rights that have been involuntarily stripped do not have price tags for those who wish to have their rights restored rather than only to be compensated for the injury suffered.

The use of a balancing doctrine, for remedy purposes, is often politically popular and has been asserted to be economically efficient. Courts began to use balancing tests more frequently in the 1930s. Some claim this was due to the strength of the legal realism movement; we think it more likely due to the economic reality of the Great Depression. In any event, strict application of property rights was weakened, and the common law courts were in something of a muddle from that time on. Some courts were strict; others took an approach more like the *Boomer* court.

Regardless of which view the courts took, they looked for evidence of real harm having been suffered. Some critics of the use of common law claims in environmental litigation allege that the technical nature of pollution actions does not lend itself to interpretation by inexperienced judges. However, court-appointed experts and masters have been relied on to oversee relief in complex environmental cases. The courts did not have to provide engineering specifics; defendants had strong incentives to find the efficient technical solution to problems given the possibility of more damages being assessed and more injunctions issued on part or all of operations.

Water Rights and the Common Law of Water Pollution

There are two basic doctrines for allocating water rights among water users: the common law of riparian rights and the (largely) statutory doctrine of prior appropriation. Although there is some overlap, riparian rights generally control in the eastern states where water supplies have historically been more abundant, whereas the prior appropriation doctrine is generally followed in the western states, where water is more scarce.

Common law riparian rights basically concern the rights of riparian water owners with respect to their usufruct rights to water in water bodies such as lakes and streams. *Riparian owners* are people or entities that possesses *riparian land*— land that includes a part of a bed of a stream or a lake or that borders on a stream or a lake.

For over a century, courts consistently have treated water pollution cases as nuisance cases. Trespass and strict liability rules have also played a role; some jurisdictions invented a tort of "pollution," but in practice it is indistinguishable from nuisance. In short, depending whether they engaged in balancing tests, riparian-rights pollution cases consider the basic nuisance issues such as which party was there first, the state of the art of technology, and extent of harm.

Under the prior appropriation doctrine, the one who first appropriates water and puts it to use acquires the right to continue to use the water against all claimants that follow—"first in time, first in right." This doctrine favors water use, even if the consumption is of trivial value, but appropriation right does not give a right to destroy water quality. Many early prior appropriation pollution cases were based on conflicts between upstream miners and downstream farmers. Those cases indicated that the general rule is that, even though a proper use of a stream for mining purposes necessarily contaminates it to some extent, such water contamination cannot inflict substantial injury on another user of the waters of the stream.

The courts intertwined common law doctrines such as nuisance with water rights. Whether courts applied balancing factors or strictly enforced water rights, cases awarded monetary damages, including punitive damages, for pollution to a variety of water bodies including creeks, groundwater, and water wells. As the court in *Branch v. Western Petroleum* (1982, 275) noted "We know of no acceptable rule of jurisprudence which permits those engaged in . . . important enterprises to injure with impunity those who are engaged in enterprises of lesser economic significance."

Some courts determined that water pollution in certain instances was best remedied by injunction. In one early case, the court heard a complaint against a manufacturer that discharged waste into a river used by a water company to provide water to a city. The court stated, "no plain, adequate, and complete remedy exists at law, and injunction will lie to restrain such discharge" (*Indiana Water Co. v. American Strawboard Co.* 1893, 976). Likewise, the court in *Sandusky Portland Cement Co. v. Dixon Pure Ice Co.* (1915) enjoined the use of stream water by an upstream cement company after finding that the use resulted in an increase of the temperature of the river (near the plaintiff's ice plant), which the court determined was sufficient to retard the formation of an ice field used by plaintiff to harvest commercial ice. In another instance, the court awarded damages to plaintiff homeowners and issued an injunction against the operation of a sewage system by a city that fouled waters passing through the plaintiffs' farm. The court cited a leading text on torts: "In deciding the right of a single proprietor to an injunction, the court cannot take into consideration the circumstance that a vast population will suffer by reason of its interference" (*Carmichael v. City of Texarkana* 1899, 573).

Common law environmentalism evolved across the states, provided a means for ordinary people to protect themselves from environmental harms, and became a key institutional player in the "marketplace" for environmental rights. As should be expected, statute writers and state regulators did not remain passive in the face of common law competition.

STATE REGULATION MATURES

With common law courts taking a harsh view of the nuisance called water pollution, a competing institution responded. States began to move on the regulatory front. Some states, including New York and Wisconsin, created conservation commissions in the 1920s to work with the departments of health in restricting pollution, but the new commissions also supplied technical advice to manufacturers on how to reduce their effluents (Tarr 1985, 1060). Other states had fish commissions that attempted to reduce industrial pollution. However, they were never granted power to take action against polluting firms (1061).

Between 1917 and 1926, three industrialized states—Connecticut, Ohio, and Pennsylvania—created boards that were responsible for controlling industrial wastes. These boards believed that abatement of industrial pollution could only be achieved through cooperation with industry. They saw themselves as suppliers of technical advice to polluting factory owners and as monitors of polluted streams. The Pennsylvania Sanitary Water Board established three classes of streams: those that were pure; those that needed pollution control; and those that were not "economical or advisable" to clean up at that time (Tarr 1985, 1061–2). Many sanitary engineers believed that Pennsylvania's actions demonstrated the ideal model for balancing the demand for environmental quality and industrial progress. The river classification scheme, which competed and interacted with orthodox common law actions, formed a piece of institutional tissue that affected the delivery of water quality.

Before World War I, a number of cases were reported involving the damaging effects of industrial pollution on water supplies. But it was not until 1922 that a widespread study of the problem was conducted. In 1923, the Committee on Industrial Wastes in Relation to Water Supply of the American Water Works Association (1923, 415–30) reported that industrial pollutants had technically damaged at least 248 water supplies in the United States and Canada. They found specifically that industrial wastes had profound effects on the color, turbidity, taste, and odor of water and had increased the expense and the level of difficulty involved with coagulation and filtration. The report provided a long list of offending industries, included sugar refining, coal mining and washing, gas and by-product coke works, wood distillation, corn products, dye and munitions manufacture, oil-producing wells and oil refining, metallurgical processes and mining, textiles, tanneries, and paper and pulp mills (Tarr 1985, 1062). Once again, enhanced scientific knowledge affected the relative positions of the institution supply curves.

During the 1920s, specialists believed that phenol wastes from gas and by-product coke works were the most acute problems associated with industrial wastes. Pollution from gas wastes was under control by the 1920s, but difficulties with phenol—primarily odor and taste—were a post-World War I phenomenon and were largely isolated in the Ohio River Basin. Concern with the effects of phenol led the U.S. surgeon general to call a conference of the state health commissioners of Ohio, Pennsylvania, and West Virginia in 1924 to explore the interstate pollution problems related to the streams in the Ohio River Basin (Tarr 1985, 1062). The conference resulted in the Ohio River Interstate Stream Conservation Agreement. By 1929, seventeen of the nineteen firms in the basin had installed phenol elimination devices, sharply reducing the most severe cases of odor and bad taste (*American Journal of Public Health*, 1929). Yet another institutional supplier had entered the picture, one that addressed a large watershed and that also provided a partial shield from common law suits. A major factor in the voluntary action by these firms was undoubtedly their concern over the possibility of legal action in the courts.

State Regulation and Federal Common Law

As incomes rose, people in urban areas moved to residential enclaves where industrial-related water pollution problems were not prevalent. Also, the 1920s saw the rise of urban land-use planning accompanied by zoning. The classification of land accompanied the classification of rivers. Land around industry was cheap; those that thought they would move in, take the polluting industries to court, and gain a windfall were told by many courts to think again when defendants were able to demonstrate that the plaintiffs had "come to the nuisance." For example, in 1928, a Cleveland industrial firm charged in a nuisance action won the suit, arguing that it had initially been located on an isolated tract; the residents that arrived subsequently could not complain about a preexisting condition (Colten 1994, 91).

Isolation was hard to maintain, however, and firms that had once enjoyed water-damaging activities in isolated areas sometimes found themselves surrounded by newly developed residential communities. The "smoking car" solution to pollution no longer worked. The courts began to impose costs of uncertainty on firms. Even when polluters located in areas isolated from residences, people could eventually move in, and firms would have to clean up or move.

The Tensions Generated by the New Property Rights

Early-twentieth-century state regulation of wastewater dischargers emphasized sewage rather than industrial wastes. Commissions of health were generally charged with promulgating and enforcing standards for their states' waterways. However, as the judicial treatment of industrial polluters more consistently enforced common law rules that favored downstream parties, industry groups sought a more comfortable institutional setting; state water-pollution-control boards began to set standards for industrial waste dischargers (Goldfarb 1988, 591). The first state legislative efforts to control pollution were classification systems of the sort used by Connecticut that categorized streams according to their uses. States would classify their dirtiest streams as "industrial use" and their trout streams as "recreational use."

The river classification systems operated in two ways: First, total pollution was constrained to avoid harmful public-health consequences. Second, the legislation was an avenue for attracting industry by inviting them to pollute in some areas—the "smoking cars"—while protecting other areas for recreational and other environmental uses. The new state water-pollution-control boards set ambient standards and administered permit programs (Goldfarb 1988, 592). Firms that abided by their permits could be shielded from common law nuisance suits. Direct dischargers that failed to obtain a permit could be charged with private and public nuisance. The older system of common law rights was partly displaced. What had been a system of private rights became public property managed by public officials.

Differing standards for water quality among states sparked competition among them. A crude environmental-trade-off market emerged with communities willing to trade water quality for economic progress. However, the law of gravity caused decisions made by upstream communities to affect the quality of waterways used by people, communities, and states downstream. In some cases, interstate disputes were adjudicated by federal common law. In others, multistate compacts were formed.

The Ohio River Compact

The success of the classification system for managing water quality depended on specialization. Some streams were assigned the role of sewage disposal, whereas others could be maintained for providing satisfactory water supplies. The problem was more complex when rivers served competing purposes. The Ohio River is one such waterway. The management of the Ohio River was complicated because eight states border its shores with varying levels of population and industrialization. Because of heavy sewage discharge, the river became a vehicle for the transmission of intestinal-borne diseases, notably typhoid fever (Cleary 1967, 25). Sewage went downstream, but typhoid could go upstream. The disease stimulated a cooperative effort to resolve the problem. By cooperating, communities along the river developed water-purifying techniques and, in the early twentieth century, installed filtration plants that ended the threat of water-borne typhoid fever.

The pollution of the river was increasing, however, and the greater concentration of sewage-associated bacteria caused engineers to question their filter plants' abilities to deal adequately with the excessive burden. Unwanted tastes and odors became intense and were found to be related to phenol compounds and to decomposed organic materials and microscopic organisms. The excessive hardness and acidity of the water during periods of low rainfall contributed to scale formation in steam boilers, corrosion of pipes, and increased fuel consumption. Finally, there were sporadic outbreaks of gastrointestinal disorders, all of which displayed characteristics of being water-borne ailments (Cleary 1967, 25).

Because unilateral action by one state would yield little benefits while incurring high costs, the most viable approach was the coordination of all states bordering the Ohio River. In 1948 the governors of Illinois, Indiana, Kentucky, New York, Ohio, Pennsylvania, Virginia, and West Virginia met in Cincinnati to bind their states to an agreement pledging cooperation in pollution abatement through the establishment of an interstate agency (Cleary 1967, 3). The governors had been empowered to do this by prior action of their legislatures and the by U.S. Congress. As a result of the effort, several thousand municipalities and industries were motivated to invest more than a billion dollars, 90 percent locally financed, in the construction of pollution-control facilities. The 1948 Ohio River Valley Water Sanitation Commission came into existence the same year that President Truman signed the Federal Water Pollution Control Act into law. The law authorized $22.5 million in annual funds designated to assist states in doing exactly what was already occurring in the Ohio River Valley. Also, two innovations specifically mentioned in President Truman's message—programming discharges in accord with variability of stream flow and continuous monitoring of river quality—were already being implemented in the regional approach adopted by those involved in the Ohio River multistate compact.

Federal Common Law: A Substitute for Compacts

States with interstate water-quality disputes that were not resolved in multistate compacts could look to the body of federal common law for a resolution. In fact, the federal efforts at statutory pollution control grew partly from a desire to control interstate pollution. The federal common law employed a neutral federal rule, needed because "each state stands on the same level with all the rest" (Heimert 1997, 458).

The 1972 case, *Illinois v. Milwaukee,* was the last major water-pollution case decided by the U.S. Supreme Court under federal common law before it was preempted by the passage of the Federal Water Pollution Control Act (Clean Water Act or CWA) that same year. In this case, Illinois sued Milwaukee and other cities in Wisconsin for dumping sewage in Lake Michigan and thus contaminating Chicago's drinking water supply. On appeal, the Supreme Court noted that federal common law looked to state common law for guidance. Therefore, a state with high water-quality standards may well ask that its strict standards be honored and that it not be compelled to lower itself to the more degrading standards of a neighbor (Heimert 1997, 464). The Court ruled that a federal district court could grant an injunction against Milwaukee's pollution.

In 1981, the Supreme Court granted certiorari to rehear *Illinois v. Milwaukee* in order to decide "the effect of [the CWA] on the previously recognized cause of action" (Heimert 1997, 464). When the case had initially been reviewed in 1972, the Court upheld the validity of federal jurisdiction to decide disputes that "deal with air and water in their ambient or interstate aspects" under federal common law. This time, however, the Supreme Court was forced to acknowledge the historical bias against federal common law and found that it was appropriate only in limited circumstances. The Court decided that the CWA had preempted the "vague and indeterminate nuisance concepts and maxims of equity jurisprudence" and supplanted them with "a comprehensive regulatory program supervised by an expert administrative agency" (Heimert 1997, 464). The monopoly position of the federal institutional supply curve was secured.

The Rise of Federal Regulation and Preemption of Interstate Common Law

The 1972 Clean Water Act brought sweeping changes to the basic pattern of pollution-control regulation embodied in the 1948 statute and effectively reduced competition from other institutional suppliers. The CWA gave federal authorities a major role in pollution control by establishing a National Pollution Discharge Elimination System (NPDES) to issue permits (Maloney and Yandle 1983, 301). In addition to nationalizing water quality in the nation's waters, the law required the administrator of the newly formed EPA to establish effluent limitations for industrial point sources based on the *best practicable technology* (BPT). This system was to be in place and operating by 1977. It also set up a timetable for standards to be tightened to a *best available technology* (BAT) basis by 1983.

The CWA preempted state standard setting and enforcement of water quality that was less stringent than the new federal standards. It required the states to develop water quality classifications for all streams, with the expectation that all streams would become swimmable and fishable. The old classification system that provided industrial havens was no longer viable. The wishes of the national interest groups overwhelmed the desires of local and state majorities. Once again, the desires of industry groups for uniform treatment coalesced with the demand for water quality. This point was summarized in the conference report on the legislation: "[T]he intent of Congress is that effluent limitations applicable to industrial plant sources within a given category or class be as uniform as possible. The Administrator is expected to be precise in his guidelines, so as to assure that similar point sources with similar characteristics, regardless of their location or the nature of the water into which the discharge is made, will meet similar effluent limitations" (Maloney and Yandle 1983, 302).

The standards defined in the 1972 law for new sources were stricter than those for existing sources. The standard defined for new sources required BAT or BPT, whereas existing polluters faced the less strict best-practicable technology standards until 1983. Also, the EPA adopted the notion of variances, which allowed a source to operate legally in violation of BPT. The granting of variances was totally under the discretion of federal authorities, who issued them not on the basis of existing water quality but on the basis of "need."

The 1977 amendments to the CWA addressed the key problem of the statutory deadlines that had been included in the 1972 legislation. These had either passed or were rapidly approaching with no hope of achievement in sight. Further, the real cost of installing new technologies had been identified, as had the realities of economic hardships associated with plant shutdowns and resulting dislocations. Technology-based standards were kept as the primary device for managing water quality, but the deadlines for achieving BPT and BAT were extended. A third category of control technologies was introduced and applied to the standards set for so-called conventional pollutants—those normally treated in publicly owned treatment works (POTWs). Huge sums of money were redistributed from taxpayers to municipalities for their construction of POTWs using *best conventional technology* (BCT) pollution abatement technologies.

The Clean Water Act was again amended in 1987, adding significant provision to the growing volume of federal water quality control. Compliance dates that were outlined in 1977 were not extended, even though they had not been met. Provisions tightened control requirement, especially for toxic pollutants and sewage sludge, and increased the penalties to be assessed against those not in compliance with the statute. Groundwork was laid for the future control of nonpoint sources of pollution, such as runoff from agriculture, forestry, construction sites, and city streets. The federal institution supplier was to be all encompassing.

COMPARING COMMON LAW WITH FEDERAL REGULATION

There are two ways to view the ultimate dominance of the federal water-quality supply curve. One way views common law rules of nuisance, trespass and water rights, and informal community actions as being more costly than federal regulation for achieving community-desired levels of environmental quality. Statutory mechanisms that centrally plan inputs are seen as being less costly and more effective for achieving environmental quality that local and state governments may fail to provide. The other view, and the one that fits the evidence, sees federal statutory dominance as less costly for special interest polluters who seek refuge from common law suits. By obtaining a permit, polluters acquire an entitlement to emit some preestablished amount of various pollutants. The federal scheme creates certainty where the unpredictability of common law and variable local standards had previously created uncertainty. In other words, in exchange for national standards on emissions that may be tougher in some cases than would emerge under common law, polluters obtain entitlements to emit set amounts of pollutants with certainty. Although statutes do preempt interstate common law nuisance suits and weaken the common law viability in intrastate controversies, thereby reducing uncertainty costs for polluters, this is not the argument often heard in defense of a statutory preemptive position. Most environmental groups argue for using the prior restraints of regulation as a deterrent to pollution. In this view, waiting for common law to remedy a pollution problem means encouraging environmental degradation. Command-and-control regulation offers the prospect of stopping pollution before it happens, not after it occurs. Reinforcing this argument is the notion that private enforcement fails because of high transaction costs. Pollution affects many people and often stems from multiple sources. For private action to achieve efficient levels of pollution, all of those affected would have to identify the precise sources of harm. By this argument, any scheme other than centralized regulation fails both to control pollution effectively and to provide citizens with a reasonable expectation of freedom from excessive pollution.

Comparing the two approaches brings the realization that common law controls are based on property rights, are location specific, and provide remedies to rightholders for real harms. Federal regulation, on the other hand, is all encompassing, provides no specific protection to rightholders, and offers no remedies for damages that rightholders may sustain. Federal law provides standing to all citizens who may complain when any part of water quality regulations is violated. Common law requires facts about the situation at hand; it is a microapproach. Federal regulation generalizes site-specific facts and forms macroimages of the world to be controlled. The two approaches are truly different and therefore, cannot be compared as though they were quite similar.

To be a good substitute for common law remedies, federal regulation would have to embody all of the facts for all of the nation's lakes, rivers, and streams, for each and every watershed, and for each and every watershed user. Then, for the federal rules to be cost-beneficial, the multitude of different situations would have to be recognized. Rivers capable of absorbing more waste would be treated differently from others that are stressed. Pollution that imposes low costs in certain areas would be allowed. The same pollution in other locations would be denied. The federal rules would have to recognize differences. Obviously, the cost of accumulating such massive amounts of bottom-up information and then administering the associated rules is prohibitively high. Because of these costs, those who support federal rules unavoidably must skim the surface of the problem being addressed, identify goals such as swimmable and fishable, which have little empirical meaning, and then focus on administratively low-cost procedures that seem to make things better, certainly not worse.

When the resulting rules are imposed, real people who live in real watersheds must find ways to adjust the rules to fit unique situations. Local institutions still matter. If these adjustment costs, or the costs of not being able to adjust, are termed "transaction costs," then there is another transaction-cost problem. Evidence of these costs is found in the history of variances, postponements of official water-quality goals, and in the fact that macromeasures of water quality show little improvement since federal programs began.

Evidence that communities have made micro-adjustments is seen in the marked improvements in water quality that has occurred for some rivers, lakes, and streams. All along, the economy being controlled has changed dramatically. What had been a smokestack economy in the 1960s, which produced relatively large levels of emissions, has become dominated by services, trade, and information. The manufacturing sector, which is larger in terms of output, is much less involved in the production of environmentally intensive goods and more involved in making sophisticated products that use less raw material. Hard, inflexible, smokestack regulations remain in force, while a fast-moving, dynamic economy moves forward.

THE FUTURE PATH OF WATER POLLUTION CONTROL: FINAL THOUGHTS

What are the lessons to be learned from this stylized review of U.S. water quality management? How can the notion of competing institutional suppliers assist in forecasting the next evolutionary stage?

By all measures, industry has made significant progress in reducing the environmental impacts of its operations, and city governments have made some progress in efforts to reduce the discharge of human waste into rivers and lakes. National environmental interest groups have much to celebrate, whereas local groups still have long action agendas. The Cuyahoga River is no longer burning, but Georgia's Chattahoochee River is heavily contaminated by the discharge from Atlanta's faulty treatment works.

To be sure, the EPA sets national standards by prescribing the technologies to be employed by industries and publicly owned treatment facilities, and individual states are mandated to enforce those standards and to grant the NPDES permits within their own political boundaries. States also have the power to set and to enforce their own standards, under federal supervision. Because federal regulators do not consider microlocations when promulgating standards, many states have imposed stricter standards on their trout streams in order to preserve them. The old river classification systems are still with us, but there are no industrial streams. The zone of control that began with states and evolved to regions has been expanded to include all waters. The water quality baseline has been raised; but given increased income levels, that would have been expected to happen anyway. We can never know the alternative that did not exist, but it is not all-or-nothing as federal control proponents indicate.

Working around the concrete of command-and-control regulation, often with federal regulator cooperation, some states and communities have discovered how to reduce the costly burden of regulation on industry, and ultimately the consumer, through watershed management and permit trading. Others, seeing the shift from smokestacks, mining, and timber cutting to high-tech activities, tourism, and recreational demand, seek to alter the fundamental institutions that affect environmental quality. In some cases, the EPA is not the chief regulator confronted. The U.S. Forest Service, Bureau of Reclamation, Park Service, and other land-based regulators that represent entrenched interests pose the most difficult challenge for accommodating changing demands for environmental quality.

The efforts to ease the evolutionary process are particularly apparent in the Pacific Northwest, where once-prevalent extractive industries no longer set the pace for economic growth. With similar forces at play across the United States, rigid regulations formed with the support of industry and of other interest groups are becoming all the more obsolete. Just as common law judges shifted between the strict enforcement of private rights and the balancing of employment and narrow economic benefits against strong protection of water rights, newly evolving regulatory institutions are again favoring a new set of interest groups.

Consider Wisconsin: The state ranks in the top two states in sales of sport fishing licenses every year. There is a strong demand for water-related recreation. Recognizing this, state legislators provided significant state funding for water quality programs during the 1970s and into the 1980s. By 1983, Wisconsin's overall compliance with the CWA stood at 95 percent; compliance by industry was 100 percent. Wisconsin was the first state to address the nonpoint-pollution problem using state taxpayer money. Today there are 150 county employees responsible for working with local landowners on water quality issues. The voluntary sign-up rate for these nonpoint control programs has risen to 70 percent. Those who volunteer receive funds that cover 80 percent of the cost of controlling pollution. Those who choose not to cooperate face the possibility of having to do so in the future with their own money. But even that statement, indicating that cooperation is high because of the threat of regulation, abuses the fact that most people are good stewards of the land and the water where they live. Carrots work better than sticks.

On another front, communities are beginning to realize that federal and state control of water quality has left environmental protection incomplete. To fill the void left by regulation, community grassroots organizations seeking to regain control of their neighborhood lakes and streams have arisen around the country. A recent search of the Internet on river associations finds at least one such non-profit, community-based organization in every state. It seems safe to say there is one for every river and stream in America.

In Atlanta, a grassroots effort to take control of the Chattahoochee River has taken hold. The American Rivers Association rates the Chattahoochee one of the three most-endangered rivers in the United States. The city of Atlanta has been paying a daily fine of $20,000 for several years for failing to meet federal regulatory guidelines for dumping waste into the Chattahoochee (Seabrook and Helton 1997, A1).

The Upper Chattahoochee Riverkeeper is a nonprofit organization founded in 1994 to protect the river. It is made up of local residents who have banded together to improve their region. Volunteers patrol the Chattahoochee, checking permits and daily monitoring reports to make sure all dischargers are in compliance. If they detect a violation, the authorities are notified. The group has also instituted community programs to heighten the public's interest in the river. Hikes, canoe trips, and river cleanup days get the neighborhood involved with the river. It is interesting that the same water pollution problems that communities have been grappling with since the advent of federal intervention are identical to those existing today, namely, raw sewage and urban runoff. Of course water quality has improved compared to what it was thirty years ago, but only the most naive would attribute the outcome to federal control of water quality.

The fact that the 1969 burning of the Cuyahoga River was not as bad as previous fires tells us that the river was actually improving. Just before the fire, Cleveland voters had approved a bond issue of one million dollars to facilitate a cleanup of that Great Lakes tributary. Other rivers were being cleaned up as well. So what explains the elusive and unenforceable standards outlined in the Clean Water Act and the difficulty faced in moving to a more flexible and effective system of environmental protection? There is no other explanation better than that provided by special-interest theories of regulation and the rent-seeking model. Competition over property rights lies at the bottom of all this. And the competition has much to do with gaining control of assets without paying and less to do with forging strong linkages that connect the cost of human action to benefits obtained.

Over the past thirty years, industrial groups have been favored in some cases, for example, by gaining certainty and shields against common law. Environmental groups have been favored in others, by gaining statutes that focus on an array of environmental degradation and that provide revenue streams for some groups. Yet other economic forces now destabilize the market for institutional control. Major advances in transportation, communication, and information delivery have opened up the global economy. Industrial firms no longer have the luxury of competing solely with those located in U.S. regions. To survive, they must compete with firms located in many nations that have nothing like the Clean Water Act.

The Evolving New Order

Given the competitive environment, U.S. industry no longer supports a one-size-fits-all standard that previously restricted output and raised costs. Instead, the push is for flexibility and freedom to find and to apply low-cost solutions to environmental problems. Instead of throwing down the gauntlet to challenge environmental groups that might seek to support the failed smokestack regulation of the past, the new global competitors will more openly negotiate for effective controls based on outcomes, not inputs. Increasing scientific environmental knowledge will assist in this. Environmental assets will be used and protected more effectively.

But will common law and other community-based suppliers regain market share,

as they did in the earlier days? Logic suggests a new division of labor that focuses again on particular watersheds, specified lakes, and well-identified shore-
lines. Armed with better information about benefits and costs than remote regulators and politicians could ever hope to have, citizens are again forming
associations and compacts for managing water quality. Well-specified property
rights will of necessity play a fundamental role in the emerging water-quality
management programs. And parties to agreements about water quality will of
necessity hold rights to the outcomes for which they bargain. Something like
common law, though tightly constrained by statutes, will emerge and become a
more important component of the complex institutional regime that will still include federal regulation of some form, along with state and local rules and regulations. In short, yet another social system will evolve, one that contains some of
the characteristics of the earlier ones.

The Supply Equilibrium

What does the future hold for water quality management? In the absence of major
economic disruptions that destroy huge amounts of wealth and income, we will
not likely see burning rivers again. The Cuyahoga's place in history will be preserved. Nor will we see a system of command and control seriously accepted as
the appropriate way to manage all the major water systems in this vast country,
though vestiges of command and control will remain as a dying characteristic of
the U.S. water-quality-management regime.

Instead, we will see a more intelligent system; after all, information is now
less costly. The new system will rely more on outcomes, continuous monitoring,
and real effects, but less on input controls, monitoring, and speculative effects.
For its operation, the new system will rely more on people closer to the waters
being managed and less on those who hold remote positions of authority in government. Market forces will be more evident, and water quality will be accepted
as a resource to be guarded along with other traditional assets that form the basis
of modern life.

But our story does not end with this picture of competing water-quality-institution suppliers providing a newly balanced system of environmental management.
Yet another supplier will enter the scheme. As the world economy becomes more
globally integrated, international providers of water-quality rights will become
more evident. The more stationary industrial firms will seek to raise the cost of
their footloose competitors. International environmental organizations will push
for world standards, and multinational environmental treaties will become a common component of the family of institution suppliers. All along, custom and tradition and common law will be ever-diminishing but still-important parts of the
institutional fabric that describes water quality control.

NOTE

We gratefully acknowledge the research assistance provided by Matt Ryan. Parts of this chapter are drawn from Thomas and Ryan (1998).

REFERENCES

American Journal of Public Health. 1929. Results Obtained in Phenolic Wastes Disposal under the Ohio River Basin Interstate Conservation Agreement. *American Journal of Public Health* 19: 758–70.

American Law Institute. 1972. *Restatement (Second) Torts.* St. Paul: West.

American Water Works Association. 1923. Progress Report of Industrial Wastes in Relation to Water Supply. *Journal of American Water Works Association* 10: 415–30.

Benson, Bruce L. 1990. *The Enterprise of Law.* San Francisco: Pacific Research Institute for Public Policy.

Blum, John M., William S. McFeely, Edmund S. Morgan, Arthur M. Schlesinger, Jr., Kenneth M. Stampp, and C. Vann Woodward. 1985. *The National Experience: A History of the United States.* 6th ed. San Diego: HBJ Publishers.

Carson, Rachel. 1962. *Silent Spring.* Greenwich, CT: Fawcett.

Cleary, Edward J. 1967. *The ORANSCO Story: Water Quality Management in the Ohio Valley under an Interstate Compact.* Baltimore: Johns Hopkins Press.

Colten, Craig H. 1994. Creating a Toxic Landscape: Chemical Waste Disposal Policy and Practice, 1900–1960. *Environmental History Review* 18(1): 85–116.

Connecticut Board of Health. Various years. *Annual Report.* Hartford.

Cumbler, John T. 1991. The Early Making of an Environmental Consciousness: Fish, Fisheries Commissions, and the Connecticut River. *Environmental History Review* 15(3): 73–91.

———. 1995. Whatever Happened to Industrial Waste?: Reform, Compromise, and Science in Nineteenth-Century Southern New England. *Journal of Social History* 29(1): 149–71.

Dirk, Joe. 1989. Fire Doesn't Still Burn on in Memories. *Cleveland Plain Dealer,* June 21.

Duffy, John. 1990. *The Sanitarians: A History of American Public Health.* Urbana: University of Illinois Press.

Ellickson, Robert C. 1991. *Order without Law.* Cambridge: Harvard University Press.

Goldfarb, William. 1988. *Water Law.* 2d ed. Chelsea, MI: Lewis Publishers.

Heimert, Andrew J. 1997. Keeping Pigs Out of Parlors: Using Nuisance Law to Affect the Location of Pollution. *Environmental Law* 27(2): 403–512.

Hill, Gladwin. 1969. Hickel's Drive on Water Pollution Is Challenged. *New York Times,* October 8.

Lipford, Jody, and Bruce Yandle. 1997. Exploring the Production of Order. *Constitutional Political Economy* 8: 37–55.

Maloney, M. T., and Bruce Yandle. 1983. Building Markets for Tradable Pollution Rights. In *Water Rights: Scarce Resource Allocation, Bureaucracy, and the Environment*, ed. Terry L. Anderson. Cambridge, MA: Ballinger Publishing, 283–315.

McChesney, Fred. 1991. Rent Extraction and Interest-Group Organization in a Coasean Model of Regulation. *Journal of Legal Studies* 20: 73–90.

Meiners, Roger E., and Bruce Yandle. 1998. Common Law Environmentalism. *Public Choice* 94: 49–66.

———. 1999. Common Law and the Conceit of Modern Environmental Policy. *George Mason Law Review* 7(4): 923–63.

Morriss, Andrew P. 1998. Miners, Vigilantes, and Cattlemen: Overcoming Free Rider Problems in the Private Provision of Law. *Land and Water Law Review* 33: 581–696.

Peltzman, Sam. 1976. Toward a More General Theory of Regulation. *Journal of Law & Economics* (August): 211–40.

Posner, Richard A. 1974. Theories of Economic Regulation. *Bell Journal* 5(Autumn): 335–58.

Priest, George L. 1977. The Common Law Process and the Selection of Efficient Rules. *Journal of Legal Studies* 6: 65–82.

Rubin, Paul H. 1977. Why Is the Common Law Efficient? *Journal of Legal Studies* 6: 51–63.

———. 1982. Common Law and Statute Law. *Journal of Legal Studies* 11: 205–23.

Seabrook, Charles, and Charmagne Helton. 1997. A Fine Mess: Sewage Runoff Puts City up the Creek, Again. *Atlanta Constitution,* March 19.

Stigler, George J. 1971. The Economic Theory of Regulation. *Bell Journal* (Spring): 3–21.

Tarr, Joel A. 1985. Industrial Wastes and Public Health: Some Historical Notes, Part I, 1876–1932. *American Journal of Public Health* 75(9): 1059–67.

Thomas, Stacie, and Matt Ryan. 1998. *Burning Rivers and Evolving U.S. Water Quality Management: Special Report.* Clemson, SC: Center for Policy & Legal Studies, Clemson University.

Tomes, Nancy. 1990. The Private Side of Public Health: Sanitary Science, Domestic Hygiene and the Germ Theory, 1870–1900. *Bulletin of the History of Medicine* (Winter): 509–631.

U.S. House. 1971 Committee on Public Works. *Hearings on Water Pollution Control Legislation.* 92nd Congress, 1st session (December 7–10).

Van Tassel, David D., and John J. Grabowski. 1996. *Encyclopedia of Cleveland History.* Bloomington, IN: Indiana University Press.

Yandle, Bruce, and Xiang Qin. 1998. *Environmental Kuznets Curves, Property Rights, and Intergenerational Learning: Special Report.* Clemson, SC: Center for Policy & Legal Studies, Clemson University.

CASES CITED

Bar Realty Corp. v. Locher, 30 Ohio St.2d 190, 283 N.E. 2d 164 (S.Ct., Ohio, 1972)

Boomer v. Atlantic Cement Co., 26 N.Y. 2d 219, 257 N.E. 2d 870, 309 N.Y.S. 2d 312 (Ct. App., N.Y., 1970)

Branch v. Western Petroleum, 657 P.2d 267 (S.Ct., Utah, 1982)

Carmichael v. City of Texarkana, 94 F. 561 (W.D. Ark., 1899)

Illinois v. Milwaukee, 406 U.S. 91, 92 S.Ct. 1385 (S.Ct., 1972)

Illinois v. Milwaukee, 451 U.S. 304, 101 S.Ct. 1784 (S.Ct., 1981)

Indiana Water Co. v. American Strawboard Co., 53 F. 970 (D. Ind., 1893)

Sandusky Portland Cement Co. v. Dixon Pure Ice Co., 221 F. 200 (7th Cir., 1915)

Village of Euclid v. Ambler Realty, 272 U.S. 365 (S. Ct., 1926)

Whalen v. Union Bag and Paper Co., 208 N.Y. 1, 101 N.E. 805 (Ct. App., N.Y., 1913)

4

Protecting English and Welsh Rivers: The Role of the Anglers' Conservation Association

Roger Bate

The prevailing view in Britain today is that the natural environment is something that the government has to protect. The preference for government-made statutory law follows this same prejudice. For decades it has been presumed that statutes are the basis of environmental protection, even though the major consequences of statutes are often unintended and painful mistakes. Fortunately, Britain also has a rich body of common law, built up over centuries, based on equitable and reasonable solutions to individual disputes. The working of these two systems in conjunction—sometimes challenging, sometimes complementary—has created a body of law pertaining to the environment and to river water quality in particular.

This chapter analyzes the Anglers' Conservation Association (ACA), providing an illustration of this joint legal process at work. Since its formation in 1948 as a private-interest, self-help group, the ACA has quietly, consistently, and successfully fought to improve and to maintain good quality rivers in England and Wales.[1] By lobbying, it has helped to form policy, and by legal action, it has helped to establish important precedents.

The basis of its legal actions is very simple. At common law, landowners have certain *riparian rights*—benefits from and duties toward water flowing across or alongside their land. They do not own the water, but they can use a "reasonable" amount of it, and they have the right to a sufficient quality and quantity of flowing water. Their duties are to ensure that the rights of neighboring riparian owners are not damaged by their own actions. Adherence to this simple-sounding principle in common law has, in the words of a former Under-Secretary of State for the Environment, Mr. Eldon-Griffiths, "been one of the main defences—and sometimes the only defence—against river pollution . . ." (*ACA Review* 1972, 19[2]:21).

In the ACA's history, there are incidents of a public water authority being successfully sued by a private individual, of an angling club stopping pollution of an estuary 40 miles downstream of the club itself, and of ACA lobbying dissuading the government from handing a license to pollute to large industries. Although they rarely make headlines, ACA cases are hugely influential. Many of its cases are settled by negotiation before they reach the courts—a very efficient process, but one that yields little publicity or recognition for the ACA as a pollution-preventing body.

Nevertheless, the ACA is probably the most efficient pollution-preventing body in Britain. This chapter details how the ACA has achieved such success and why the idea that individuals cannot or do not want to protect the environment is wrong. To be able to understand the ACA's approach, it is essential to know the legal and historical basis for its formation.

COMMON LAW

Water and Riparian Rights

The common law of England, as it developed over many centuries, allowed the owner of land adjoining a river or watercourse the entitlement to protect it from pollution and excess abstraction. This is the entitlement known as a riparian right. Meiners, Thomas, and Yandle (2000) discuss this development in the United States. Lord Wensleydale in *Chasemore v. Richards* summarized the law in 1859 as follows: "[The landowner] has the right to have it come to him in its natural state, in flow, quantity and quality, and to go from him without obstruction, upon the same principle that he is entitled to the support of his neighbour's soil for his own in its natural state" (*Chasemore v. Richards* 1859).

Hence, the riparian owner has the right to have water flowing past his land in its natural state of purity. If water is polluted by a proprietor higher upstream, causing damage to the lower riparian proprietor, he has a good cause for action against the upper proprietor.

The principle that the waters of a natural stream must not be polluted applies also to tidal waters, to water that percolates discontinuously either on the surface or through underground strata, to wells (by water percolating through the earth), and to ponds and inland lakes. A riparian owner also has a right to the ordinary abstraction (use) of the water flowing past his land. The definition of *ordinary abstraction* is problematic because there is no simple, standard definition of where *extraordinary* abstraction begins. Domestic and agricultural use (with the exception of modern spray irrigation) are considered ordinary—indeed, if the purpose is connected to the land, it is generally considered ordinary. Any other abstraction that reduces the flow of water is in principle actionable by a lower riparian owner (Wisdom 1979, 104). Furthermore, the ownership rights are so strong that it was established in 1867 (*Crossley v. Lightowler* 1867) that if a person wished to exercise a riparian right (e.g., to stop pollution of a river), it was only necessary for him to own a tiny fraction of the bank of the stream.

Fisheries

A riparian owner who fishes (or a lessee whose fishery is severed from owner-ship of the soil) has the right of action for an injunction and damages against anyone who unlawfully does any act that disturbs the enjoyment of the fishery (e.g., *Dulverton R.D.C. v. Tracy* 1921). Specifically, every fishery owner is en-titled to the free passage of fish up and down the river from the sea to the source. Where the fishery owner's entitlement is separated from the ownership of the soil (an incorporeal hereditament), the entitlement is slightly weaker than that of the riparian owner. A riparian owner may restrain any degree of pollution, whereas a fishery owner or tenant who is not a riparian owner must show that the pollution is sufficient to damage his right of fishing or to render it less enjoyable.

Actions: Nuisance

The main common law action in tort (that is, civil wrong) used by landowners and angling lessees is nuisance. Simply defined, *nuisance* is a use of property that interferes with the rights of others to enjoy their own property. In nuisance, (subject to defenses) all that is required for a successful action is proof of a causal connection between the polluter and the harm. Claims for nuisance have been made in cases that go back at least as far as 1611. Then, damages and an injunction were granted to plaintiffs whose air had been "infected and corrupted" by the odors from a defendant's pigsty (*William Aldred's Case* 1611, cited in Juergensmeyer 1972, 216). Actions for negligence, trespass, and loss of fishing are also possible but far less common.

Remedies: Damages and Injunctions

The two remedies (with numerous variations) available in successful common law actions are injunctions and damages. Together, these remedies are very powerful. Strict interpretation could impose a severe burden on a defendant, such as forcing him or her out of business.

Injunctions are the traditional relief from nuisance, that is, stopping the tort from happening again. A liable defendant is required to stop the nuisance he is causing. The injunction may be suspended to allow time for compliance, or it may be qualified, in that the nuisance will be allowable at certain times (see *Kennaway v. Thompson* 1980). It is not a part of the court's duty to inquire how the defen-dant is to comply with the injunction and remove the nuisance. However, the court may well grant a suspension of the injunction if the removal of the nuisance is physically impossible (at least in the short run). If a suspension is granted, the defendant must satisfy the court that during that time everything in his or her power has been done to stop the pollution. If the defendant cannot comply within the time allowed, he or she must ask for an extension of time. Extensions are usually only given if the defendant can prove that he or she is not responsible for the default. The plaintiff is entitled to damages during this period. If the extension is not given or if the time period elapses and the pollution continues, then the defendant is in contempt of court, the penalty for which can be imprisonment and confiscation of property.

Damages are payable to the plaintiff approximating the value of the property damaged and for loss of any enjoyment of the property. Equity damages may be payable for future harm (often if an injunction is awarded but suspended).

Defenses: Prescription, Statutory Authority

There are two key defenses to a common law action that affect river pollution. These are (1) prescription and (2) conduct permitted by statute.

Pollution by custom, or plaintiffs granting pollution rights, is unusual. A *prescriptive right* is deemed to exist when a nuisance caused by the defendant has been continuing for a long period to the full knowledge of the plaintiff without complaint (see *Sturges v. Bridgman* 1879). Most important, if the defendant has secretly enjoyed the alleged easement to pollute and the plaintiff was unaware that pollution was occurring, then a prescriptive right is not granted. Interpretation of what is *unintentionally allowed by conduct permitted by the state* is varied, and hence may include pollution as a byproduct of a necessary approved activity. It is, therefore, the most frequent defense.

Injunction or Equity Damages

At the height of industrial growth, there was a general feeling that the national interest was best served by giving businesses greater freedom to pollute (Brenner 1974). Since the Lord Cairns Act of 1858, courts have been able to grant damages in lieu of an injunction. This was an attempt to "balance the interests" of the parties involved in a dispute by giving compensatory damages to put the plaintiff "in the position he would have been in if the wrong had not been committed" (Ogus and Richardson 1977, 307).

It should be obvious that the water environment is harmed if the plaintiff has to accept equity damages for future chronic pollution, rather than the pollution being enjoined. This act is, therefore, material to this chapter because it, rather than a fundamental legal deficiency, gave rise to a serious problem for common law enforcement of property rights and hence environmental protection.

A BRIEF HISTORY OF RIVERS, WATER, AND STATUTORY LAW

Prior to 1876 the attorney general could take action if pollution was so gross as to constitute a public health danger—a public nuisance. Acting against polluters for small nuisances was not considered a public duty. Action to prevent water pollution was historically taken by riparian proprietors. Indeed, "prior to 1876 a pollution action was a recognised method of liquidating a trade rival" (Gerrish 1973, 9). Nevertheless, a High Court action is expensive, so few riparian owners could afford it. Risking one's capital for an attractive riverbank was probably beyond most landowners, and it became more so after the uncertainty induced by the Lord Cairns Act. Because riparian owners were unlikely to do the job and because the acts of Parliament to that point had been inadequate, various new acts were designed to reduce pollution.

The first act of Parliament (ignoring certain purely local acts) that was passed ostensibly to stop pollution was the 1875 Public Health Act. This act specifically dealt with pollution from sewage works and gas works.

It was quickly followed by the Rivers Pollution Prevention Act of 1876, which attempted to alleviate the problem of the expense of private action. However, it failed primarily because the potential prosecutor under the act was usually the polluter itself (a local authority) or another local authority. In the case of industrial pollution, the consent for an action had to be given by the Minister of Health, who refused permission if the polluter could demonstrate that there was, as yet, no means of purifying the effluent. "It paid industry handsomely not to discover new methods of effluent treatment" (Gerrish 1973, 8). The perception following the act was that polluters could escape liability if they used the latest technology. The result of this assumed defense for pollution was that between 1876 and 1948 riparian owner actions were so rare that most polluters were unaware of the rights retained by the riparian landlord (9).

The 1876 act also established river boards; but the powers given to them under this and later acts were limited, and the impact of the boards was weak. One reason for this situation was the boards' lack of finance. The river boards had to raise money by selling licenses to fishermen and by levying fines from successful prosecutions. However, they rarely had enough finance to risk a prosecution, and when they were successful, the fines were minimal. Also, fishermen were unlikely to buy licenses in rivers that were already, or likely to become, polluted.

The next major statute to address water pollution was the Public Health (Drainage of Trade Premises) Act of 1937. This act allowed industries to discharge their effluents into sewers (subject to certain safeguards) and threw the onus of purifying them on to the local authorities. In effect, polluters were able to pump effluents into rivers, as the sewerage system simply could not cope with the volumes and the concentration of the discharges. Following a successful common law action, the courts would not compel a local authority to stop its pollution overnight—

drowning the local inhabitants in their own sewage—and the practice, where the matter was not remedied instantly, was for the court to suspend the operation of an injunction. Over time, courts made the distinction between local authorities and large corporations that were not acting in the "public interest." The corporation had less chance of having the injunction suspended for any considerable time unless the court considered the business to be of some importance. This was the position up to 1948.

THE BIRTH OF THE ANGLERS' CO-OPERATIVE ASSOCIATION

In the mid-1940s, an angler and a lawyer, John Eastwood, OBE, KC, analyzed the sixteen acts of Parliament then in force for the protection of rivers and decided "that none of them was any good" (*ACA Review* 1953, 5[1]:65). He saw that the quality of water in a river was highly dependent on the purpose to which the water in that river was put. For example, good salmon fishing could be found on rivers like the Test, which supported little industrial activity; whereas industrial production near rivers like the Derwent and Trent meant that water quality (and the fishing) was far poorer in these rivers. According to Eastwood, there was apparently no real effort to stop any polluter from releasing effluent into those British rivers used to support industrial activity. Any statutory action on these industrial rivers had been either ineffectual or even damaging. Eastwood was undeterred. As a lawyer, he was aware of the riparian rights enjoyed under English common law and considered that, in principle, no other right or regulation would be needed to protect British inland waterways. But he was concerned that riparian rights were not being enforced due to a lack of money and to the inability to finance any action. Eastwood wanted to know how to overcome the difficulties of enforcing these rights.

He came up with the novel idea of an association designed to spread the risk of an action in common law. His correspondence from 1946 showed the first germ of the idea: "Did I tell you that I have been working on a new scheme to protect our rivers against pollution? It is rather original and aims at enrolling 500,000 anglers on co-operative lines . . . it is my own idea."[2] According to Eastwood's wife, in the two and a half years prior to the formation of the Anglers' Co-Operative Association (ACA), he wrote three thousand letters (in longhand) to drum up support for the scheme. He also wrote numerous articles, attended many meetings, gave interviews, and journeyed all over the country. On February 6, 1948, the first meeting of the temporary committee of the ACA was held in a little room in Lincoln's Inn Fields in London's legal district. The ACA was incorporated soon after as ACA Trustees Ltd.

It is interesting to note that John Eastwood used the term *co-operative* to describe his idea. Co-operative (self-help) movements were far more prevalent prior to the formation of the welfare state. At that time it was not unusual that finances for medical attention and unemployment insurance were provided through co-operative associations (see Green 1994). It is unlikely that any environmental interest group in England would use that title today, even though the basis of many environmental ideals is co-operation. This compares with the United States where co-operatives (local food markets, for example) have flourished in the 1990s. But, in 1994 the co-operative name was dropped in favor of *conservation*—the Anglers' Conservation Association. What was fundamental to the design of the organization in 1946 has lost its social relevance today.

Eastwood's appeal was not to a notion of public service (i.e., as a duty to help keep rivers clean, as most environmental groups do today), but to *all* anglers' self-interest. "Remember—every mile of water which is restored to angling means a dozen fewer people competing for your own fishing . . . however sure you may be of your fishing, others have had theirs ruined in next to no time" (*ACA Review* 1950, 1[1]:7).

He also made it clear in his letters that the ACA would only support common law actions of those riparian owners and angling associations who were paid-up members of the ACA. To be able to free ride, one had to be sure that an ACA member or a riparian owner was on the same stretch of river. The incentive to join was not, however, that strong, given that in principle only one member per river was required to act as a deterrent to polluters and many rivers are very long. Nevertheless the membership fee was only £1, and nonmembership did preclude receiving any compensation if pollution, then quite frequent, occurred.

How the ACA Works

The primary aim of the ACA was to help anglers and riparian owners finance common law actions against polluters. This was achieved through the ACA trustees who set up a Guarantee Fund that could be drawn on to give financial aid to the ACA members who owned the right to fish.

The clubs and individuals pay a membership fee to the ACA, which indemnifies them against the legal costs of bringing an action under common law. In Britain, unlike the United States, a plaintiff who loses an action is generally liable for the defendant's legal fees. This indemnity is therefore critical. If a pollution incident occurs and harms the fishing or other riparian property rights of anglers and/or landowners who are ACA members, the ACA will "maintain" (financially support) the action in court. In other words, being a member of the ACA entitles you, subject to agreement from the ACA solicitors, to sue a polluter without incurring any of the cost, other than your membership fee. The fee is like an annual insurance premium for anglers. The ACA's solicitors analyze the strength of each case and usually finance a single action, sometimes bringing together numerous plaintiffs to act together. Successfully acting for one plaintiff will often induce the defendant to settle with other residual claimants.

The ACA advises the angling clubs to obtain a lease from the riparian owner so that the clubs have a proprietary interest, which is needed for any common law action. In its early days, the ACA found that many cases were not actionable because angling clubs did not have the proper proprietary interest. The clubs often had only verbal consents from riparian owners. As the ACA became more prominent and their advice to anglers to obtain a proprietary interest was more widely heard, so the number of cases where no action could be taken fell. At the end of the first year, twenty-nine clubs had asked for help, but only five had proper leases; whereas, over the next decade, there were fewer than ten clubs that asked for help without proper leases. The ACA also explained the advantages of obtaining long leases. If pollution occurred and an injunction was suspended, a claim could be made over the life of the lease until the pollution was stopped.

Cases Brought by the Anglers' Conservation Association

Some of the cases briefly presented here set precedents as new applications of the common law.[3] The other cases mentioned were of some special interest because of their economic, financial, or environmental significance.

Lord Brockton v. Luton Corporation, 1946

When the ACA was still in formation in 1946, Lord Brockton as plaintiff financed the ACA's first action. The Luton Corporation had to maintain certain effluent quality objectives, standards considered acceptable to the government of the day. They were not strictly breaking the standards, but, as there was not enough dilution for their effluent, pollution resulted. In World War I, the Luton Corporation produced one million gallons of sewage a day. This was reasonably well diluted by a daily flow of six million gallons of river water. By 1939, they were producing seven million gallons of sewage a day, but the amount of river water used was the same. Pollution was inevitable. The corporation as defendant had an injunction placed on it for polluting the River Lea in Hertfordshire.

However, the Luton Corporation continued polluting for months after they were found liable. Judge Vaisey commented, when explaining that the injunction would not be suspended indefinitely: "It was no use for the defendants to say that they could not purify their effluent to a higher standard as the Metropolitan Water Board were actually taking this effluent and turning it into drinking water" (*ACA Review* 1950, 1[4]: 83).

The case gave the ACA "a try-out against determined opposition and proved its efficiency in action" (*ACA Review* 1950, 1[1]: 10). It showed that the ACA would not shy from conflict or controversy to achieve its goal. The case also epitomized the cases that the ACA would encounter later—local authorities disregarding common law rights, effluent quality objectives that were useless at preventing pollution, and the lack of dilution for effluents being ignored.

Upton v. Great Torrington Corporation, 1951

One of the more interesting cases that the ACA undertook was a nuisance action brought against the Great Torrington Corporation for sewage pollution. The Borough of Great Torrington was founded over one thousand years ago by Alfred the Great, who, like those that followed him, made no provision for sewage disposal. The resulting pollution was obviously made worse by an expanding population. The Great Torrington Corporation capitulated three days before the trial and submitted to an injunction. *Upton v. Great Torrington* set a standard that alarmed local authorities and polluting industries: "The duty of anyone who turns effluent into a stream is to regulate his discharge so that it does not pollute the stream . . . The real test is whether pollution occurs when the flow of the stream is at its minimum and when the discharge of effluent is at its maximum volume and worst quality" (*ACA Review* 1951, 2[4]: 51).

Pride of Derby et al. v. British Celanese Ltd., 1952

The ACA's most famous case, usually referred to simply as the *Pride of Derby*, and the one that alerted the author to the existence of the ACA involved a major pollution of the River Derwent. Eight miles of the Derwent and three miles of the Trent (at the confluence of the two rivers) were deoxygenated. The riverbed was covered with fungus and foul black sludge, and the temperature of the water was high. There was no life in the river. The case lasted seventeen days, still the longest of all the ACA legal battles.

The key point of this case was that the Derby Corporation had statutory authority to provide sewage works for the region and claimed this as its defense against the action of the plaintiffs, in effect claiming that it was entitled to pollute the river. The judge gave an injunction and set a precedent that any statutory authority had to have explicit pollution rights written into it to resist a common-law action. Derby Corporation did not have that explicit authority. Nevertheless, the issue was not resolved immediately. By 1956 the Derby Corporation still had not properly updated its sewage works; and because of the increased sewage and decay to its facilities, the costs of compliance were estimated to be fourfold greater than had it done the work in 1952 (*ACA Review* 1967, 16[9]:15). Over the next few years, the works were updated, and all pollution abated.

Myddleton and Others v. J. Summers and Sons Ltd., 1954

This was an important test case. Salmon and trout are anadromous fish that swim upriver to spawn. Fishery owners enjoy the right that fish can move freely up and down the river. Anything that substantially interferes with this right is potentially actionable.

Myddleton claimed that salmon smolts were being killed in the River Dee estuary and that his fishery, 35 to 40 miles upstream, was being harmed. There was no course of action except for claiming harm to the free movement of fish. A finding for the plaintiff would therefore set a useful precedent for the ACA. The ACA knew this would be an important case and asked for increased guarantees from their members in case the action took a long time to present. Additional guarantees were put up by the netsmen of the Dee estuary, who were losing their livelihood because of estuarial pollution.

Justice Roxburgh found that cyanide pollution by the defendant created a material obstruction to the free passage of salmon through the estuary. This pollution was an interference with the right of the fishery owners on the river and thus "there should be judgement for the plaintiff in the form of an injunction and damages" (Justice Roxburgh quoted in *ACA Review* 1955 6[1]:5). The sum awarded for damages was £6,000.

The Dee was the first river on which an injunction was granted to upstream fishery owners to restrain pollution in tidal waters. *Myddleton* was a new and singularly unambiguous application of the law. The ACA pointed out that the estuaries of the Tyne, Tees, Usk, Wyke, Taw, and Torridge were in a similar condition to the Dee. It therefore wondered whether an action similar to *Myddleton* could be used to save those estuaries. However, the impact of this case was uncertain—no similar cases were reported in future issues of the *ACA Reviews*.

ACA Trustees Ltd v. Northumbrian Water Authority, 1983

In October 1983, 13,500 liters of flux oil leaked into the River Tees upstream of Darlington. The oil killed fish over a 20-mile stretch of the river. To flush the oil away, the Northumbrian Water Authority (NWA) used water from Kielder Reservoir by operating tunnels that connect the Tyne, Wear, and Tees. Acting on behalf of the Tees Fisheries Action Committee, which represented fifty-two claimants, the ACA negotiated two interim payments of £20,000 from NWA, which was spent on restocking the river. In October 1987, a final settlement was obtained that lifted the total figure to a record £352,684.85 (*ACA Review* 1988, 10–11).

Golden Hill Fishing Club v. Wansford Trout Farm, 1986

In 1986 the ACA achieved one of its most notable legal victories with its first action against a trout farm. A trout farm was polluting the West Beck, one of the best chalk streams in Britain. It also was abstracting large quantities of water, which at times cut off all instream flows to the Beck.

The fish farm claimed the right to abstract and to pollute by easement because it had been farming trout since 1955. The ACA challenged the defense by claiming that the level of abstraction and pollution had increased over time. As evidence they cited the sales revenue for the Wansford Trout Farm, which was £58,907 in 1973 but which had hugely increased to £616,329 by 1981. Negotiations broke down and action in the High Court followed. The ACA's costs, had they lost, would have been in excess of £80,000. Nevertheless, when the ACA's Pollution Subcommittee met in London, they unanimously voted to go to the High Court. In front of the judge, the trout farm backed down and agreed to remedy the conditions and to pay costs and damages of £32,500 to the Golden Hill Club.

Five years later the trout farm again polluted the West Beck, causing harm to rights of the Golden Hill Fishing Club. The pollution in 1990–91 was held to be contempt of court because the farm had an injunction against them following their pollution in 1986. Justice Henry fined them £500 each for each breach of covenant (fourteen breaches in total). The managing director of the trout farm did not have his property sequestered nor was he sent to jail "because of the efforts the company was now making to counter the pollution" (*ACA Review* 1991, 3:1–2). The trout farm put into operation pumps that cost £46,500 and a biological filter that cost £50,000.

ACA Trustees Ltd v. Thames Water Authority, 1987

In 1987, the ACA mounted its "first-ever statutory prosecution to highlight the fact that those charged with preventing pollution are often polluters themselves" (*ACA Review* 1988, 10). In mid-May the magistrates at Aylesbury heard six specimen charges of pollution against the Thames Water Authority (TWA). The charges alleged that on September 11, 1986, and on five subsequent dates, the TWA caused sewage effluent to enter the River Thames, breaching the conditions of Consent no. 1365 of section 32 (1) of the Control of Pollution Act (COPA), 1974, Part II.

The ACA brought this criminal prosecution to highlight specific pollution problems with respect to sewage treatment, or the lack of it. Section 32 of the act was not implemented until August 1985, and it was not until May 1987 that this first action was brought.

The TWA pleaded guilty to the charges and was fined £1,000 on each of the counts. In addition to this, it was ordered to pay £800 costs. The ACA's successful prosecution of the Thames Water Authority had widespread coverage in the national press, met with enthusiastic approval by anglers, and led to future prosecutions, such as that against the Anglian Water Authority in 1988.

Case History Summary

In the fifty years since the prescient John Eastwood founded the ACA, the various solicitors and barristers acting on the behalf of its members have probably brought over two thousand actions against polluters, losing only three. Of these, 920 cases have been collated so far by the author in an expanding database; more will be added over the coming years.

The cases presented in the preceding section were probably the most important in establishing the rights of anglers. In particular, *Myddleton v. Summers* and the *Pride of Derby* were truly path-breaking. The ACA did not discriminate in favor of or against any particular group. All polluters were targeted for action in the most single-minded campaign against pollution that any nation has seen from a voluntary organization. Approximately 40 percent of the cases were brought against local authorities or companies operating with statutory authority (government approval for its actions). Private companies were defendants in 47 percent of the cases, farmers were defendants in about 7 percent, with a small miscellaneous remainder.

From the author's database, there are thirty-four recorded injunctions (most before 1966) and damages and costs totaling considerably more than £1 million against defendants. Having clearly established anglers' rights, few cases brought direct challenges. Once the defendant's lawyers became aware of the strength of the ACA case, most disputes were settled out of court, and therefore not reported. The ACA reported that "large, undisclosed settlements" were being achieved from the late 1960s onward (*ACA Review* 1974, 20: 1). There are probably far more injunctions, court orders, and verbal agreements made than this author has unearthed. Furthermore, the settlements are probably nearer £10 million because settlements often remain undisclosed—most defendants wish to keep their names out of the press.

Most cases were never tried in court; and of those, only a handful were reported in law reports or journals, such as some of those mentioned in the preceding section. Legal representatives for the ACA became adept at negotiating settlements by the threat of action. A team of three lawyers (working part-time for the ACA) and an ACA staff of four (who were also working on membership and other matters) were able to maintain an average of forty cases a year, a remarkable achievement of efficiency and simplicity.

GOVERNMENT ACTION AND LEGISLATION

"Strangely enough the lamentable amount of pollution existing today is due largely to the various Acts of Parliament that have been passed ostensibly to stop pollution" (Stratton Gerrish quoted in *ACA Review* 1973, 6).

This section briefly discusses the efficacy of water quality legislation (and those charged with its implementation) and the impacts that ACA lobbying has had on legislation since 1948. The ACA has consistently lobbied for the ability to use English common law to prevent pollution over the past fifty years. Were it not for ACA lobbying, common law actions against pollution would have become a historical topic of study, rather than a practical remedy for harm.

Rivers Boards

The government's river boards were never a success. Part of the problem was the background of their decision-making committees, whose members had an interest in the water environment but mainly from a commercial angle. Most were from local business, such as farmers and industrialists, or from local government. Few, if any, were from fisheries, although some may have been wealthy landowners. Therefore, many members of the river boards were themselves potential polluters. It is not surprising that the boards were unsuccessful in preventing pollution. Nevertheless, a lack of finance for the river boards certainly contributed to their failure.

It became obvious where the allegiances of river board members lay from their influence on the initial drafting of the Rivers Prevention of Pollution Bill of 1951. Subsections 4 and 5 of clause 4 were adopted with river board approval. In essence, these subsections stated that, provided a polluter kept to the standards set by the river boards, the polluter was safe not only from criminal prosecution but from civil action as well. This suggests a direct response to ACA actions brought in the common law.

Uniform Emission Standards

The standards set by the Rivers Prevention of Pollution Act of 1951 were called uniform emission standards (UES), and they applied to the quantity and the quality of the effluent emitted. When originally set, the UES took notice of the impact that effluent would have on the receiving environment. In other words, it was not simply the amount or the type of effluent that mattered, but also the amount of water in the river. However, in practice, the assimilative capacity of the receiving environment was ignored. The operation of the UES omitted half the equation. It provided certainty for the polluter, but it would lead to pollution. Fortunately, as the UES were never given statutory authority and were interpreted as a guideline, common law actions could proceed.

In addition to standard setting, the river boards were also responsible for the issue of abstraction licenses, and it became clear that too many licenses were issued, causing serious depletion of instream flow and exacerbating the problems of the UES. Being unable to retract licenses once given, the river boards demanded more powers to deal with the very problems that they had themselves created (*ACA Review* 1960, 11[4]: 60). The river boards, when abolished in 1963, had prosecuted no one under the Rivers Prevention of Pollution Act of 1951.

Because of business and local government lobbying aimed at ensuring that the UES should protect polluters, the ACA maintained a running campaign against such statutory protection. The ACA spent considerable sums reminding government officials that the UES, if defined as a statutory authorization by government, would stop any common law action against a polluter complying with their UES, regardless of the pollution caused.

Acknowledging the power of the interests against it and in favor of the UES, the ACA suggested a compromise to the government. The common law should remain as it was (hence the UES was not a statutory authorization and would not undermine the common law); but in any case where national economic interests might have been affected by any common law action, the attorney general could apply to the court for an extension of time before the order of the court (such as an injunction) became operative. Most politicians supported this amendment, and in the end, the minister withdrew the subsections undermining common law. This was the first instance that the ACA successfully influenced public policy.

Rivers Prevention of Pollution Act, 1961

This act brought into existence many of the recommendations of the Trade Effluents Subcommittee of the Central Water Authority Committee (1960), usually referred to as the Armer Committee, so named for its chairman. This period marks the lowest point of relations between government and the ACA. The influence and success of the ACA were becoming a threat to nationalized interests, which were of paramount importance to the government of the day.

It is interesting that the largest representation for change in the common law came from sections of the Federation of British Industry (now Confederation of British Industry), mainly the British Iron and Steel Federation. The Gas Council and the National Coal Board also supported the proposed changes. In their deposition, the Federation of British Industry cited the ACA's first case, *Lord Brockton v. Luton Corporation* (1946), saying that generally the business community could not comply with injunctions, and hence the common law should not be allowed to work. In *Brockton*, the designers of the sewage works said that they could not comply with the Royal Commission standards (Bate 1994).

The ACA was invited to give evidence before the Armer Committee. Although the ACA's advice was heeded, the committee still recommended that the rights of riparian owners and anglers should be attenuated if it could be shown "that the operation of the common law was unduly onerous, or had led to the closing of industrial works, or had raised the cost of production" (quoted in *ACA Review* 1960, 11[1]: 2). This seems to indicate that the committee was not aware of the importance of external costs (i.e., pollution), resulting from the production process. However it is more likely that the committee was responding to special interests—polluting businesses and communities that did not want to bear the full costs of fully enforced property rights. In effect, the committee was saying that external costs should not be internalized by common law action, such as judges making companies pay for their pollution. In short, the Armer Committee was saying that business shouldn't have to pay for its pollution and that the common law should be changed accordingly. The committee noted that the "common law remedy had been invoked more frequently in recent years under the influence of the ACA . . . and that some pressure had been put on polluters in consequence" (quoted in *ACA Review* 1960, 11[1]: 2).

The Armer Committee had also recommended that statutory UES be set for each individual effluent. This would have made the common law impotent.

The Armer Committee also seemed to want to completely undermine the common law's ability to combat excess abstraction. "Abstraction of water from streams on the surface or from underground sources should be subject to a licence [which confers] a statutory right to reduce the flow of the river . . . and should override all common law rights of riparian owners or anglers" (*ACA Review* 1962, 13[2]: 17, citing the Armer Committee). This proposal made common law action against abstractors even more difficult. It was also inequitable. For example, if an abstractor reduced the flow of a river, an emitter of effluent might inadvertently cause pollution and be liable to prosecution, whereas the abstractor would go free. As the ACA put it, "Abstraction . . . is the handmaiden of pollution" (*ACA Review* 1973, 19[4]: 6).[4]

The River Prevention of Pollution Act of 1961 did instruct officials to design individual abstraction-licensing systems as recommended by the Armer Committee. But, under lobbying pressure by the ACA, it did not take away the possibility of common law actions by making the UES a statutory authority (Bate 1994).

In 1965, river boards were superseded by River Authorities, which were to assess the acceptable minimum "instream" flow for each river. (It was apparent that the government was finally acknowledging the significance of dilution.) Because of the decision to set instream flow requirements, the ACA supported the new River

Authorities (*ACA Review* 1965, 16: 1). But, yet again, the Ministry of Health adopted effluent standards that ignored the dilution factor. Over the next few years, sewage multiplied rapidly with increases in industrial development and the demands for domestic use, and the dilution factor became so low that pollution incidents led to increased ACA legal actions.

Water Resources Act, 1968

Under the Rivers Prevention of Pollution Acts of 1951 and 1961, the river boards had to impose conditions on discharges of effluent and had to license discharges that complied with their conditions, which in turn had to be related to the amount of clean diluting water available. But "under proposals for the new Water Resources Act the Minister must license abstractions of clean water regardless of the effect that they may have on the pollution of the river by reducing the volume of clean diluting water" (*ACA Review* 1969, 16[13]: 8). ACA lobbying forced changes in these provisions. Had this act passed in its original form without amendment, it would have undermined all the previous work of the ACA.

Control of Pollution Act, 1974

The buildup to the Control of Pollution Act (COPA), 1974, highlights the powerful political position that anglers, and the ACA in particular, were creating for themselves. From the nadir of the Armer Committee, the ACA was now enjoying very good relations with government. The ACA even boasted that: "we have helpful contacts at both government and parliamentary level" (*ACA Review* 1976, 22[1]: 3). In 1972, the ACA was called in for negotiations with the Under-Secretary of State for the Environment, Eldon-Griffiths. According to an ACA editorial, this call came because of substantial pressure from ACA members who wrote to their members of Parliament and demanded changes in government policies toward anglers. In November 1972, Eldon-Griffiths announced in Parliament: "I have met the Anglers' Conservation Association. As a result we have been able to accept some suggestions for revision of the proposals relating to Common Law rights" (*ACA Review* 1972, 19[2]: 6).

The overriding concern of the ACA was that, in some cases, the vital decision as to whether a fishery had suffered damage would have been made by various government nominees and officials instead of by the High Court. Similarly, the same nominees and officials would have fixed the amount of compensation payable. Fortunately, because of ACA persistence, Eldon-Griffiths agreed that rights to bring common law actions for damages against all dischargers of effluents would remain absolutely as they stood, "*whether or not* the discharger in question had complied with a water authority's 'consent'" (*ACA Review* 1972, 19[2]: 6, emphasis in original). However, on August 5, 1975, the UK Department of the Environment announced that implementation of Part II of the Control of Pollution Act was to be postponed indefinitely. As all the more effective statutory measures to contain or to reduce pollution were included in Part II, this was a major setback.

The ACA was even more dismayed when, in the following year, the government announced an easing of emission standards. It would have been politically embarrassing to introduce Part II when 30 percent of discharges to rivers did not comply with the existing legal standards. According to the ACA, the "consent conditions are being revised, just to make sure that there aren't any embarrassing legal actions" (*ACA Review* 1978: 3). It is likely that this measure was intended to ensure that Part II of COPA, 1974, could be brought into effect. COPA, Part II, was still not fully implemented ten years after Part I, and the ACA concluded that:

> when it is (if it is), factories that have been polluting Britain's rivers for decades will carry on polluting. They will either be exempt from the Act's controls, or they will have obtained what are known as "deemed consents." One of the main aims of the legislation was to enable members of the public to prosecute any firm or individual who failed to keep the consent conditions. There is little possibility of that happening for the simple reason that "consents" have been tailored to fit polluters' requirements. In short, the Act will legalise pollution. (*ACA Review* 1984, 3)

Privatization

In the discussion leading up to water privatization in 1989, Environment Secretary John Patten wrote an article in the *ACA Review* to attempt to convince anglers that privatization was not a bad idea. He wrote, "In future, quality objectives for our rivers will be set on a statutory basis—by the Authorities themselves. There will be new powers to ensure that Authorities give effect to environmental policies—and a new government inspectorate to advise on their exercise of environmental functions and to check the quality of their own effluent discharge" (*ACA Review* 1989, 11).

Members of the ACA were unconvinced by Patten's statement. They criticized unfulfilled government promises to clean up rivers and to enforce existing legislation. The ACA was particularly scathing in its critique of the eleven-year wait for the enforcement of COPA, Part II, noting that even after eleven years "some parts of the Act have never been implemented" (*ACA Review* 1989, 11).

The ACA thought that the National Rivers Authority (NRA), the new government inspectorate, was a step in the right direction. However, it was concerned that the NRA, like the river boards, would be ineffectual: "At present there is nothing [the NRA] can do, because in order to make a success of water privatisation the Government gave legal permission to the water authorities to discharge sewage into rivers pending the building of adequate sewage works, so the NRA, like an army awaiting its supplies of ammunition, will only be able to tackle the problem when the Government's derogations expire in a few years' time" (*ACA Review* 1990, 4).

Nevertheless, the ACA cooperated in several actions with the NRA. The NRA quickly developed a good reputation for combating pollution of English rivers and continued to cooperate with the ACA until the NRA became part of the Environment Agency in the late 1990s.

CONCLUSIONS

English common law, as it relates to pollution, is working at its best when it has nothing to do—when the deterrent effect is complete. The preventative power of an ex post liability system relies on the threat of action. Where rights are clearly defined, as with anglers and rivers, potential polluters know quite well what they can and cannot do. There is no doubt that in its heyday, the ACA used common law as a significant threat to would-be polluters. Although an estimation of how much pollution it prevented is impossible to calculate, its more famous cases show that it cleaned up (and kept clean) hundreds of miles of English rivers in industrial areas, such as the Derwent, the Trent, and the Dee (Estuary).

However, the ACA as an organization has been a victim of its own success. The extremely successful and efficient out-of-court settlement of disputes means that the ACA's public profile is very low. It is obvious from the writing in the *ACA Reviews* (an extensive newsletter that kept members informed of ACA activities) that it was always a struggle for the ACA staff to maintain membership. When the ACA was bringing actions (and receiving newspaper coverage), their membership increased from 1,500 in 1950 to 10,000 in 1966. As the powerful common law deterrent became widely known among local authority and business circles, any disputes were quickly settled in the anglers' favor. Even members who had directly benefited from ACA actions forgot to renew their subscriptions because the threat of pollution had been removed so effectually. Membership declined until the notable actions of the 1980s, when it rose to its current 16,500.

The ACA rarely failed, but it was increasingly hampered as more polluters, and especially local councils, were given statutory authority for their activities in the 1960s and 1970s. There were also instances when there were so many polluters in an area that identifying the guilty party became impossible. Under these circumstances, antipollution government regulation was the only solution, but it was not until COPA, Part II, actually came into effect in the mid-1980s that regulation really began to tackle pollution with some of the same effect that the common law could have generated.

Almost as remarkable as the ACA legal action was its lobbying activity. Working within its specific brief to establish and to maintain clean rivers, the ACA became a successful environmental watchdog long before the major environmental groups were even formed. Had it not been for ACA lobbying, government acts between 1951 and 1985 would have protected nationalized industries from all liability of pollution action. It is extremely doubtful that government, national or local, would have prevented gross pollution of English and Welsh rivers.

Modern environmental organizations have grown to resemble the large corporations that they attack. They rely on orchestrated publicity events to raise donations to support massive staffs. They lobby support from large donors and have all but forgotten the individual supporter on whom the movements were founded. They rarely rely on common law property-rights protection. Rather, they usually call for ever more statutory intervention to address the latest real or imagined environmental problem. The ACA, which has never had more than five employees, has resisted the temptation to do this. The ACA occasionally reviews the latest scares (acid rain, pesticide residues, global warming), but it recognized that these topics were tangential to its main aim, and the review editors always treated the issues sensibly.

It is likely that the ACA is probably the most efficient and determined, member-led, environmental organization in Britain. It is potentially a model, a template for other interest groups to follow. But can that potential be realized? Part of the success of the ACA is that it relies on a system of law whereby the individual's rights are narrowly defined and can be strictly upheld. Actions of the ACA are, on the whole, specific actions against individual polluters, not general citizen suits against threats to the environment. Thus, only in countries where similar rights exist and are exercised, such as any country with a tradition of English common law, could the bold specific approach of the ACA be followed.

There were over 1.1 million anglers registered in England and Wales in 1998 (and over 500,000 when the ACA was formed). This is a massive user base from which to draw support, and an ever-vigilant membership to spot pollution. It is unlikely that any other interest group would have as many potential members with a similar goal. Although only a fraction of the anglers paid dues to the ACA, the free rider problem that is supposed to prevent such organizations from ever succeeding did not deter members. Private citizens acting together to protect common property rights can achieve great results without centralized commands from the legislature.

Therefore, the ACA model could be extended to other common law countries with large angling interests. It is possible that other user groups with large regional or local membership in common law countries could follow its approach. Whether the approach could be taken by angling groups in non-common law countries is a topic for future research.

NOTES

This chapter is based on a longer book manuscript in progress. Contact the author at 101627.2464@compuserve.com for further details.

1. The Anglers' Conservation Association produced an extensive newsletter to keep its members informed of the association's activities. The newsletter, originally published quarterly, then biannually, and now annually, is hereinafter cited as the *ACA Review*. ACA mailing address: Anglers' Conservation Association, Shalford Dairy, Shalford Hill, Aldermaston, Reading, Berkshire RG7 4NB UK.

2. Dorothea Eastwood, quoted in *ACA Review* (1955, 7[3]: 54), in remembrance of her husband, John Eastwood, who died in 1950.

3. Additional cases are described in the in-progress manuscript noted earlier.

4. The names and dates are a bit different, but the experience is much the same as in Canada and the United States.

REFERENCES

ACA Review. Various years. Reading, UK: Anglers' Conservation Association.

Bate, Roger N. 1994. English and Welsh Rivers: A Common Law Approach to Pollution Prevention. Master's thesis, Cambridge University.

Brenner, Joel. 1974. Nuisance Law and the Industrial Revolution. *Journal of Legal Studies* 3: 403–33.

Gerrish, C. Stratton. 1973. *Pollution: The ACA Handbook.* Bury St. Edmunds, U.K.: ACA.

Green, David. 1994. *Reinventing Civil Society.* London: Institute of Economic Affairs.

Juergensmeyer, Jens. 1972. Common Law Remedies and Protection of the Environment. *University of British Columbia Law Review* 6: 215–36.

Meiners, Roger E., Stacie Thomas, and Bruce Yandle. 2000. Burning Rivers, Common Law, and Institutional Choice for Water Quality, this volume.

Ogus, Anthony I., and G. M. Richardson. 1977. Economics and the Environment: A Study of Private Nuisance. *Cambridge Law Journal* 36(2): 284–325.

Wisdom, Arthur S. 1979. *The Law of Rivers and Watercourses.* London: Shaw & Sons Ltd.

CASES CITED

Cases marked with an asterisk are those that are only reported in the ACA's records.

ACA Trustees Ltd. v. Northumbrian Water Authority (1983)*

ACA Trustees Ltd. v. Thames Water Authority (1987)*

Chasemore v. Richards, 7 H.L. Cas. 349 (1859)

Crossley v. Lightowler, 16, L.T. 438 (1867)

Dulverton R.D.C. v. Tracy, 85, J.P. 217 (1921)

Golden Hill Fishing Club v. Wansford Trout Farm (1986)*

Kennaway v. Thompson, 3 All ER 329 (1980)

Lord Brockton v. Luton Corporation (1946)*

Myddleton and Others v. J. Summers and Sons Ltd. (1954)*

Pride of Derby and Derbyshire Angling Association Ltd. and Earl of Harrington v. British Celanese Ltd., the Derby Corporation, the British Electrical Authority and Midland Tar Distillers, 1 All ER 179 (1952); Court of Appeal, 1 All ER 1326 (1953)

Sturges v. Bridgman, 11 Ch. D. 852, 865 (1879)

Upton v. Great Torrington Corporation (1951)*

William Aldred's Case, 9 C Rep 57 77 Eng. Rep. 816 (K.B. 1611)

Part III

The Institutions of the Common Law

5

The Institution of Property

David Schmidtz

The evolution of property law is driven by an ongoing search for ways to internalize externalities: positive externalities associated with productive effort and negative externalities associated with misuse of commonly held resources. In theory, and sometimes in practice, costs are internalized over time. Increasingly, people pay for their own mistakes and misfortunes, and not for the mistakes and misfortunes of others.

One general kind of justification has to do with law's role in internalizing externalities. Property enables would-be producers to capture the benefits of productive effort. It also enables people to insulate themselves from negative externalities associated with activities around the neighborhood. Property law is not perfect. To minimize negative externalities that neighbors might otherwise impose on each other, people resort to nuisance laws and zoning laws. People turn to institutions like the Environmental Protection Agency (EPA) for the same reasons they turn to central planners in other parts of the world; they think that decentralized decision making is chaos and that with chaos comes a burgeoning of negative externalities.

What is the reality? The reality is that decentralization may or may not be chaos. It depends on institutional structure. An open-access commons decentralizes decision making in one way; private property decentralizes it in another way, with systematically different results.

ORIGINAL APPROPRIATION: THE PROBLEM

Philosophers speak of the ideal of society as a cooperative venture for mutual advantage (Rawls 1971). To be a cooperative venture for mutual advantage, though, society must first be a setting in which mutually advantageous interaction is possible. In the parlance of game theorists, society must be a positive-sum game.

What determines the extent to which society is a positive sum game? This essay explains how property institutions convert negative-sum or zero-sum games into positive-sum games, setting the stage for society's flourishing as a cooperative venture.

The term *property rights* is used to refer to a bundle of rights that could include rights to sell, to lend, to bequeath, and so on. In what follows, I use the term to refer primarily to the right of owners to exclude nonowners. Private owners have the right to exclude nonowners, but the right to exclude is a feature of property rights in general rather than the defining feature of private ownership in particular. The National Park Service claims a right to exclude. Communes claim a right to exclude nonmembers. This chapter does not settle which kind or which mix of public and private property institutions is best. Instead, it asks how we could justify *any* institution that recognizes a right to exclude.

The right to exclude presents a philosophical problem, though. Consider how full-blooded rights differ from mere liberties (Hohfeld 1919). If I am at liberty to plant a garden, that means that my planting a garden is permitted. That leaves open the possibility of your being at liberty to interfere with my gardening as you see fit. Thus, mere liberties are not full-blooded rights. When I stake a claim to a piece of land, though, I claim to be changing other people's liberties—canceling them somehow—so that other people no longer are at liberty to use the land without my permission. To say I have a right to the land is to say I have a right to exclude.

From where could such rights have come? There must have been a time when no one had a right to exclude. Everyone had liberties regarding the land, but not rights. (Perhaps this does not seem obvious, but if no one owns the land, no one has a right to exclude. If no one has a right to exclude, everyone has liberties.) How, then, did we get from each person having a liberty to someone having an exclusive right to the land? What justifies original appropriation, that is, staking a claim to previously unowned resources?

To justify a claim to unowned land, people need not make as strong a case as would be needed to justify confiscating land already owned by someone else. Specifically, because there is no prior owner in original appropriation cases, there is no one from whom one can or needs to get consent. Following Locke (1690, sec. 25), some say we start out holding the earth in common, perhaps as a gift from God. But holding earth in common does not mean we own it (in the sense of having a right to exclude). Holding is merely holding. Locke himself (sec. 25) distinguished between holding the earth in common and owning it. Locke is rebutting the absolute monarchist Robert Filmer, who failed to make this distinction and thus incoherently assumed that the situation preceding the land's initial acquisition is a situation in which people (as a group) already own it, and therefore already have a veto—a right to exclude. Filmer (1652, 234) said that "if but one man in the world had dissented, the alteration had been unjust, because that man by the law of nature had a right to the common use of all things."

What, then, must a person do? Locke's idea seemed to have been that any residual (perhaps need-based) communal claim to the land could be met if a person could appropriate it without prejudice to other people, in other words, if a person could leave "enough and as good" for others. This so-called Lockean Proviso (Nozick 1974) can be interpreted in many ways, but an adequate interpretation will note that this is its point: to license claims that can be made without making other people worse off.

We also should consider whether the "others" who are to be left with enough and as good include not just people currently on the scene but latecomers as well, including people not yet born. John Sanders (1987, 377) asked, "What possible argument could at the same time require that the present generation have scruples about leaving enough and as good for one another, while shrugging off such concern for future generations?" Most theorists accept the more demanding interpretation. It fits better with Locke's idea that the preservation of humankind (which includes future generations) is the ultimate criterion by which any use of resources is assessed. Aside from that, we surely have a more compelling defense of an appropriation when we can argue that there was enough left over not just for contemporaries but also for generations to come.

Of course, when we justify original appropriation, we do not in the process justify expropriation. Indeed, McDonald (1976, 27–48) argued that to endorse Nozickian property theory is to be committed to endorsing aboriginal rights and aboriginal claims to land taken from them without consent. Some say institutions that license expropriation make people better off; I think our histories of violent expropriation are ongoing tragedies for us all. Capitalist regimes have tainted histories. Communist regimes have tainted histories. Europeans took land from native American tribes, and before that, those tribes took the same land from other tribes. We may regard those expropriations as the history of markets or of governments or of Christianity or simply as the history of the human race. It makes little difference. This chapter discusses the history of property institutions, not because their history can justify them, but rather because their history shows how some of them enable people to make themselves and the people around them better off.[1] Among such institutions are those that license original appropriation (and not expropriation).

ORIGINAL APPROPRIATION: A SOLUTION

Private property's philosophical critics often have claimed that justifying original appropriation is the key to justifying private property, frequently offering a version of Locke's Proviso as the standard of justification. Part of the Proviso's attraction for such critics was that it seemingly could not be met. Even today, philosophers generally conclude that the Proviso is, at least in the case of land appropriation, logically impossible to satisfy and, thus, that (private) property in land cannot possibly be justified along Lockean lines.

The way Judith Thomson (1990, 330) put it is, if "the first labor-mixer must literally leave as much and as good for others who come along later, then no one can come to own anything, for there are only finitely many things in the world so that every taking leaves less for others." To say the least, Thomson is not alone:

"We leave enough and as good for others only when what we take is not scarce" (Fried 1995, 230n).

"The Lockean Proviso, in the contemporary world of overpopulation and scarce resources, can almost never be met" (Held 1980, 6).

"Every acquisition worsens the lot of others—and worsens their lot in relevant ways" (Bogart 1985, 834).

"The condition that there be enough and as good left for others could not of course be literally satisfied by any system of private property rights" (Sartorius 1984, 210).

And so on. If we take something out of the cookie jar, we *must* be leaving less for others. This appears self-evident. It has to be right.

Appropriation Is Not a Zero-Sum Game

But it is *not* right. First, it is by no means impossible—certainly not logically impossible—for a taking to leave as much for others. Surely we can at least imagine a logically possible world of magic cookie jars in which, every time you take out one cookie, more and better cookies take its place.

Second, the logically possible world I just imagined is the sort of world we actually live in. Philosophers writing about original appropriation tend to speak as if people who arrive first are luckier than those who come later. The truth is that first appropriators begin the process of resource creation; latecomers get most of the benefits. Consider America's first permanent English settlement, the Jamestown Colony of 1607. (Or, if you prefer, imagine the lifestyles of the first people to cross the Bering Strait from Asia.) Was their situation better than ours? How so? Is it that they never worried about being overcharged for car repairs? Never awoke in the middle of the night to the sound of noisy refrigerators, leaky faucets, or flushing toilets? Never had to change a light bulb? Never agonized over the choice of long-distance telephone companies?

Philosophers are taught to say, in effect, that original appropriators got the good stuff for free, while latecomers have to pay for ugly leftovers. But in truth, original appropriation benefits latecomers far more than it benefits original appropriators. Original appropriation is a cornucopia of wealth, but mainly for latecomers. The people who got here first never dreamt of things we latecomers take for granted. The poorest among us have life expectancies exceeding theirs by several decades. This is not political theory. It is not economic rhetoric. It is fact.

Original appropriation diminishes the stock of what can be originally appropriated, at least in the case of land; but that is not the same thing as diminishing the stock of what can be owned. (Is it *fair* for latecomers to be excluded from acquiring property by rules allowing original appropriation? Sanders [1987, 385] noted that latecomers "are *not* excluded from acquiring property by these rules. They are, instead, excluded from being the first to own what has not been owned previously. Is *that* unfair?") On the contrary, in taking control of resources and thereby removing those particular resources from the stock of goods that can be acquired by originally appropriation, people typically generate massive increases in the stock of goods that can be acquired by trade. The lesson is that appropriation typically is not a zero-sum game. It normally is a positive-sum game.[2] As Locke stressed, appropriation creates the possibility of mutual benefit on a massive scale. Locke (1690, sec. 40, sec. 43) estimated that at least 99 percent of the value of products of the earth is attributable to labor inputs. When we add this to the premise (implicit in Section 35) that parceling the commons allows labor to multiply the products of the earth, we can infer that, in contemporary terms, appropriation is a positive-sum game: it creates the possibility of society as a cooperative venture.

The argument is not merely that enough is produced in appropriation's aftermath to compensate latecomers who lost out in the race to appropriate. The argument is that the bare fact of being an original appropriator is not the prize. The prize is prosperity, and latecomers win big, courtesy of those who got here first. If anyone had a right to be compensated, it would be the first appropriators.

The Commons before Appropriation Is Not Zero-Sum Either

The second point is that the commons before appropriation is not a zero-sum game either. Typically it is a negative-sum game. Let me tell two stories. The first comes from the coral reefs of the Philippine and Tongan Islands. People who once fished those reefs with lures and traps have recently caught on to a technique called bleach-fishing, which involves dumping bleach into the reefs. Fish cannot breathe sodium hypochlorite. Suffocated, they float to the surface where they are easy to collect. More recently, Nash (1996) claimed that fishermen pump 330,000 pounds of cyanide per year into Philippine reefs.

The problem is that the coral itself is composed of living animals. The coral suffocates along with the fish, and the dead reef is no longer a viable habitat. (Another technique, blast-fishing, involves dynamiting the reefs. The concussion produces an easy harvest of stunned fish and dead coral.) You may say people ought to be more responsible. They ought to preserve the reefs for their children. That would miss the point, which is that individual fishermen lack the option of saving the coral for their children. Individual fishermen obviously have the option of not destroying it themselves, but what happens if they elect not to destroy it? What they want is for the reef to be left for their children; what is actually happening is that the reef is left for the next blast-fisher down the line. If a fisherman wants to have anything at all to give his children, he must act quickly, destroying the reef and grabbing the fish himself. It does no good to tell fishermen to take responsibility. They *are* taking responsibility—for their children. Existing institutional arrangements do not empower them to take responsibility in a way that would save the reef.

Under the circumstances, they are at liberty to not destroy the reef themselves, but they are not at liberty to do what is necessary to save the reef for their children. To save the reef for their children, fishermen must have the power to restrict access to the reef. They must claim a right to exclude blast-fishers. Whether they stake that claim as individuals or as a group is secondary, so long as they actually succeed in restricting access. But one way or another, they must claim and effectively exercise a right to restrict access.

The second story comes from the Cayman Islands.[3] The Atlantic Green Turtle has long been prized as a source of meat and eggs. The turtles were a commonly held resource and were being harvested in an unsustainable way. In 1968, when by some estimates there were as few as three thousand to five thousand left in the wild, a group of entrepreneurs and concerned scientists created Cayman Turtle Farm and began raising and selling captive-bred sea turtles. In the wild, as few as one-tenth of one percent of wild hatchlings survive to adulthood. Most are seized by predators before they can crawl from nest to sea. Cayman Turtle Farm, though, boosted the survival rate of captive-bred animals to well over 50 percent. At the peak of operations, they were rearing in excess of a hundred thousand turtles. They were releasing one percent of their hatchlings into the wild at the age of ten months, an age at which hatchlings had a decent chance of surviving to maturity.

In 1973, commerce in Atlantic Green Turtles was restricted by the Convention on International Trade in Endangered Species and, in the United States, by the Fish and Wildlife Service, the Department of Commerce, and the Department of the Interior. Under the newly created Endangered Species Act, the United States classified the Atlantic Green Turtle as an endangered species, but Cayman Farm's business was unaffected, at first, because regulations pertaining to commerce in Atlantic Green Turtles exempted commerce in captive-bred animals. In 1978, however, the regulations were published in their final form; and although exemptions were granted for trade in captive-bred animals of other species, no exemption was made for trade in turtles. The company could no longer do business in the United States. Even worse, the company no longer could ship its products through American ports, so it no longer had access via Miami to world markets. The farm exists today only to serve the population of the Cayman Islands themselves. The Atlantic Green Turtle's future is, once again, in doubt.

What do these stories tell us? The first tells us we do not need to justify failing to preserve the commons in its pristine, original, unappropriated form because preserving the commons in pristine original form is not an option. The commons is not a time capsule. Leaving resources in the commons is not like putting resources in a time capsule as a legacy for future generations. In some cases, putting resources in a time capsule might be a good idea. However, as the second story reminds us, there are ways to take what we find in the commons and preserve it—put it in a time capsule—but before we can put something in a time capsule, we have to appropriate it. (A private nonprofit organization, the Nature Conservancy, pursues such a strategy. Although not itself an original appropriator, it has acquired over a billion dollars' worth of land in an effort to preserve natural ecosystems, including habitats for endangered species that have no market value.)

Justifying the Game

Note a difference between justifying institutions that regulate appropriation and justifying particular acts of appropriation. Think of original appropriation as a game and of particular acts of appropriation as moves within the game. Even if the game is justified, a given move within the game may have nothing to recommend it. Indeed, we could say (for argument's sake) that any act of appropriation will seem arbitrary when viewed in isolation, and some will seem unconscionable. Even so, there can be compelling reasons to have an institutional framework that recognizes property claims on the basis of moves that would carry no weight in an institutional vacuum. Common law implicitly acknowledges morally weighty reasons for not requiring original appropriators to supply morally weighty reasons for their appropriations (Rose 1986). Rose (1985) argued that a rule of first possession, when the world is notified in an unambiguous way, induces discovery (and future productive activity) and minimizes disputes over discovered objects. Particular acts of appropriation are justified not because they carry moral weight but because they are permitted moves within a game that carries moral weight.

Needless to say, the cornucopia of wealth generated by the appropriation and subsequent mobilization of resources is not an unambiguous benefit. The commerce made possible by original appropriation creates pollution, and other negative externalities as well. (I will return to this point.) Furthermore, there may be people who attach no value to the increases in life expectancy and other benefits that accompany the appropriation of resources for productive use. Some people may prefer a steady-state system that indefinitely supports their lifestyles as hunter-gatherers, untainted by the shoes and tents and safety matches of Western culture.

If original appropriation forces such people to participate in a culture of which they want no part, then from their viewpoint, the game does more harm than good.

Here are two things to keep in mind, though. First, as I said, the commons is not a time capsule; it does not preserve the status quo. For all kinds of reasons, quality of life could drop after appropriation. However, pressures that drive waves of people to appropriate are a lot more likely to compromise quality of life when those waves wash over an unregulated commons. In an unregulated commons, those who conserve pay the costs but do not get the benefits of conservation, while overusers get the benefits but do not pay the costs of overuse. Therefore, an unregulated commons is a prescription for overuse, not for conservation.

Second, the option of living the life of a hunter-gatherer has not entirely disappeared. It is not a comfortable life—it never was—but it remains an option. There are places in northern Canada and elsewhere where people can and do live that way. As a bonus, those who opt to live as hunter-gatherers retain the option of participating in Western culture on a drop-in basis during medical emergencies, to trade for supplies, and so on. Obviously, someone might respond, "Even if the hunter-gatherer life is an option now, that option is disappearing as expanding populations equipped with advancing technologies claim the land for other purposes." Well, probably so. What does that prove? It proves that in the world as it is, if hunter-gatherers want their children to have the option of living as hunter-gatherers, then they need to stake a claim to the territory on which they intend to preserve that option. They need to argue that they, as rightful owners, have a right to regulate access to it. If they want a steady-state civilization, they need to be aware that they will not find it in an unregulated commons. They need to argue that they have a right to exclude oil companies, for example, which would love to be able to treat northern Canada as an unregulated commons (Tully 1994).

When someone says appropriation does not leave enough and as good for others, the reply should be, "Compared to what?" Compared to the commons as it was? As it is? As it will be? Often, in fact, leaving resources *in the commons* does not leave enough and as good for others. The Lockean Proviso, far from forbidding appropriation of resources from the commons, actually requires appropriation under conditions of scarcity. Moreover, the more scarce a resource is, the more urgently the Proviso requires that it be removed from the negative-sum game that is the unregulated commons.

I have made this point before (Schmidtz 1991, ch. 2). A correspondent asked: "If we take the Proviso seriously—and assume it actually is enforced—then why would there be a tragedy of the commons? . . . If the Proviso precluded the taking of the property in the first place, then it doesn't seem as if the resource would be overutilized." My answer is that although the Proviso morally precludes bleach-fishing, the practice continues. Enforcement is a variable; it cannot be assumed. Real world Tongan fishermen operate against a background of Proviso violations, but a moral fisherman still needs to ask how to leave enough and as good for others. The background of violations does not change the question, but it does change the answer. Specifically, when the burden of common use exceeds the resource's ability to renew itself, the Proviso comes to require, not merely to permit, people to appropriate and regulate access to the resource. Even in an unregulated commons, some fishermen will practice self-restraint, but something has to happen to incline the group to practice self-restraint in cases in which it already has shown that it has no such inclination in an unregulated commons.

Removing goods from the commons stimulates increases in the stock of what can be owned and limits losses that occur in tragic commons. Appropriation replaces a negative-sum game with a positive-sum game. Therein lies a justification for social structures enshrining a right to remove resources from the unregulated commons: when resources become scarce, we need to remove them if we want them to be there for our children. Or anyone else's.

WHAT KIND OF PROPERTY INSTITUTION IS IMPLIED?

I have defended appropriation of, and subsequent regulation of access to, scarce resources as a way of preserving (and creating) resources for the future. When resources are abundant, the Lockean Proviso permits appropriation; when resources are scarce, the Proviso requires appropriation. It is possible to appropriate without prejudice to future generations. Indeed, when resources are scarce, it is leaving them in the commons that is prejudicial to future generations.

Private property enables people (and gives them an incentive) to take responsibility for conserving scarce resources. It preserves resources under a wide variety of circumstances. Private property is the preeminent vehicle for turning negative-sum commons into positive-sum property regimes. However, it is not the only vehicle. Evidently, it is not always the best vehicle, either. Public property is ubiquitous, and it is not only rapacious governments and mad ideologues who create it. Sometimes it evolves spontaneously as a response to real problems, enabling people to remove a resource from an unregulated commons and to take responsibility for its management. The following sections discuss research by Martin Bailey, Harold Demsetz, Robert Ellickson, and Carol Rose, showing how various property institutions help to ensure that enough and as good is left for future generations.

The Unregulated Commons

An unregulated commons need not be disastrous. An unregulated commons will work well enough so long as the level of use remains within the land's carrying capacity.[4] However, as use nears carrying capacity, there will be pressure to shift to a more exclusive regime. As an example of an unregulated commons evolving into something else as increasing traffic began to exceed carrying capacity, consider Harold Demsetz's (1967) account of how property institutions evolved among indigenous tribes of the Labrador peninsula.[5] As Demsetz tells the story, the region's people had, for generations, treated the land as an open-access commons. The human population was small. There was plenty to eat. Thus, the pattern of exploitation was within the land's carrying capacity.[6] The resource maintained itself. In that situation, the Proviso, as interpreted earlier, was satisfied. Original appropriation would have been permissible, other things equal, but it was not required.

With the advent of the fur trade, though, the scale of hunting and trapping activity increased sharply. The population of game animals began to dwindle. The unregulated commons had worked for a while, but now the tribes were facing a classic tragedy. The benefits of exploiting the resource were internalized but the costs were not, and the arrangement was no longer viable. Clans began to mark out family plots. The game animals in question were small animals like beaver and otter that tend not to migrate from one plot to another. Thus, marking out plots of land effectively privatized small game as well as the land itself. In sum, the tribes converted the commons in nonmigratory fur-bearing game to family parcels when the fur trade began to spur a rising demand that exceeded the land's carrying capacity. When demand began to exceed carrying capacity, that was when the Proviso came not only to permit but to require original appropriation.

One other nuance of the privatization of fur-bearing game: although the fur was privatized, the meat was not. There was still plenty of meat to go around, so tribal law allowed trespass on another clan's land to hunt for meat. Trespassers could kill a beaver and take the meat, but they had to leave the pelt displayed in a prominent place to signal that they had eaten and had respected the clan's right to the pelt. The new customs went to the heart of the matter, privatizing what had to be privatized, leaving intact liberties that people had always enjoyed with respect to other resources where unrestricted access had not yet become a problem.

The Communal Alternative

We can contrast the unregulated or open-access commons with communes. A commune (Ellickson 1993) is a restricted-access commons. In a commune, property is owned by the group rather than by individual members. People as a group claim and exercise a right to exclude. Typically, communes draw a sharp distinction between members and nonmembers and regulate access accordingly. Public property tends to restrict access by time of day or year. Some activities are permitted; others are prohibited.

Ellickson believes a broad campaign to abolish either private property or public and communal property would be ludicrous. Each kind of property serves social welfare in its own way. Likewise, every ownership regime has its own externality problems (Ellickson 1993, 1326). Communal management leads to overconsumption and to shirking on maintenance and improvements, because people receive only a fraction of the value of their labor and bear only a fraction of the costs of their consumption. To minimize these disincentives, a commune must intensively monitor people's production and consumption activities.

In practice, communal regimes can lead to indiscriminate dumping of wastes, ranging from piles of unwashed dishes to ecological disasters that threaten whole continents. Privately managed parcels also can lead to indiscriminate dumping of wastes and to various other uses that ignore spillover effects on neighbors. One advantage of private property is that owners can buy each other out and reshuffle their holdings in such a way as to minimize the extent to which their activities bother each other. But it does not always work out so nicely, and the reshuffling itself can be a waste. There are transaction costs. Thus, one plausible social goal would be to combine private property and public property in a way that reduces the sum of transaction costs and the cost of externalities.

LOCAL VERSUS REMOTE EXTERNALITIES

Is it generally best to convert an unregulated commons into smaller private parcels or to manage it as a commune with power to exclude nonmembers? It depends on the kind of activities in which people tend to engage. Ellickson (1993, 1325) separates activities into three categories: small (like cultivating a tomato plant), medium (like damming part of a river to create a pond for ducks), and large (like using an industrial smokestack to disperse noxious fumes). The distinction is not meant to be sharp. As one might expect, it is a matter of degree. It concerns the relative size of the area over which externalities are worth worrying about. Small events affect one's own property. Medium events affect people in the immediate neighborhood; their external effects are localized. Large events affect people who are more remote. Ellickson says private regimes are clearly superior as methods for minimizing the costs of small and medium events. When it comes to large events, though, there is no easy way to say which mix of private and public property is best. On the one hand, the problem suggests a need for a matching of jurisdictional responsibility to the size of the problem (Macey and Butler 2000). On the other, the multifaced nature of the problem suggests that an effective match can be achieved only by a "portfolio" of overlapping jurisdictions (Meiners, Thomas, and Yandle 2000).

Small Events

Small events are not much of a problem for private regimes. When land is parceled out, the effects of small events are internalized (Ellickson 1993, 1327). Neighbors do not care much when we pick tomatoes on our own land; they care a great deal when we pick tomatoes on the communal plot. In the former case, we are minding our own business; in the latter, we are minding theirs. Ellickson credits that point to Demsetz, adding that much of the internalization process has to do with changing monitoring costs. Private owners need only monitor border crossings, whereas communal owners need to monitor people's movements in much more elaborate and intrusive ways. As Ellickson put it, "detecting the presence of a trespasser is much less demanding than evaluating the conduct of a person who is privileged to be where he is." Guard dogs and motion detectors can detect trespassers; detecting shirkers is not so easy. Compared to private regimes, monitoring costs associated with small events in communes are prohibitive. Private parcels do require monitoring, to be sure, but the cost of monitoring small events is lower, and the kind of monitoring that has to be done is less intrusive. In short, "when land uses have no spillover effects, individual ownership directly and precisely punishes land misuse and rewards productive labor" (Ellickson 1993, 1327).

Medium Events

In contrast, the effects of medium events tend to spill over onto one's neighbors and, thus, can be a source of friction. Nevertheless, privatization has the advantage of limiting the number of people having to be consulted about how to deal with the externality, which reduces transaction costs. Instead of consulting the entire community of communal owners, each at liberty with respect to the affected area, one consults a handful of people who own parcels in the immediate area of the medium event. Regarding medium events, then, a virtue of privatization is that it reduces the number of people with whom one needs to negotiate or coordinate one's effort (Demsetz 1967, 356–57).

Regarding medium events, Ellickson mentions two further benefits of privatization. First, privatization increases the extent to which interactions are of a repeating character. It tends to put people in long-term, face-to-face, binary relations with neighbors. It thereby increases the extent to which people's dealings are with familiar and friendly faces, which is valuable in its own right and also insofar as it puts the resolution of externality problems from medium events into the hands of people who are most likely to have ongoing relationships and, thus, to be most motivated to cooperate (Ellickson 1993, 1331). Second, privatization puts decisions in the hands of people most familiar with local circumstances. There will be disputes, of course, and there is no guarantee that familiar faces will be friendly faces. (Those who want friendly neighbors sometimes need to change neighborhoods.) Still, in a private regime, disputes arising from medium events tend to be left in the hands of people in the immediate vicinity, who tend to have a better understanding of local conditions and, thus, are in a better position to devise resolutions without harmful unintended consequences.

They are in a better position to foresee the costs and the benefits of a medium event.

Large Events

Large events involve far-flung externalities among people who do not have face-to-face relationships. The difficulties in detecting such externalities, tracing them to their source, and holding people accountable for them are difficulties for any kind of property regime. There is no general answer to the question of which regime best deals with them (Ellickson 1993, 1335). It is no easy task to devise institutions that encourage pulp mills to take responsibility for their actions while simultaneously encouraging people downstream to take responsibility for their welfare and to avoid being harmed by negative externalities.

Private regimes respond to negative externalities in various ways: through contract law, tort law, regulatory statutes (nuisance laws, zoning restrictions), and a matrix of conventions about neighborliness. All such responses are imperfect. One alternative is to return the land to the commons, and that too is imperfect.

A large event will fall into one of two categories. Releasing toxic wastes into the atmosphere, for example, may violate existing legal rights or community norms. Or such laws or norms may not yet be in place. Most of the problems arise when existing customs or laws fail to settle who (in effect) has the right of way. That is not a problem with parceling land per se but rather with the fact that key resources like air and waterways remain in a largely unregulated commons.

So privatization exists in different degrees and takes different forms. Different forms have different incentive properties. Simply parceling out land or sea is not always enough to stabilize possession of resources that make land or sea valuable in the first place. Suppose, for example, that fish are known to migrate from one parcel to another. In that case, owners have an incentive to grab as many fish as they can whenever the school passes through their own territory. Thus, simply dividing fishing grounds into parcels may not be enough to put fishermen in a position collectively to avoid exceeding sustainable yields. It depends on the extent to which the sought-after fish migrate from one parcel to another and on conventions that are continuously evolving to help neighbors deal with the inadequacy of their fences (or other ways of marking off territory).

There are multiple examples. Temporal parceling of time-share condominiums, for example, is an open invitation to shirk responsibility for cleaning up; the mess one leaves is someone else's problem. Clearly, not all forms of privatization are equally good at internalizing externalities. Privatization per se is not a panacea, and not all forms of privatization are equal.

There are obvious difficulties with how private property regimes handle large events. The nature and extent of the difficulties will depend on the details. So, for purposes of comparison, Ellickson looked at how communal regimes handle large events.

JAMESTOWN AND OTHER COMMUNES

The Jamestown Colony is North America's first permanent English settlement. It begins in 1607 as a commune, sponsored by London-based Virginia Company. Land is held and managed collectively. The colony's charter guarantees to each settler an equal share of the collective product regardless of the amount of work personally contributed (Ellickson 1993, 1336). Of the original group of 104 settlers, two-thirds die of starvation and disease before their first winter is over. New shiploads replenish the population, but the winter of 1609 cuts the population from 500 to 60. In 1611, visiting Governor Thomas Dale finds living skeletons bowling in the streets, waiting for someone else to plant the crops. Their main food source is wild animals such as turtles and raccoons, which settlers can hunt and eat by dark of night before neighbors can demand equal shares. In 1614, Governor Dale has seen enough. He assigns three-acre plots to individual settlers, which reportedly increases productivity sevenfold. The colony converts the rest of its land holdings to private parcels in 1619.

Why go communal in the first place? Are there advantages to communal regimes? One advantage is obvious. Communal regimes can help people spread risks under conditions in which risks are substantial and in which alternative risk-spreading mechanisms, like insurance, are unavailable. But as communities build up capital reserves to the point at which they can offer insurance, they tend to privatize, for insurance lets them secure a measure of risk-spreading without having to endure the externalities that afflict a communal regime.

A communal regime might also be an effective response to economies of scale in large-scale public works that are crucial in getting a community started. To build a fort, man its walls, dig wells, and so on, a communal economy is an obvious choice as a way of mobilizing the teams of workers needed to execute these urgent tasks. But again, as these tasks are completed and community welfare increasingly comes to depend on small events, the communal regime gives way to private parcels. At Jamestown, Plymouth, the Amana colonies, and Salt Lake, formerly communal settlers "understandably would switch to private land tenure, the system that most cheaply induces individuals to undertake small and medium events that are socially useful" (Ellickson 1993, 1342–3). (The legend of Salt Lake says that the sudden improvement in the fortunes of once-starving Mormons occurred in 1848 when God sent seagulls to save them from plagues of locusts, at the same time as they coincidentally were switching to private plots. Similarly, the Jamestown tragedy sometimes is attributed to harsh natural conditions, as if those conditions suddenly changed in 1614, multiplying productivity sevenfold while Governor Dale coincidentally was cutting the land into parcels.)

Of course, the tendency toward decentralized and individualized forms of management is only a (strong) tendency, and, in any case, there are trade-offs. For example, what would be a small event on a larger parcel becomes a medium event under more crowded conditions. Loud music is an innocuous small event on a ranch but an irritating medium event in an apartment complex. Changes in technology or in population density affect the scope or the incidence of externalities. The historical trend, though, is that as people become aware of and concerned about a medium or large event, some of them seek ways of reducing the extent to which the event's cost is externalized. Social evolution is partly a process of perceiving new externalities and devising institutions to internalize them.

Historically, the benefits of communal management have not been enough to keep communes together indefinitely. Perhaps the most enduring and successful communes in human memory are the agricultural settlements of the Hutterites, dating in Europe back to the sixteenth century. There are now around twenty-eight thousand people living in such communities in many countries. Hutterites believe in a fairly strict sharing of assets. They forbid the possession of radio or television sets, to give one example of how strictly they control contact with the outside world.

Hutterite communities have three special things going for them (Ellickson 1993, 1347–60):

1. *A population cap*: When the population of a settlement reaches one hundred twenty, a portion of the community must leave to start a new community. The cap helps them retain a close-knit society.

2. *Communal dining and worship*: People congregate several times a day, which facilitates a rapid exchange of information about individual behavior and a ready avenue for supplying feedback to those whose behavior deviates from the norm.

3. *A ban on birth control*: The average woman bears nine children, which more than offsets the trickle of emigration.

We might add that Hutterite culture and education leave people ill-prepared to live in anything other than a Hutterite society, which surely accounts in part for the low emigration rate.

Ellickson also discusses kibbutzim and other examples of communal property regimes. But the most pervasive example of communal ownership in America, Ellickson says, is the family household. American suburbia consists of family communes nested within a network of open-access roadways (Ellickson 1993, 1395). Families tacitly recognize that there are limits on how far they can go in converting common holdings into individual parcels. Consider your living room. You could fully privatize, having one household member own it while others pay user fees. The fees could be used to pay family members or outside help to keep it clean. In some respects, it would be better that way. The average communal living room today, for example, is notably subject to overgrazing and shirking on maintenance. Yet the family puts up with it. No one charges user fees to household members. Seeing the living room degraded by communal use may be irritating, but it is better than treating it as one person's private domain.

Some institutions succeed while embodying a form of ownership that is essentially collective. History indicates, though, that members of successful communes internalize the rewards that come with that collective responsibility. In particular, they reserve the right to exclude nonmembers. A successful commune does not run itself as an open-access commons.

GOVERNANCE BY CUSTOM

Many commons (such as our living rooms) are regulated by custom rather than by government; so saying there is a role for common property and saying there is a role for government management of common property are two different things. As Ellickson (1993, 1335) noted, "Group ownership does not necessarily imply government ownership, of course. The sorry environmental records of federal land agencies and Communist regimes are a sharp reminder that governments are often particularly inept managers of large tracts."[7] Carol Rose told of how, in the nineteenth century, public property was thought to be owned by society at large. The idea of public property often was taken to imply no particular role for government beyond whatever enforcement role is implied by private property. Society's right to such property was held to precede and to supersede any claim made by government. Rose said, "Implicit in these older doctrines is the notion that, even if a property should be open to the public, it does not follow that public rights should necessarily vest in an active governmental manager" (Rose 1986, 720). Sometimes, the rights were understood to be held by an "unorganized public" rather than by a "governmentally organized public" (736).

Along the same lines, open-field agricultural practices of medieval times gave peasants exclusive cropping rights to scattered thin strips of arable land in each of the village fields. The strips were private only during the growing season, after which the land reverted to the commons for the duration of the grazing season. Thus, ownership of parcels was usufructuary in the sense that once the harvest was in, ownership reverted to the common herdsmen without any negotiation or process of formal transfer. The farmer had an exclusive claim to the land only so long as he or she was using it for the purpose of bringing in a harvest.

The scattering of strips was a means of diversification, reducing the risk of being ruined by small or medium events: small fires, pest infestations, and so forth. The post-harvest commons in grazing land exploited economies of scale in fencing and tending a herd. The scattering of thin strips also made it harder for a communal herdsman to maneuver the herd into dropping a disproportionate amount of manure on his own cropland (Ellickson 1993, 1390).

According to Martin Bailey (1992, 192), the pattern observed by Rose and Ellickson also was common among aboriginal tribes, that is, tribes that practiced agriculture treated the land as private during the growing season, and often treated it as a commons after the crops were in. Hunter-gatherer societies did not practice agriculture, but they too tended to leave the land in the commons during the summer when game was plentiful. It was during the winter, when food was most scarce, that they privatized. The rule among hunter-gatherers is that where group hunting's advantages are considerable, that factor dominates (191). But in the winter, small game is relatively more abundant, less migratory, and evenly spread. There was no feast-or-famine pattern of the sort one might expect to see with big-game hunting. Rather, families tended to gather enough during the course of the day to get themselves through the day, day after day, with little to spare. Even though this pattern corroborates my own general thesis, I confess to being a bit surprised. I might have predicted that it would be during the harshest part of the year that families would band together and throw everything into the common pot in order to pull through. Not so. It was when the land was nearest its carrying capacity that they recognized the imperative to privatize.

Customary use of medieval commons was hedged with restrictions limiting depletion of resources. Custom prohibited activities inconsistent with the land's ability to recover (Rose 1986, 743). In particular, the custom of "stinting" allowed the villagers to own livestock only in proportion to the relative size of their (growing season) land holdings. Governance by custom enabled people to avoid commons tragedies.[8] Of course, no one thinks governance by custom automatically solves commons problems. Custom works when local users can restrict outsider access and monitor insider behavior; but those conditions are not always met, and tragedies like those discussed earlier continue to occur.

Custom is a form of management unlike exclusive ownership by either individuals or governments. Custom is a self-managing system for according property rights (Rose 1986, 742). For example, custom governs the kind of rights-claims you establish by taking a place in line at a supermarket checkout counter. Rose believes common concerns often are best handled by decentralized, piecemeal, and self-managing customs that tend to arise as needed at the local level. So, to the previous section's conclusion that a successful commune does not run itself as an open-access commons, we can add that a successful commune does not entrust its governance to a distant bureaucracy.

THE HUTTERITE SECRET

I argued that the original appropriation of (and subsequent regulation of access to) scarce resources are justifiable as a mechanism for preserving opportunities for future generations. There are various means of exclusive control, though. Some mechanisms internalize externalities better than others, and how well they do so depends on the context. My argument does not presume that there is one form of exclusive control that uniquely serves this purpose. Which form is best depends on what kind of activities are most prevalent in a community at any given time and on the extent to which public ownership implies control by a distant bureaucracy rather than by local custom.

As mentioned earlier, I have heard people say Jamestown failed because it faced such harsh natural conditions. But communal (and noncommunal) settlements typically face harsh natural conditions. Jamestown had to deal with summer in Virginia. Hutterites dealt with winter on the Canadian prairie. It is revealing, not misleading, to compare Jamestown to settlements that faced harsher conditions more successfully. It also is fair to compare the two Jamestowns: the one immediately before and the one immediately following Governor Dale's mandated privatization. What distinguished the first Jamestown from the second was not the harshness of its natural setting but rather the thoroughness with which it prevented people from internalizing externalities.

Sociologist Michael Hechter (1983, 21) considered group solidarity to be a function of (1) the extent to which members depend on the group and (2) the extent to which the group can monitor and enforce compliance with expectations that members will contribute to the group rather than free ride upon it. On this analysis, it is unsurprising that Hutterite communal society has been successful. Members are extremely dependent, for their upbringing leaves them unprepared to live in a nonHutterite culture. Monitoring is intense. Feedback is immediate. But if that is the secret of Hutterite success, why did Jamestown fail? They, too, were extremely dependent on each other and had nowhere else to go. Monitoring was equally unproblematic. Everyone knew who was planting crops (no one) and who was bowling (everyone). What was the problem?

The problem lay in the guarantee embedded in the Jamestown Colony's charter. Jamestown's charter entitled people to an equal share regardless of personal contribution, which is to say it took steps to ensure that individual workers would be maximally alienated from the fruits of their labors. The charter ensured that individual workers would think of their work as disappearing into an open-access commons.

Robert Goodin (1985, 1) said, "Working within the constraints set by natural scarcity, the greatest practical obstacle to achieving as much justice as resources permit is, and always has been, the supposition that each of us should cultivate his own garden."[9] However, Jamestown's charter did not suppose each of us should cultivate his or her own garden. It supposed the opposite. Colonists abided by the charter. And while they languished, people in other colonies were tending their own gardens, and thriving.

We should applaud institutions that encourage people to care for each other. But telling people they are required to tend someone else's garden rather than their own does not encourage people to care for each other. It does the opposite. It encourages spite. The people of Jamestown reached the point where they would rather die, bowling in the street, than tend the gardens of their free-riding neighbors, and die they did.

NOTES

This essay is a revised version of "The Institution of Property," *Social Philosophy and Policy* 11, no. 2 (Summer 1994): 42–62. Reprinted with the permission of Cambridge University Press.

1. Regarding the difference between justifying an institution by looking at how it emerged versus looking at how it functions, see Schmidtz (1990). I spend a chapter on what might be involved in making people better off, discussing the philosophical concept and also what might serve as rough economic measurements thereof, in Schmidtz (1995).

2. There are different kinds of things over which one can establish possession, however, and they have different welfare implications. See Lueck's (1995) distinction between capturing a flow (like a barrel of oil) and appropriating a stock (like an oil field). There also are different ways to establish first possession. Anderson and Hill (1990) compare first possession by squatting, by homesteading, and by government auction. Homesteading rules require people to expend resources merely for the sake of signaling title to them, whereas under an auction system people leave the land alone until the cost/benefit of exploitation becomes favorable. But see Allen's (1991) defense of homesteading as a way of inducing settlers to rush by the thousands into a given area and settle down in numbers sufficient to enable them to form effective mutual protection associations and thereby reduce the cost to the government of enforcing property rights.

3. I thank Peggy Fosdick at the National Aquarium in Baltimore for correspondence and documents. See also Fosdick and Fosdick (1994).

4. A resource's carrying capacity is the level of use the resource can sustain. See Hardin (1977, 112–125).

5. Demsetz has been criticized. "The essence of all the criticism is that Demsetz ignores how value-laden might be the processes that lead from common to private ownership," according to Dukeminier and Krier (1993, 61). Their overview, however, is favorable on the whole, and generally corroborate Demsetz's account. See Dukeminier and Krier (1993, 62) for a list. See also Bailey (1992).

6. So I accept Dukeminier and Krier's (1993, 62) warning against forming "an unduly romantic image of Native American culture prior to the arrival of 'civilization.' There is considerable evidence that some American Indian tribes, rather than being natural ecologists who lived in respectful harmony with the land, exploited the environment ruthlessly by overhunting and extensive burning of forests."

7. See also Brubaker (1998, 87–119) and especially Zywicki (2000) in this volume.

8. See Ostrom, Gardner, and Walker (1994) for more examples.

9. Goodin and I debate the issue at length in Schmidtz and Goodin (1998).

128   *David Schmidtz*

REFERENCES

Allen, Douglas W. 1991. Homesteading and Property Rights; Or, How the West Was Really Won. *Journal of Law and Economics* 34(April): 1–23.

Anderson, Terry L., and Peter J. Hill. 1990. The Race for Property Rights. *Journal of Law and Economics* 33(April): 177–97.

Bailey, Martin J. 1992. Approximate Optimality of Aboriginal Property Rights. *Journal of Law and Economics* 35(1): 183–98.

Bogart, J. H. 1985. Lockean Provisos and State of Nature Theories. *Ethics* 95(4): 828–36.

Brubaker, Elizabeth. 1998. The Common Law and the Environment. In *Who Owns the Environment?* ed. Peter J. Hill and Roger E. Meiners. Lanham, MD: Rowman & Littlefield.

Demsetz, Harold. 1967. Toward a Theory of Property Rights. *American Economic Review* 57(May): 347–59.

Dukeminier, Jesse, and James E. Krier. 1993. *Property.* 3d ed. Boston: Little, Brown & Co.

Ellickson, Robert C. 1993. Property in Land. *Yale Law Journal* 102(April): 1315–1400.

Filmer, Robert. [1652] 1991. *Patriarcha and Other Writings.* Reprint, ed. J. P. Sommerville. Cambridge: Cambridge University Press.

Fosdick, Peggy, and Sam Fosdick. 1994. *Last Chance Lost?* York, PA: Irvin S. Naylor Publishing.

Fried, Barbara. 1995. Wilt Chamberlain Revisited: Nozick's "Justice in Transfer" and the Problem of Market-Based Distribution. *Philosophy and Public Affairs* 24(3): 226–45.

Goodin, Robert E. 1985. *Protecting the Vulnerable: Toward a Reanalysis of Our Social Responsibilities.* Chicago: University of Chicago Press.

Hardin, Garrett. 1977. The Ethical Implications of Carrying Capacity. In *Managing the Commons,* ed. Garrett Hardin and John Baden. San Francisco: W. H. Freeman.

Hechter, Michael. 1983. A Theory of Group Solidarity. In *Microfoundations of Macrosociology,* ed. Michael Hechter. Philadelphia: Temple University Press, 16–57.

Held, Virginia. 1980. Introduction. In *Property, Profits, and Economic Justice,* ed. Virginia Held. Belmont, CA: Wadsworth, 1–11.

Hohfeld, Wesley Newcomb. 1919. *Fundamental Legal Conceptions.* New Haven: Yale University Press.

Locke, John. [1690] 1960. *Second Treatise of Government.* Reprint, ed. P. Laslett. Cambridge: Cambridge University Press.

Lueck, Dean. 1995. The Rule of First Possession and the Design of the Law. *Journal of Law and Economics* 38(2): 393–435.

Macey, Jonathan R., and Henry N. Butler. 2000. Federalism and the Environment, this volume.

McDonald, Michael. 1976. Aboriginal Rights. In *Contemporary Issues in Political Phi-*

losophy, ed. William Shea and John King-Farlow. New York: Science History Publications.

Meiners, Roger E., Stacie Thomas, and Bruce Yandle. 2000. Burning Rivers, Common Law, and Institutional Choice for Water Quality, this volume.

Nash, J. Madeleine. 1996. Wrecking the Reefs. *Time*, September 30, 60–62.

Nozick, Robert. 1974. *Anarchy, State, and Utopia*. New York: Basic Books.

Ostrom, Elinor, Roy Gardner, and James Walker. 1994. *Rules, Games, and Common Pool Resources*. Ann Arbor: University of Michigan Press.

Rawls, John. 1971. *Theory of Justice*. Cambridge: Harvard University Press.

Rose, Carol. 1985. Possession as the Origin of Property. *University of Chicago Law Review* 52(1): 73–88.

———. 1986. The Comedy of the Commons: Custom, Commerce, and Inherently Public Property. *University of Chicago Law Review* 53(3): 711–87.

Sanders, John T. 1987. Justice and the Initial Acquisition of Private Property. *Harvard Journal of Law and Public Policy* 10(2): 367–99.

Sartorius, Rolf. 1984. Persons and Property. In *Utility and Rights*, ed. Ray Frey. Minneapolis: University of Minnesota Press, 207–45.

Schmidtz, David. 1990. Justifying the State. *Ethics* 101(1): 89–102.

———. 1991. *Limits of Government*. Boulder: Westview Press.

———. 1995. *Rational Choice and Moral Agency*. Princeton: Princeton University Press.

Schmidtz, David, and Robert E. Goodin. 1998. *Social Welfare and Individual Responsibility*. New York: Cambridge University Press.

Thomson, Judith Jarvis. 1990. *The Realm of Rights*. Cambridge: Harvard University Press.

Tully, James. 1994. Aboriginal Property and Western Theory: Recovering a Middle Ground. *Social Philosophy and Policy* 11(2): 42–62.

Zywicki, Todd J. 2000. Industry and Environmental Lobbyists: Enemies or Allies?, this volume.

6

Lessons for Environmental Law from the American Codification Debate

Andrew P. Morriss

Environmental law today is largely a creature of statutory law. Common law principles, which predominated as recently as the 1960s, have been displaced by lengthy, complex statutes and regulations. (The basic federal environmental statutes, like the Clean Air Act and the Clean Water Act, are hundreds of pages long, and the regulations implementing them are thousands more.) The size and complexity of the regulatory regime created by these statutes stands in stark contrast to the simplicity of common law principles (Zywicki 2000; Morriss 2000). Although supporters and opponents of particular pieces of environmental legislation vigorously debated the merits of particular provisions of these laws, the transformation of the common law into a complex statutory regime in the 1970s took place with little discussion of the relative merits of the two systems.

This lack of debate stemmed in part from the crisis atmosphere surrounding passage of the foundational environmental statutes in the early 1970s. Earth Day in 1970 was only one of the most visible manifestations of the politicization of environmental issues. One Nixon aide, for example, described the atmosphere in Washington in 1969 as "hysteria" over environmental issues, with Congress "producing environment-related bills by the bushel" and Nixon worried about being "left behind" (Whitaker 1976, 27). The Clean Air Act Amendments of 1970 rewrote the air pollution laws despite there having been too little time to evaluate the rewrite of those same laws three years earlier by the Air Quality Act of 1967. Instant success was the only politically acceptable outcome, and *success* was defined as federal legislation. In such an atmosphere, relying on court cases was obviously too slow.

Americans have debated the relative merits of statutory law and common law, however. Throughout the nineteenth century, both lawyers and nonlawyers across the United States debated replacing the common law entirely with a codified legal system. The debate stretched across the country, from New York to California, and across the century. It involved many of the best legal minds of the nineteenth century, including Joseph Story, David Dudley Field, and James Coolidge Carter. Many of the disagreements between code and common law proponents remain directly relevant to the debate today over the appropriateness of the statutory approach to environmental law. Moreover, several states (California, the Dakotas, Georgia, and Montana) adopted huge statutes intended to be versions of code-based systems embedded within common law systems.[1] The experience with those statutes is directly relevant to understanding the interaction between the growing body of statutory environmental law and the larger legal system.

THE U.S. CODIFICATION DEBATE

In 1811, English utilitarian philosopher and reformer Jeremy Bentham wrote to President James Madison offering to draft "a *complete body* of proposed law, in the form of Statute law, say in one word a *Pannomion*—including a succedaneum to that mass of foreign law, the yoke of which in the *wordless*, as well as boundless, and shapeless shape of *common*, alias *unwritten* law, remains still about your necks" (Bentham 1988, 182).

While waiting for Madison's reply, which was delayed by the War of 1812, Bentham discovered that the United States was a federal system and that the "yoke" of the common law actually rested on the "necks" of the states, rather than on the federal government's "neck." He then wrote to the various state governors, making the same offer (Cook 1981, 100–101). Only New Hampshire's governor showed any interest; even that state failed to follow through and accept Bentham's proposal (101–2).[2]

Bentham's advocacy of *codification* (a word he coined) and the success of the Napoleonic Code forced on France's conquests during Napoleon's campaigns sparked the imaginations of reformers on both sides of the Atlantic. For example, Joseph Story was commissioned by the Massachusetts legislature to produce a report on codification for that state in 1836. Perhaps the most important impact of the early-nineteenth-century codification movement, however, was the winning over of a young New York lawyer, David Dudley Field.

Field succeeded in gaining the insertion of a provision into New York's 1846 constitution calling for a code commission "to reduce into a written and systematic code the whole body of the law of this state, or so much and such parts thereof as to the said commissioners should seem practicable and expedient" (Cook 1981, 190). Field was not appointed to the commission because his views were considered too radical, although he did gain appointment to a commission to revise the procedural rules. Field's first project was thus reforming the rules of civil procedure, and he led his commission in producing a radical restructuring of court practice in 1848 (191). The resulting "Field Code" of civil procedure was copied widely across the United States in the years that followed.

The 1846 constitution's code commission languished for several years, producing little, before Field finally succeeded in having himself appointed to it in 1857. Along with fellow commissioners William Curtiss Noyes and Alexander Bradford, Field set about producing a complete set of codes for New York: a Political Code to include all the laws relating to government; a Penal Code to cover criminal law; and a Civil Code to cover private law. The commission produced a draft Political Code in 1859, a draft Penal Code in 1864, and a draft Civil Code in 1862. After circulating the drafts to attorneys and judges throughout the state for comments, final drafts were published in 1860, 1865, and 1865, respectively (Coe and Morse 1942, 243–45). The commission also produced a Criminal Procedure code. All three draft codes included numerous changes in New York's laws, but the Civil Code was the most revolutionary. Section six declared "There is no common law in any case where the law is declared by the Five Codes."[3]

The combination of the codes' radical changes and the disruptions of the Civil War left the commission's final reports largely ignored in New York. The reports circulated around the United States, however, and interest in them developed farther west. At least one copy of the draft codes ended up in Dakota Territory (present-day North and South Dakota) where it "came into the possession of the Supreme Court of the Territory." The judges were "favorably impressed" by the codes and "the bench and bar of the territory united upon recommending" repeal of the existing laws adopted in 1862 and adoption of the New York drafts in their place (Kingsbury 1915, 430). After a careful comparison of the 1865 New York draft Civil Code and the 1866 Dakota Territorial Civil Code, I found only minor changes (like substituting "Territory" for "State") in the civil code provisions. The records of the 1866 Territorial Legislature being understandably sparse, we cannot know exactly what it intended. Nonetheless, this lack of modification, the hasty adoption, and Dakota's later dissatisfaction with the New York–based 1866 codes suggest less than careful consideration of the codes' content. The Dakota Territorial Legislature's prompt request for federal funds to pay for maintenance of the codes suggests that they appreciated at least some of the benefits of codification, however (Morriss 1995, 374, n59).

Farther west, Field's proposals also found support in California. David Dudley Field's brother, Stephen, traveled to California as a forty-niner and rose to prominence, serving on the California Supreme Court before he became a U.S. Supreme Court Justice. Stephen used his position in California to promote David's law-reform ideas there.

Stephen Field's task was made easier because California's laws reflected that state's chaotic birth and growth. By the end of the 1860s, determining the law on any particular subject required multiple searches through session law volumes (Kleps 1954, 771). After a series of failed attempts at compiling the existing laws into a single source, the legislature authorized a code commission to address the problems. The commission took a broader view of its mandate, however, and created an entirely new system based on the New York drafts. Following publication of the code commission's drafts in 1871 and review by an advisory commission, the California legislature adopted Civil, Political, Civil Procedure, and Penal Codes based on the New York drafts, although with extensive changes (Parma 1929, 15). One crucial change was the elimination of section six's abolition of the common law, although the result was to add to the confusion over where to find the law. California left her courts adrift with respect to the rules governing interpretation, and as a result "California judges wandered between expansive construction and traditional strict construction, lingering at every point in between—sometimes all in the course of the same opinion" (Natelson 1990, 41).

Although California undertook a far more extensive process of examination and reexamination than Dakota had, as well as making much more extensive changes in the codes' text, there was little real debate over the codes. The state's newspapers from the period show little coverage of the code bills, particularly in comparison to other issues in the same legislature. Passage of the codes did not even merit mention in the *Sacramento Reporter*'s summary of the legislative session, for example. Even staunch code supporters found the process too rushed— Code Commission Chairman Charles Lindley resigned over the failure of the commission to adequately review the drafts, detailing his complaints in a letter he later published as part of a work on how to interpret the new codes (Lindley 1874, app. v).

Dakota, meanwhile, was experiencing some difficulties with integrating new legislation into her codes and with discovering some of the disadvantages of a legal system built for a state with quite different history and institutions. As a nineteenth-century historian later noted, the copying of the New York drafts left in Dakota's laws "many repugnant provisions" (Tilton 1898, 90–91). In 1875, therefore, the Dakota Territorial Legislature appointed a commission to revise the codes. Working largely from the California codes this time, the commission produced a new set of codes in 1877, which the legislature then adopted with almost as little discussion as the earlier set.

Back in New York, David Dudley Field's code-drafting efforts remained largely unappreciated. Not much more might have come of Field's codes there except for the combination of Field's enormous wealth and political influence with his vanity. Field had a high opinion of his talents, an opinion sufficiently shared by clients like William "Boss" Tweed and Jay Gould to make him one of the wealthiest lawyers in the United States (van Ee 1986, 251–52). His skills on his clients' behalf were underappreciated by the public and the bar, however. Similarly, his attempts at public service through a political career did not find public favor (he served only a partial term in Congress in 1877). He therefore saw his legacy to the ages as wrapped up in his codes. (His ambitions were not limited to reforming New

York's laws—he also drafted an international law code in the 1860s.) Gratifying as California's and Dakota's adoptions of the complete set were, New York's failure to adopt more than his procedure code was galling. Even worse, in the 1870s, a revision commission headed by prominent lawyer Montgomery Throop proposed such extensive changes to the procedure code that it would no longer be recognizably Field's.

Field managed to block the adoption of a crucial portion of the Throop proposals in the 1879 legislative session. This maneuver threatened chaos in the legal system, leaving the procedural rules in a state of disarray. To gain Field's support for the full set of Throop proposals, revision proponents offered Field a bargain. If he would drop his opposition, they would ensure passage of the remaining codes. Field accepted (van Ee 1986, 329–31). The legislature then adopted the Throop amendments and all the Field codes. The compromise came undone a short time later, however, when the governor signed the Throop amendments but vetoed the Field codes, calling for more careful study before making such a radical change.

Later legislatures adopted the Penal Code and portions of the Political Code. The crown jewel of Field's efforts, the Civil Code, never became law in New York, however. Although Field traveled to Albany for each session of the legislature for more than a decade afterward, relentlessly revising the proposed Civil Code to meet objections and sometimes persuading one house or the other to pass the code bills, he never succeeded in gaining adoption of the Civil Code.

Despite the heated debates spanning more than a decade in New York, the details of the Field codes were hardly better known there than in the other states. Code opponents like the Association of the Bar of the City of New York claimed that after the 81–3 assembly vote in favor of the Civil Code in 1881, "the result of many inquiries was an inability to find any member of the Assembly who was willing to admit that he had *read* [the proposed code], although one member did admit that he himself had *voted* for it, in order to rid the Assembly of its presence as an element of disturbance" (Association of the Bar 1881, 5). Even discounting for the claim's source, it seems likely that few members of both houses of the legislature voting either way knew the details of the proposed Civil Code in any of the many votes in New York taken during the 1880s. Despite his failure to win adoption in New York, Field's codes continued to be discussed in the west. In Montana Territory decades of partisan conflict, neglect, indifference, and mistakes combined to make the territorial statutes a shambles (Morriss 1995, 378–80). In response to continuing pressure from the territorial bench and the bar, the territorial legislature created a code commission. Although the commission was told to produce drafts by the next session of the legislature, statehood came later that year bringing a new legislature before the codes were completed. Working mostly from the California version of Field's drafts, the commission reported draft codes two and a half years later, in time for consideration by the 1893 legislature. That legislature deadlocked over the selection of a United States senator, however, and so took no action on the proposed codes (Morriss 1995, 384–85).

Two years later, with a new Republican majority in control of both houses of the Montana legislature, the code bills quickly passed through the legislature with little debate and few changes from the commission proposals. Indeed, the legislature changed only a few provisions, all of which directly related to its own power. For example, the legislature deleted a provision banning members from accepting free railroad passes and restored their own authority to choose the state's school textbooks, a provision that a Montana newspaper referred to as a rich source of "boodle" (Morriss 1995, 391). A patronage scandal brewing over the legislature's hiring of less-than-competent, young, single, female "clerks" was also averted by the need to copy out the massive code bills by hand to officially "enroll" them (Morriss 1995, 395–97).

This abbreviated history of the Field codes in New York, Dakota Territory, California, and Montana suggests a striking similarity to modern American environmental legislation. Both the codes and modern environmental statutes are complex and physically large statutes. The Clean Air Act Amendments of 1970, for example, totaled more than one hundred printed pages; the Montana codes included more than 784,000 words. Similarly, when the next wave of clean air amendments came to the floor of the Senate late in the 1976 session, opponents pointed to the state of the draft bill and the committee report—covered with penciled changes and corrections—and to the absence of a printed version as proof that no one understood what was being voted on. Not surprisingly, therefore, both the codes and modern environmental statutes overwhelmed the legislative mechanisms for review, leaving legislators voting with little understanding of the bills (Morriss 2000).

Moreover, this complexity is not accidental. Both the codes and modern environmental legislation represent attempts to restructure the law through a centralized, planned process. Both attempt to short-circuit the common law's evolutionary process and to deliver a complete set of laws addressing a problem at once.[4] Thus the 1866 Dakota legislature sought to give itself a complete body of law with a single bill, just as the Congress sought to solve air pollution problems in 1970, 1977, and 1990 with increasingly complex Clean Air Act amendments.

Both codes and modern environmental statutes also represent attempts to substitute a vision of law held by a small group for the decentralized common law process in which precedent gains authority across jurisdictions through its persuasive power rather than by fiat. David Dudley Field, as both his supporters and opponents recognized, attempted a virtually one-man revolution in the law. The New York Civil Code was Field's draft; and although he made use of assistants and recruited allies, no one doubted that it represented his vision. For code supporters, Field's genius was further reason to adopt "his" codes. For code opponents, it was conclusive evidence of the flawed nature of Field's project that it could be attributed to one man, regardless of that man's talents. No one man, they argued, could possibly draft an adequate code covering the entire legal system (Morriss 1999b).

Environmental legislation is similar in many respects. The Air Quality Act of 1967 and the Clean Air Act Amendments of 1970, for example, are widely acknowledged to be the work primarily of Maine's Senator Edmund Muskie (Morriss 2000). Given their size and complexity and the air of crisis surrounding passage of virtually every major environmental statute, all represent the work of small groups of members of Congress and their staffs, administration representatives, and lobbyists. "Persuasion" in such circumstances turns on demonstrating political clout or trading changes in one section for other changes in another. For example, the arguments of Senator Robert Byrd of West Virginia (particularly while he was majority leader) were not "persuasive authority" because of his eloquence but rather because of his power.

Legislation need not be quite so centralized, of course. The Uniform Law Commissioners, for example, regularly produce proposed state laws to assist state legislatures in resolving problems. Some of these Uniform Acts deal with minor problems, such as the Uniform Simultaneous Death Act, which provides rules governing the effect on wills of the near-simultaneous deaths of the testator and a beneficiary (as when both spouses are fatally injured in a car crash and their wills leave their estates to each other). Other acts deal with problems of much wider scope, such as the Uniform Commercial Code (UCC). The lengthy drafting process, involving widespread debate, that accompanies proposed revisions of the UCC and the requirement that amendments gain separate approval from each state make it quite different from the midnight votes and closed-door-conference meetings so common to environmental statutes. Indeed, the Uniform Acts operate more as a constraint on legislatures, forcing them to justify departures from the proposals and so reducing their freedom of choice, than as an inducement to rent seeking.

The similarities do not end there. The Western codifiers succeeded where Field failed in New York because they were able to portray codification as a one-shot solution to legal chaos. Dakota in 1866 had almost no written law of any sort, and statute law in California in 1871, Montana in 1895, and Dakota in 1877 was in chaos (largely because of previous legislatures' mistakes, of course). Codification would solve their problems, the code proponents claimed, by gathering all the disparate laws into a single, comprehensive, organized, and planned body of law. Like the Western codifiers, the proponents of the modern environmental statutes claimed (and still claim) that the inadequacies of earlier patchwork statutory solutions and the common law left a vacuum that required a comprehensive approach. Each successive layer of ever-more-complex statutory law is designed to solve the problems created by the previous statute. Thus, in almost biblical fashion, the

Clean Air Amendments of 1970 begat tall stacks, which begat attempts to limit them, which begat protectionist measures for coal from the eastern United States in the Clean Air Amendments of 1977, which begat acid rain, which begat the Clean Air Amendments of 1990.

Finally, despite the size and the complexity of the codes and modern environmental legislation, both were pushed through the respective legislative bodies with little or no public debate or examination. Public debate over the codes largely concerned nonquestions, such as whether one's state was to be "forward looking," whether a state would assume its "rightful place" among progressive states, and so forth. The extent of debate over modern environmental statutes has often been similar, with the question becoming whether one is "for or against" the environment. This is not surprising: the packaging of so many changes in the law offered many opportunities for coalition building but left little opportunity for public understanding. In both cases, one of the main results of the passage of the comprehensive reform was the creation of a vast demand for modifications of it, to constantly adjust the details of the law.

These similarities suggest why the issues in the codification debate remain relevant to understanding the transition from common law to statutory law in the environmental area. I next turn to examining the issues raised by code opponents in their attacks on the codes and by code proponents in their defense of codification.

COMMON LAW AND CODIFIED LAW

The consensus that accompanied the creation of modern environmental statutes in the late 1960s and early 1970s was that the common law was too slow and incoherent to deal effectively with environmental issues. Nuisance law, one of the common law's primary means of addressing externality problems, was (and often still is) dismissed as "incapable of any exact or comprehensive definition" and as embodying "the familiar tendency of the courts to seize upon a catchword as a substitute for any analysis of a problem" (Keeton et al. 1984, 616–17). What was needed, many reformers argued, was a comprehensive, scientific, and thorough legislative solution—precisely what Field thought the common law in general required a hundred years earlier. There was a right answer to how to solve environmental problems, and getting it in place was just a matter of rolling up our collective sleeves and doing it. Much as the United States had put a man on the moon, the argument went, we would develop low-emission or zero-emission cars, stop water pollution, and so forth. This analysis largely buys into Field's view of the common law, a view rejected in the earlier debate. In this section, I describe the contrasting views of the common law and the codified law of the nineteenth-century codification-debate participants and then discuss how their ideas can be used to reexamine environmental law today.

Defining the Systems

The participants in the late-nineteenth-century U.S. codification debate disputed virtually every point concerning the relative merits of the common law and code systems. Although their debates over particular code sections' accuracy and adequacy need not concern us, their discussions about the nature of the two systems is relevant. On the one hand, code opponents argued that the common law system provided a set of largely unwritten principles that were applied by courts in individual cases. (To the extent legislatures added statutory rules to this body of principles, those rules were a minor part of the overall system.) On the other hand, code proponents argued that code systems provided (or at least attempted to provide) comprehensive, organized bodies of written rules.

Environmental statutes today are similar in many respects to the code systems proposed by Field and others. Although they do not purport to govern every aspect of every transaction of human existence as Field's codes did, they do attempt to cover the environmental aspects. Given the broad definitions of "the environment" popular among environmentalists and environmental statute drafters alike, this attempt comes uncomfortably close to Field's ambition. Moreover, the heavy reliance on rulemaking over adjudication in implementing environmental statutes increases the resemblance to the codification process.

Two main questions drove the codification debate: Is it possible to reduce the common law to a code? And, if that is possible, Is it desirable to do so? The division over the possibility of codification derived from differences in the two sides' views of case law. The code proponents saw case law as, at best, a long-winded way of stating rules. In an address to the Law Academy of Philadelphia, David Dudley Field summed up this view: "Suppose the members of this well-equipped academy were to take for a thesis one of the most important decisions upon your common law, and formulate the rule of law there discussed and applied. If you can do it, the rule so formulated can stand in a code; if you can not formulate it, the case is valueless as authority for any future case" (Field 1886a, 250). This view led directly to Field's claim that codification would significantly reduce the volume of legal materials without affecting the content of the law.

By stripping the common law process of the context of decisions that apply actual controversies, Field reduced it to a list of holdings, much as a first-year law student today might "brief" cases in a casebook, searching for black-letter law. Not surprisingly, today's law students often prefer commercial outlines of subjects that present clear statements of doctrine to case analysis. So, too, Field sought to reduce the common law to a vast outline.

This led in turn to Field's four arguments for codification: First, it is necessary to prevent judicial lawmaking, an antidemocratic alternative to legislative action. Second, "they who are required to obey the laws should all have the opportunity of knowing what they are." Third, discovering the law would be easier and more efficient if it were reduced to a single source. Fourth, "no people, which has once exchanged an unwritten for a written law, has ever turned back" (Field 1886b, 239–41).[5]

Given Field's view of case law, these arguments were persuasive. If establishing a common law rule was merely the process of selecting the appropriate rule from the universe of possible rules, there could be little quarrel with providing a fixed set of possible rules in advance. Moreover, a code would allow virtually anyone who could read to find the rules. A code would thus check the power of judges and make the law more certain.

Field's view of the common law was by no means universal, however, even in his day. The common law in the latter half of the nineteenth century was at its zenith in many respects. Judges and lawyers alike worked in an environment in which at least the formal emphasis was on discovery, not the creation, of the law. Although subsequently legal realists claimed that the common law lawyers failed to grasp that nineteenth-century U.S. judges were creating the law, embodying their own class prejudices in legal doctrines (Horowitz 1992), the writings of the common law lawyers, both in judicial opinions and elsewhere, suggest that the realist criticism misses the mark. These writings suggest that nineteenth-century U.S., common law lawyers believed that their search for legal principles was not simply a search for the "best" rule from a policy perspective but that their analysis was constrained by the principles of the common law.

As noted earlier, the primary U.S. opponent of codification was New York lawyer James Coolidge Carter. At the invitation of Harvard president Charles Eliot in 1904–05 to speak at his (Carter's) alma mater, Carter (1907) prepared a set of lectures, although he died before he could deliver them. In those lectures, Carter set out his theory of law, which had informed his decades-long struggle against Field and codification in New York. As this theory underlies his more specific objections to codification, a brief sketch is necessary.

Much like Hayek (1973) and Leoni (1991) did later, Carter divided the products of the legal system into law and legislation. Carter began his lectures by drawing together definitions of law offered by various thinkers, including Hobbes, Bentham, Austin, and Cicero. From these he drew two opposing tendencies: One, natural law, he described as "an ideal tendency seeking to enthrone over human affairs a rule of absolute Right" (Carter 1907, 9). The other was Austin's (which Carter attributed to Field as well), which went "to the opposite extreme and refuse[d] the name of law to everything which is not prescribed in definite language by the sovereign power of the State" (12). Natural law did not satisfy Carter because it depended on "hypothesis," as we could not observe the foundational

Law of Nature. Similarly, Austin's identification of law with force was unsatisfying because "when we ascribe all law to the command of the supreme power in a State we are simply contenting ourselves with an assumption"—that the sovereign has adopted the vast unwritten law that governs society as his commands (13–14).

Rejecting both tendencies, Carter sought a third definition of the law. Law, Carter wrote, "is the *form* in which human conduct—that is, human life—presents itself under the necessary operation of the causes which govern conduct. It is the fruit of the myriads of concurring judgments of all the members of society pronounced after a study of the consequences of conduct touching what conduct should be followed and what should be avoided" (Carter 1907, 129–30).

Legislation, on the other hand, "is simply the formal written expression of the *will* of the Sovereign State" (Carter 1907, 229). Legislation was useful, according to Carter (228–29), when used to "perfect the organization of the state" through organizing government and when, where several states had recently been united into a single state, it was used to harmonize differing customs.

Generalizing from his review of the successes and the failures at creating law through legislation, Carter created rules governing when legislation might be legitimately used:

- "The State may, by an expression of its will, simply *do* something, in which case all that it has directly in view is accomplished by such expression: for instance, it may grant the public franchise of building and operating a railroad" (Carter 1907, 233).

- "The State may *command* something to be done by others; for instance, it may command one of its officers to cause a prison, a courthouse, or other public building to be constructed" (Carter 1907, 234).

- The State may issue "commands which do affect the conduct of all the members of society, as where a law is enacted defining and punishing a crime" (Carter 1907, 235).

Carter (1907, 228–29) heavily qualified this last category, noting that legislators rarely shared "the same elevated purposes" of reformers, but "at heart [they] often have only their own personal interests and ambitions, or they have been elected through the patronage and money of some powerful pecuniary interest and are faithful alone to that influence." The scope of legislation must therefore be kept relatively narrow.

Applying his views to codification, Carter rejected the code proponents' claims of advantages for the code system. Thus, for example, in considering the claim that rules must be known before they can be applied, Carter conceded that this was an important point but argued that proponents tended to exaggerate its importance. Most people, he noted, never read the existing laws and, indeed, ignored existing books written to explain the law to laymen. "What good reason have we for a belief that laymen would, to any considerable degree, seek to learn the law from statutes, when they wholly neglect the means already in their hands for gaining that knowledge?" (Carter 1889, 20).

More important, however, Carter argued that all these claimed advantages ultimately turned on whether it was possible to create a code (Carter 1889, 22). Putting in writing the rules of private law required the same efforts, across a wider range of cases, that a judge would apply to a single case. In contrast to Field's view of judges making law by selecting among the entire universe of possible rules, Carter saw judges engaged in classifying cases according to the facts of the cases and limited by both those facts and the structure of the common law. Thus, in Carter's example, a judge confronted by a contract made by an infant would assign it to the class of voidable contracts. When confronted with a new situation, a contract made by an infant but ratified after the infant reached legal age, the judge would first determine whether the new feature (ratification) was a material one that justified moving the contract from the voidable class to a new class. The first judge to confront this problem had no precedent to guide him but was obliged to determine the issue himself. "And what was the real problem which he had to solve? Simply this: what does justice require? He was to apply to the case the social standard of justice; not to simply repeat what had been done before, but to make an original application of it" (Carter 1889, 26–27).

Those writing comprehensive statutes must engage in the same process, without the advantage of facts to assist them.

> We may indeed *imagine* future transactions, and, by classifying them, make the law for them; but the world we thus deal with is an imaginary world, and the law we thus create should be regarded as imaginary law. If we attempt to make it *real* law by *enacting* it, it will prove just and efficient in its operation precisely in proportion as our imaginary world shall correspond with the real one as the future reveals itself; and I need not argue to intelligent minds that it will not be likely to thus correspond in any instance. We may indeed attempt to force this imaginary law upon the future transactions of an actual world; but it will not be law in any just or respectable sense. It will not be justice. It will be a mere arbitrary rule. (Carter 1889, 29)

Most important, Carter argued, it was the impossibility of knowing the future that rendered the codification project impossible. "The notion that society has reached, or ever will reach, a state of equilibrium and rest, so that the transactions of tomorrow will be mere repetitions in substance of the transactions of today, is a vain illusion. There is no part of the universe which is not forever under the dominion of change, and nowhere does it proceed with such activity as in the realm of man" (Carter 1889, 36).

The nineteenth-century American-codification debate thus turned on much more than whether Field's drafts were well written, although Carter and his allies were emphatic that the drafts were poorly done. The common law's defenders articulated a sophisticated rationale for the system, relying heavily on its evolutionary approach and the impossibility of predicting future circumstances when drafting statutes. Only by waiting for the facts to develop, they argued, could a decision maker understand the context of a dispute requiring a decision. The code proponents, on the other hand, sought rationalization of the law and freedom from the mass of reports. Their position was echoed by the proponents of environmental statutes in more recent years, who sought both to rationalize and to expand environmental regulation beyond the constraints of the common law.

Perhaps the most significant difference between proponents and opponents of codification was their understanding of the role of law in society. Codifiers like Field sought to use law reform as a means of restructuring society. Not only the substance of the reforms but the appearance mattered—the chance to claim a place as a modern state undoubtedly attracted Western code proponents. Common law advocates like Carter took a more restricted view of the role of law. Creating a system within which individuals could privately order their lives was the goal. Eschewing global reforms, they sought to develop stable rules through experience and process, not through the force of their intellect.

REINVIGORATING THE DEBATE TODAY

If we missed the opportunity to examine the common law in the rush to quickly "solve" environmental problems with statutes during the 1960s and 1970s, there is no reason why the periodic and seemingly endless attempts to redesign those statutes should not include consideration of common law alternatives as well. To do so first requires being clear about what the common law alternative to statutory environmental law is and what it is not.

The common law is not a particular set of rules in the sense that the Clean Water Act or the Clean Air Act is. Rather, the common law is best seen as an evolutionary process, which produces relatively slowly (although with periodic innovations) changing rules out of the resolution of specific disputes. Whereas academics may propose unifying theoretical schemes as a guide to understanding the common law, the common law itself consists only of the actual decisions and the principles articulated in them.

Moreover, despite the legal realist critique, the common law is not simply a series of unconstrained choices by judges, elected or not. When judges attempt to resolve a case under the common law, the decision is constrained both by the facts of the case before the court and by the existing body of common law rules.

The facts of the case before a court constrain its decision in several ways: First, the facts of a particular dispute limit the scope of the decision. A judge may speculate about how he would decide other cases based on the same principles, but the decision is binding only with respect to the actual case and within the jurisdiction where it was made. With regard to all other jurisdictions or cases with different facts, a decision's authority is persuasive only.

Second, by limiting the scope of the decision, the facts prevent the development of a larger political bargain. Unlike legislation, where coalitions can form around such trade-offs, the common law process hinders such bargaining. "I'll scratch your back if you'll scratch mine" is harder to enforce when only my back is susceptible to scratching in the present case. Thus a coalition like the one between high-sulfur coal producers and environmental pressure groups that produced the "dirty coal" provisions of the Clean Air Act Amendments of 1977 and prevented a shift by coal users to lower-sulfur coal would not be possible (Ackerman and Hassler 1981).

In addition to constraining the parties, the factual structure of a common law suit also creates incentives for the parties to discover the appropriate facts. By focusing the court on resolving a specific dispute involving a factual record created by the parties, the factual circumstances produce incentives for parties to develop that record. Lawyers who are good at developing facts have an entrepreneurial opportunity that continues over time to discover techniques that produce facts that will persuade a decision maker. If, for example, the problem is discovering the source of a pollutant that could potentially come from several sources, the plaintiffs and the "innocent" defendants have incentives to develop information that will establish who the responsible party is. (The source responsible for the pollution, of course, has an incentive to obscure the record.) Moreover, unlike the mix of generalities and anecdotes that predominate in congressional testimony, courtroom testimony is focused and on point, at least if the attorneys and the judge are doing their jobs. An attorney or an expert witness who develops a means of solving a causation or other proof problem can earn significant returns by marketing his or her expertise.

At the same time, the common law process restricts the incentives for investing in rent seeking. Although outsiders can attempt to influence the courts through amicus briefs (Morriss 1999a) or by financing a party's litigation or settlement, they cannot bring the same level of lobbying resources to bear on a case. Interest groups cannot prevent another case from arising tomorrow on the same issue, for example; and so even if they are able to "buy out" one case, as civil rights groups did in *Piscataway Township Board of Education v. Taxman* (1997), they cannot prevent another from arising tomorrow.

The case law also constrains the development of the law in a healthy way. A common law judge who takes judging seriously must fit his decisions within the existing framework of decisions. Whereas the first common law judges *may* have experienced relatively little constraint in this regard,[6] common law courts today (and as recently as the nineteenth-century) face an enormous structure of existing law within which their decisions must fit.

Courts can, of course, change court-made rules. Common law court decisions reveal a strong bias against overturning earlier decisions, however, where those decisions have entered into the fabric of the law. Thus, for example, courts considering abrogating common law tort immunities during the second half of the twentieth century often resisted change to offer legislatures the opportunity to examine the question, even when the courts concluded that they would not create the immunity in question if considering the issue for the first time (Morriss 1999c).

Nonetheless, the framework of existing rules is a powerful constraint because it forces courts to explain how their decision in a particular case fits within the framework. To the extent that a court's explanation is not persuasive, other jurisdictions will not follow it, and even courts within the same jurisdiction will limit its applicability by distinguishing it.

Consider, for example, how the common law court system dealt with the aberrant decision of the Oklahoma Supreme Court in *Peeveyhouse v. Garland Coal* (1962). As almost every former law student knows, in that case the Oklahoma court overturned a contract damages award to landowners for a mining company's refusal to fulfill its contractual obligation to restore the landowner's property to its original condition after completing strip-mining for coal. Finding that the damages awarded were far in excess of the land's objective value as restored, the Oklahoma court awarded the landowners only the difference in value between the unrestored land and the restored land ($300) instead of the $29,000 it would take to restore the land. Spending the money to restore the land would be wasteful, the court concluded, and so the defendant could not be required to pay it.

The most that can be said for this decision is that it is flat wrong and the result of poor reasoning. A more likely explanation, however, is that the Oklahoma Supreme Court that made the decision was profoundly corrupt. Shortly after the *Peeveyhouse* decision, a corruption investigation uncovered more than thirty years of routine bribery of several of the court's members (Maute 1995). Remarkably, one of the justices who confessed noted that he was unable to identify all the cases in which he had taken bribes because they were so numerous.

How did the common law system handle the *Peeveyhouse* decision? The decision was roundly criticized (and continues to be criticized in many first-year contracts casebooks and law and economics textbooks). No other state followed the reasoning of *Peeveyhouse*, and even Oklahoma appears to have abandoned the rule (*Rock Island Improvement v. Helmerich & Payne* 1983). An almost worst-case example (a terrible rule on the merits that was likely procured by corruption) produced very little harm (except, of course, to Willie and Lucille Peeveyhouse, the landowners in the case itself).

Compare this to "mistakes" in environmental statutory law. Early pesticides were substances that were found to kill pests through trial and error. Arsenic, for example, was a popular early pesticide. The initial pesticide laws in the United States focused on forcing use to overcome free-riding orchard owners. Gradually the statutory focus shifted to ensuring that pesticides were efficacious with respect to the pests they targeted and not acutely toxic to the users (Morriss 1997b).

The next generation of pesticides, sparked by the accidental discovery of DDT's effectiveness, included organophosphates and other broad-spectrum pesticides. The problems with these pesticides were caused by their excessive effectiveness with respect to multiple species. After the discovery of the externalities caused by the use of the second-generation, broad-spectrum pesticides, federal pesticide laws were amended to include as goals protecting the environment and preventing chronic human health impacts.

The increased data requirements of the expanded regulatory review sharply increased the cost of developing new pesticides, however. Moreover, these data requirements' cost meant that review of existing pesticides would take years, even under the best circumstances. Of course, pesticide manufacturers also successfully sought to prolong the review process to extend the franchise of their existing products. The net effect of the regulatory process was to slow introduction of a third generation of more narrowly targeted, less broadly lethal pesticides. Moreover, because the pesticide law was a federal law, there was comparatively little room for states to experiment (Morriss 1997b). Resolving these problems is a continuing process; even today, federal registration of pesticides still suffers from these types of problems.

Although code systems like those used today in civil-law systems and those proposed by the nineteenth-century U.S. code advocates can also provide constraints on legislatures, by requiring rules to be written at the most general level and by insisting that each rule fit within the overall conceptual framework, modern environmental laws provide no similar constraints. Conceptual coherence does not appear to be even a theoretical goal, with each major media (air, water, land) subject to wildly different regulatory schemes. Even within a single statute, there is little evidence that the drafters attempted more than ad hoc drafting of provisions to deal with each problem separately. Moreover, the total regulatory scheme, including the administrative regulations, is so complex that coherence would be impossible. Indeed, under the Clean Air Act, the vitally important State Implementation Plans are often not kept in a physical format that permits anyone to grasp their provisions (Morriss 2000). Mistakes in environmental laws, if noticed, breed not corrective changes but new layers of statutes and regulations.

In summary, our turn toward statutory solutions for environmental problems points us toward Field's vision of the law. Comprehensive statutes like the Clean Air Act are just as much attempts to restructure society as Field's codes were. Carter's analysis of the proper role of statutory law provides a good starting point for thinking about how to restructure environmental law today. As discussed earlier, four jurisdictions adopted versions of Field's civil code. I now turn to examining how the introduction of massive amounts of codified law affected their legal systems.

THE EFFECT OF CODIFIED LAW IN A COMMON LAW SYSTEM

The codifications in California, the Dakotas, and Montana offer another area in which we can learn about the impact of displacing the common law by statutory enactments. All four states experienced a massive injection of new statutory rules, which at least purported to systematically state the law that governs a large part of society. Similarly, the passage of the ever-growing list of federal and state environmental statutes since the 1960s (at least) threatens to overwhelm the common law today. What can we learn about the impact of such injections on the common law?

As discussed earlier, Field originally proposed to simply do away with the common law in any area in which his codes stated the law. His original draft and his New York drafts until late in the 1880s thus contained straightforward provisions eliminating the common law. The Western codifiers were not prepared to go quite so far (with the exception of the Dakota codifiers who copied, and then largely ignored, Field's language.) In place of total displacement, they substituted provisions making partial displacements. As Professor Robert Natelson (1990) has described, the partial-displacement approach was even less satisfactory than complete displacement might have been.

In some respects these partial displacements are similar to the effect of statutory environmental law today, which is premised on the ability of the judicial system to integrate the complex environmental statutes with existing law. Thus, for example, the particularly appallingly drafted Comprehensive Environmental Response, Compensation, and Liability Act (CERCLA) imposes strict liability on "owners" of land on which hazardous waste is found. Are owners of easements over such land liable under CERCLA? Easement owners can exercise a high degree of control over their easements (think of railroads and utilities). The question remains unresolved.[7]

Codification had three major impacts on the common law. First, the codes crowded out common law rules. Second, even where the codes did not crowd out the common law, the presence of the code rules skewed the evolution of common law rules by forcing judges to adapt the common law to the statutory rules. Third, the code rules reduced the evolutionary pressure on the common law by redirecting resources into seeking statutory changes.

Crowding Out

Statutes crowd out the common law much as government investment crowds out private investment. To the extent that the codes were successful in providing a rule that at least appeared to govern for most transactions (and they were not always successful in doing so), there was no need for courts to engage in the common law classification process described by Carter. To the extent that the codes overdetermined the result, by providing more than one rule that appeared to govern a transaction, courts and lawyers devoted resources to fitting the transaction into the appropriate code classification, not to common law reasoning.

Skewing Evolution

Even when a code provision did not directly address an issue, it might still affect the development of the common law by altering the legal analysis. Any common law rule selected would have to coexist with the code rules on related subjects. A court might, therefore, change its interpretation of the common law to prevent conflicts. If it did not, it would create a contradiction in the law, inducing parties to attempt to persuade future courts to allocate their dispute to either the common law or the code rule, as their own interests dictated. This effort would then prompt additional expenditure of resources on developing rules to distinguish when the code would apply and when the common law rule would apply.

An example of such a change is the well-known 1972 California case *Willard v. First Church of Christ, Scientist*. In that case, the California Supreme Court abandoned the common law rule that one cannot "reserve" an interest in property to a stranger. (This is a technical rule whose details thankfully do not concern us here.) The rule's origins are the feudal requirements for land transfer; the justification for maintaining the rule (or at least for relying on the legislature to change it) is that people may have relied on this rule in purchasing property and its abolition would upset their expectations.

In *Willard*, the California court examined the rule's origins and quickly rejected them as a basis for maintaining the rule. It then dismissed the expectations issue as well. Finally, the court noted that "in some situations the rule conflicts with section 1085 of the Civil Code" (*Willard v. First Church of Christ, Scientist* 1972, 990), although there was no conflict in this case. Based on these conclusions, the court then abandoned the rule entirely.

Section 1085 provides that a "present interest, and the benefit of a condition or covenant respecting property, may be taken by any natural person under a grant, although not named a party thereto." (It did not apply in *Willard* because the Church was not a natural person.) The conflict with the common law rule, which dated back to an 1860 case in California, existed from the Civil Code's adoption in 1872. That it was first discussed one hundred years later in a 1972 case suggests the possibilities for such conflicts to lurk beneath the surface of the law for extended periods.

It may be that feudal notions of property transfer play no useful role in our modern society and that legal rules based on them therefore should be vigorously rooted out of the legal system. That is certainly the view of many commentators on this rule. Not all courts (or even most), however, have made the same choice; New York, for example, recently reaffirmed the common law rule on stability grounds (*Estate of Thomson v. Wade* 1987). In rejecting the California court's view, New York's highest court wrote

> Although application of the stranger-to-the-deed rule may, at times, frustrate a grantor's intent, any such frustration can readily be avoided by the direct conveyance of an easement of record from the grantor to the third party. The overriding considerations of the "public policy favoring certainty in title to real property, both to protect bona fide purchasers and to avoid conflicts of ownership, which may engender needless litigation" persuade us to decline to depart from our settled rule. We have previously noted that in this area of law, "where it can reasonably be assumed that settled rules are necessary and necessarily relied upon, stability and adherence to precedent are generally more important than a better or even a 'correct' rule of law." (*Estate of Thomson v. Wade* 1987, 509 NE 2d at 310, internal citations omitted)

Thus, the choice between the rule adopted in *Willard* and the rule rejected in *Willard* is not simply a choice between feudal property rules and modern property rules. It is also a choice about how the law should balance the need for "good" rules with the cost of upsetting settled expectations.

It may be that the California Supreme Court was determined to abandon the common law rule even without the code provision; the California court was an extremely activist court during the 1970s. As the New York court noted, the change was an important one with serious consequences for security of title, which many consider the single most important policy of property law. That the existence of a potential conflict with a relatively obscure code provision, which the court conceded had never been previously cited in an opinion, provided a justification for such a change in the law is significant.

REDIRECTING RESOURCES

Creating a complex statute usually requires a significant investment of resources, although, as the example of Dakota Territory in 1866 suggests, copying can reduce those costs substantially. Maintaining such a statutory scheme requires additional resources, often more than the initial investment. Although codification propaganda often implied that adoption of a set of principles would lead to stability in the law, the experience of all four Western states suggests otherwise. Indeed, their experience with the codes is evidence supporting Carter's rejection of statute law—as Westerners found that their "imagined" world did not correspond to reality, they were forced to constantly adjust the codes to compensate. Moreover, because the codes were designed to be interdependent bodies of law, an adjustment in one area often had implications for other provisions.

The costs of maintaining the Western codes were thus substantial, too substantial for the codes to survive as comprehensive, logical statements of the law. Although the codifiers succeeded in building their statutory structures, they could not maintain them. In none of the four Western states do the codes today occupy the position imagined by their authors. No one reads the codes to learn their legal rights and duties. Code provisions and annotations have swollen the codes themselves far beyond the size at which they might comfortably rest on the bedside table, alongside the Bible and the dictionary, as some codifiers envisioned. Indeed, the conceptual structure itself has been largely abandoned, with California relying on an alphabetical arrangement. The abandonment of the attempt to maintain the codes as codes means that the code states themselves thus ultimately found the costs of codification exceeded the benefits.

The Codes in Practice

The codes in practice offer numerous examples of the problems described earlier. In the interests of brevity, let me discuss only one, the Montana Supreme Court's 1929 decision in *Barth v. Ely*. The decision involved a relatively routine business transaction: the plaintiff-landlord owned a hotel and leased it to the defendant-tenant, the defendant failed to pay the rent, and the plaintiff sued for the reasonable value of the premises.[8] The lease included a provision that the rent was payable in advance and gave the landlord a lien on the tenant's personal property in the hotel "in the same manner as in the case of chattel mortgages on default thereunder" (*Barth v. Ely* 1929, 278 P. at 1003).

Two code sections covered remedies that might apply to the contract: (1) Civil Code section 8233 provided that "the existence of a lien, as security for the performance of an obligation, does not affect the right of a creditor to enforce the obligation without regard to the lien." This provision codified the rule that efforts to gain additional protection by the creation of a lien should not reduce a creditor's options, enabling credit markets to function more easily. (2) Section 9467 of the Code of Civil Procedure provided that "there is but one action for the recovery of a debt, or the enforcement of any right secured by mortgage upon real estate or personal property, which action must be in accordance with the provisions of this chapter." This section was adopted for the sensible purpose of simplifying the complex set of common law and equitable remedies for default on mortgages. The two code provisions thus were both eminently sensible rules standing alone and neither appears to have been the result of interest group lobbying in the pejorative sense.

After an extensive survey of the policies underlying the two sections and origins of each, the court turned to determining how they fit together. Looking back at its earlier decisions interpreting section 9467, the court first noted that those decisions had held that section 9467 prohibited any action other than that provided by the statute for foreclosure of a mortgage and that a creditor could waive a mortgage and sue on the underlying debt. Its earlier interpretation, the court concluded, "would be unhesitatingly approved, were it not for the existence of section 8233. . . ." (*Barth v. Ely* 1929, 278 P. at 1006).

The court admitted, however, that none of these earlier decisions mentioned section 8233. This failure was most likely because no one had raised the issue and because section 9467 was clear on its face—there was no reason to look for additional code provisions. The failure meant that if section 8233 required a change in interpretation of section 9467, the court would have to disturb a long-standing interpretation, on which parties had undoubtedly been relying.

Nonetheless, section 8233 both existed and clearly conflicted with the earlier interpretation of section 9467. Worse, the court concluded that "were it not for our decisions above, or had section 8233 been enacted after those decisions were rendered and the question was now presented as one of first impression, we would as unhesitatingly hold that the latter section impliedly repealed the former and permits a mortgagee to waive his mortgage security and sue upon the mortgage debt 'without regard to the lien'" (*Barth v. Ely* 1929, 278 P. at 1006–7).

Section 8233 had been enacted after section 9467, of course, seemingly solving the court's problem. The normal technique of statutory interpretation, examining the dates of passage of the two conflicting statutes, was not available here, however. Although section 8233 was first adopted over thirty years after section 9467, the court could not consider that fact. Section 9467 was first passed in 1864, one of Montana's earliest statutes, but it was included in the Civil Code passed in 1895. Section 8233 first appeared in the 1895 Code of Civil Procedure. As an aid to interpretation of the codes, the codes provided that they "must be construed as though each had been passed on the last day of the session during which they were passed" (*Barth v. Ely* 1929, 278 P. at 1007). Hence the court was required to treat them as if they were passed simultaneously.

Nor could the court consider the location of section 8233 in the procedure code and the location of section 9467 in the Civil Code to resolve the difference. Another code-interpretation provision provided that in the case of conflicts, both provisions must prevail as to all matters and questions arising out of the subject matter of such chapter in "like manner." Therefore, the court concluded, "it must be presumed that the Legislature intended that both should be operative and each should govern as to the title in which it is found, and it becomes our duty to construe them together and reconcile them, if possible." The solution the court chose was to limit section 8233 to "the general subject of the chapter in which that section is found, 'Liens,' other than mortgage liens" (*Barth v. Ely* 1929, 278 P. at 1007). This is not quite the end of the story because the new rule had to be applied to the case at hand.

Even if section 8233 applied only to liens "other than mortgage liens," however, the court still had to determine "what is meant by the term 'mortgage.'" The court resolved this issue by looking to earlier decisions interpreting section 9467, decisions that had not considered the issue of the applicability of section 8233. It found that its prior decisions interpreting section 9467 supported a view that section 9467 applied to securities "in the form of a mortgage, or, adopting the most liberal view, to be what the law would deem the equivalent of a mortgage" (*Barth v. Ely* 1929, 278 P. at 1007). Thus despite that the contract in question "treats the lien as something other than a chattel mortgage and provides for satisfaction 'in the same manner as' in the case of a chattel mortgage" (powerful evidence that the parties did not believe they had created a mortgage), the court found that it must be a mortgage. The court also rejected the plaintiff's argument that the statute contemplated formal mortgages (i.e., those that the parties understood to be mortgages) rather than mortgages generally, noting that the existence of a code definition of *mortgage* prevented the court from "read[ing] in" the word *formal*.

The reader may be tempted to ask, "So what?" Why is a 1929 decision of a court from a relatively unimportant state worth all this effort? I have two justifications for asking for your time in pondering *Barth*. First, it is precisely the ordinariness of the transaction that makes this decision important. As is the case with the environmental laws today, the significance of the code approach lay in its comprehensiveness—it sought, not always successfully, to apply to almost every legal issue. Code rules thus lurked as traps for the unwary, suggesting that with the proper investment in legal talent, one might discover a conflict or a provision that rationalized one's position. The regular appearance of news stories today about unwary landowners' surprise at discovering they have violated environmental statutes, even if we discount for the self-serving nature of the surprise, suggest this remains a problem.

Second, the decision illustrates the trap for the law provided by complicated, comprehensive laws. The conflict between these two code provisions lay waiting to be discovered for thirty-four years. During that time the Montana Supreme Court decided at least six cases interpreting section 9467 without reference to section 8233.[9] Undoubtedly, individuals entered into transactions during that time in reliance on both sections. The potential for major changes in interpretation hangs over all transactions—in this case those who relied on section 9467 prevailed, whereas those who relied on section 8233 found themselves suddenly with less valuable rights. That we do not know how many exist on either side prevents an explicit cost-benefit analysis. It does not prevent the instability from undermining the benefits of clear rules.

Environmental Law

Modern environmental law is even more subject to these problems than the codes. Environmental law today is primarily an exercise in statutory and regulatory interpretation, and the common law has been already largely crowded out of environmental law. The sheer volume of statutes and rules makes it impossible for all but the dedicated specialist, at most, to understand the system as a whole. Gaining permits and other indicia of regulators' permission to operate and negotiating penalties for regulatory violations have become the primary focus of environmental lawyers.

The skewing of the law is readily apparent in environmental and administrative law. Consider the landmark case *Seacoast Anti-Pollution League v. Costle* (1978). This case turned on administrative procedures used to resolve the issue of the thermal sensitivity of the soft-shelled clams living near the Seabrook nuclear reactor's cooling-tower outflow pipes and whether the Environmental Protection Agency (EPA) had accurately assessed the impact of increases in water temperature. Of course the real issues in dispute that led to the *Seacoast* opinion were a combination of concerns over the appropriateness of nuclear power in general and the siting of a nuclear plant in a densely populated region lacking evacuation routes in particular. Challenging the EPA's method of review of data on the thermal sensitivity of soft-shelled clams was merely one among many attempts to block the plant; yet the legal issues surrounding the challenge played a major role not just in that case but for future, unrelated cases in which agencies had to evaluate technical evidence. Devoting resources to technicalities in administrative law may be worthwhile on its own merits in some instances, but it is a poor way to develop substantive law or policy.

The redirection of resources is readily apparent in the EPA's heavy investment in producing regulations that serve little purpose other than satisfying the formal requirements imposed by statutes. Thus the EPA engages in an expensive "review" of state "special local need" pesticide registrations that adds almost no substantive review (Morriss 1997b). In a similar way, the "double key" approach to state implementation plans under the Clean Air Act requires the plans to go through notice and comment-rule making at both the state and the federal levels. This requires the EPA to invest significant resources in processing routine amendments to state master plans without improving the quality of air (Morriss 2000). Not only the EPA redirects resources to maintaining the complex Rube Goldberg structure of environmental law, of course. Lobbyists and lawyers for various interest groups consume vast resources in lobbying and litigation over adjustments to the regulatory regime.

LESSONS FOR ENVIRONMENTAL LAW TODAY

Criticism of the modern reliance on complex statutes to deal with environmental law is growing. The nineteenth-century U.S. codification debate and the subsequent experience of the four Western code states suggest some reasons for giving serious attention to this criticism.

On a theoretical level, the debate between code proponents like David Dudley Field and code opponents like James Coolidge Carter has much to recommend it with regard to modern environmental law. In Field's and Carter's competing visions of the role of the law, we can see some of the differences underlying disagreements over how to deal with environmental problems. Field saw the law as the command of the sovereign and the fundamental problem of law as ensuring that the right commands were issued, understood, and obeyed. The common law's inefficiency at accomplishing all three tasks, because of its slow evolution, difficult presentation in case reports, and obscurity, motivated Field to attempt to replace the common law with a more suitable set of commands. In a similar way, the modern environmental law reforms are far-reaching attempts to restructure society premised on the notion that we simply need the right orders from EPA to clean up the environment, the proper understanding of our responsibilities, and the existence of a big enough club for EPA to use to coerce us into obedience.

The nineteenth-century defenders of the common law resisted codification for reasons beyond the flaws they found in many of the specific rules embodied in Field's drafts. More important to their argument was a vision of the common law as an intellectual process. That process is vanishing from the United States today in many areas. The proportion of statutory law to common law generally has risen to new heights; worse than that, modern courts have unmoored the common law from the principles that once constrained judges. In the environmental area, the common law process is almost completely lost. What might we recover from the U.S. codification debate? What could the common law process bring to environmental law if environmental law grew out of case law instead of regulatory agencies?

We would certainly find that the resulting rules were imperfect. The common law process is unlikely to produce results as consistent and as clear as a well-drafted code. The opportunity to consider linkages between areas of the law, for example, is more generally available to the authors of a systematic body of law than to a judge considering a single claim. This disadvantage is offset, however, by two factors. First, modern environmental laws hardly qualify as examples of clear drafting. Compared to what we actually have, the common law rules do not look quite so bad. Second, the evolutionary nature of the common law allows it to always be growing toward the appropriate rule, whereas the discontinuous process of enactment and amendment characteristic of statutes ensures that even the best-drafted statute is soon out of sync with changed conditions (Rubin 1992, 11).

If we consider the law in general and environmental law in particular as a process of evolving appropriate rules to govern particular forms of social interaction, then the common law's advantages become clear. Our current system relies heavily on the foresight of the small group of Congresspeople, congressional staff, lobbyists, and administration representatives that produce sporadic revolutions in environmental statutes. Working under intense political pressure in a situation where the common currency is political clout, without access to the facts of actual transactions, it is no surprise that even the most talented statute writers fall short in imagining how the future will turn out. The decentralized processing of the common law is slower, to be sure, but its lack of speed is not always a vice. What it lacks in speed compared to the statutory process in moments of crisis, the common law often regains over the long haul. Fifty state court systems continuously processing environmental cases, even if they process slowly, may well have an advantage over one legislative body fitfully considering environmental subjects.

Moreover, the environment is far too important to be abandoned to the political process. The common law is much superior to statutory law in controlling the role of interest groups. The statutory/regulatory approach puts a premium on lobbying and manipulation of the drafting/rule-making process. This fosters the creation of interest groups capable of organizing resources to engage in such activities. The common law process, by contrast, is far less predictable. Even though interest groups might seek to assist either plaintiffs or defendants in nuisance suits, for example, with expert assistance or funding, such assistance is much more likely to take the form of market purchases of expert or legal services than the creation of the type of staff-based organizations common to both sides in Washington, D.C. A common law system for environmental issues would significantly change the structure of interest groups on all sides of environmental issues for the better.

Potentially even more important to realizing the public choice problems of environmental legislation would be the shift to a generalist forum for dispute resolution. Because the common law decisions are made by generalist courts, the "prize" of agency capture would be significantly reduced (Morriss 1997a, 158–61). Lobbying for appointment of "green" judges, for example, would be less intense than lobbying over EPA appointments if only because much of the judges' time would continue to be taken up with other issues.

CONCLUSION

When repeatedly confronted with the chance to replace the common law with "a *complete body* of proposed law, in the form of Statute law, say in one word a *Pannomion*" in the nineteenth century, Americans largely turned away, despite the projects' backing by intellectual giants like Bentham and Field. When they took hesitating steps down the path toward codification, as they did in California, Dakota Territory, and Montana, nineteenth-century Americans quickly retreated. Today, however, we have swallowed statutes whose complexity and scope would likely befuddle even men like Bentham and Field.[10] By recovering some of the intellectual history of the earlier debate, we can shed some light on why these statutes seem to be causing such indigestion today. Most important, by reflecting on these earlier debates, we can rediscover the virtues of the common law.

NOTES

1.   Louisiana, of course, also has a mixed system. The development of that system is sufficiently different that I will not address it here.

2.   Those interested in a more complete description of the process of codification in the Western states should examine Morriss (1995) and the sources cited therein. Works in progress address California, Dakota, and New York in greater detail.

3.   The "fifth" code was the code of Criminal Procedure.

4.   The nineteenth-century codifiers were slightly more ambitious, seeking to rewrite the entire legal system; but authors of present-day environmental statutes still attempt to produce systems by handling an extensive range of problems within a single statute. Indeed, one of the criticisms leveled at modern environmental law is that it is insufficiently complex, "solving" only one media (air, water, solid waste) per statute and neglecting the interactions between them.

5.   This historical argument rested in part on some peculiar ideas shared among nineteenth-century codifiers about Roman law and the "codification" of Emperor Justinian. These, mercifully, are too obscure to discuss here. I explore one Montana codifier's views on the subject in Morriss (1998).

6.   I use the term "may" here because it appears to me that at least most early common law judges viewed themselves as constrained by principles of natural law.

7.   Compare *Wells Fargo Bank v. Goldzband* (1997), review denied (1997), extending liability to easement owner and declining to extend *Long Beach Unified School Dist. v. Dorothy B. Godwin California Living Trust* (1994), exempting easement owner because easement owner's pipeline did not contribute to problem. This example came to my attention in Dukeminier and Krier (1993).

8.   There were some other minor issues that need not concern us, such as whether the tenant was holding over or present under a lease.

9.   The court lists these opinions at 278 P. 1006.

10.   Well, maybe not Bentham—he'd just want to rewrite them himself.

REFERENCES

Ackerman, Bruce A., and William T. Hassler. 1981. *Clean Coal, Dirty Air.* New Haven, CT: Yale University Press.

Association of the Bar of the City of New York. 1881. [First Annual] *Report of the Special Committee to "Urge the Rejection of the Proposed Civil Code."* New York: Association of the Bar of the City of New York.

Bentham, Jeremy. 1988. *The Correspondence of Jeremy Bentham*, ed. Timothy L. S. Sprigge. London: Athlone Press.

Carter, James Coolidge. 1889. *The Provinces of the Written and Unwritten Law.* New York: Banks Brothers.

————. 1907. *Law: Its Origin, Growth and Function.* New York: G. P. Putnam's Sons.

Coe, Mildred V., and Lewis W. Morse. 1942. Chronology of the Development of the David Dudley Field Code. *Cornell Law Quarterly* 27: 238–45.

Cook, Charles M. 1981. *The U.S. Codification Movement: A Study in Legal Reform.* Westport, CT: Greenwood Press.

Dukeminier, Jesse, and James E. Krier. 1993. *Property.* 3d ed. Boston: Little, Brown & Co.

Field, David Dudley. 1886a. Address before the Law Academy of Philadelphia, April 15, 1886. Reprinted in vol. 3 of *Speeches, Arguments, and Miscellaneous Papers of David Dudley Field,* ed. Titus Munson Coan. New York: D. Appleton & Co., 1890, 244–58.

————. 1886b. Codification. Reprinted in vol. 3 of *Speeches, Arguments, and Miscellaneous Papers of David Dudley Field,* ed. Titus Munson Coan. New York: D. Appleton & Co., 1890, 238–44.

Hayek, Friedrich A. 1973. *Law, Legislation and Liberty.* London: Routledge & Kegan Paul.

Horowitz, Morton J. 1992. *The Transformation of U.S. Law, 1870–1960.* Oxford, England: Oxford University Press.

Keeton, W. Page, Dan B. Dobbs, Robert E. Keeton, and David G. Owens, eds. 1984. *Prosser & Keeton on the Law of Torts.* 5th ed. St. Paul: West Publishing Co.

Kingsbury, George W. 1915. *History of the Dakota Territory.* Vol. 1. Chicago: S. J. Clarke Publishing.

Kleps, Ralph N. 1954. The Revision and Codification of California Statutes, 1849–1953. *California Law Review* 42: 766–802.

Leoni, Bruno. 1991. *Freedom and the Law.* 3d ed. Indianapolis: Liberty Fund Inc.

Lindley, Charles H. 1874. *California Code Commentaries.* Self-published, San Francisco.

Maute, Judith L. 1995. *Peeveyhouse v. Garland Coal & Mining Co.* Revisited: The Ballad of Willie and Lucille. *Northwestern University Law Review* 89: 1341–473.

Morriss, Andrew P. 1995. This State Will Soon Have Plenty of Laws: Lessons from One Hundred Years of Codification in Montana. *Montana Law Review* 56: 359–450.

————. 1997a. Specialized Labor and Employment Law Institutions in New Zealand and the United States. *California Western International Law Journal* 28: 145–66.

————. 1997b. Pesticides and Environmental Federalism: An Empirical and Qualitative Examination of Special Local Needs Registrations. In *Environmental Federalism,* ed. Terry L. Anderson and Peter J. Hill. Lanham, MD: Rowman & Littlefield, 133–74.

————. 1998. Decius Wade's *The Common Law. Montana Law Review* 59: 225–74.

————. 1999a. Private Amici and Supreme Court's 1997–1998 Term Employment Law Jurisprudence. *William and Mary Bill of Rights Journal* 7: 823–911.

————. 1999b. Right Answers and Codification. *Chicago-Kent Law Review* 74, forthcoming.

————. 1999c. The Evolution of Post-New Deal Immunity and Warranty Law. Paper presented at Applications of Public Choice Theory to Economic History conference at Wake Forest University, Winston-Salem, NC, April 9–10.

———. 2000. Clean Air and the Politics of the Clean Air Act. In *Political Environmentalism*, ed. Terry L. Anderson. Palo Alto, CA: Hoover Institution Press, forthcoming.

Natelson, Robert G. 1990. Running with the Land in Montana. *Montana Law Review* 51: 17–93.

Parma, Rosamond. 1929. The History of the Adoption of the Codes of California. *Law Library Journal* 22: 8–21.

Rubin, Paul. 1992. Growing a Legal System in the Post-Communist Economies. *Cornell International Law Journal* 27: 1–47.

Tilton, Horace G. 1898. History of the Dakota Codes. *Monthly South Dakotan* 1: 90–93.

van Ee, Daun. 1986. *David Dudley Field and the Reconstruction of the Law*. New York: Garland Publishing.

Whitaker, John C. 1976. *Striking a Balance—Environmental and Natural Resources Policy in the Nixon-Ford Years*. Washington, DC: American Enterprise Institute.

Zywicki, Todd J. 2000. Industry and Environmental Lobbyists: Enemies or Allies?, this volume.

CASES CITED

Barth v. Ely, 85 Mont. 310, 278 P. 1002 (1929)

Estate of Thomson v. Wade, 69 N.Y. 2d 570, 509 N.E. 2d 309, 516 N.Y.S. 2d 614 (1987)

Long Beach Unified School Dist. v. Dorothy B. Godwin California Living Trust, 32 F.3d 1364 (9th Cir. 1994)

Peeveyhouse v. Garland Coal Co., 382 P.2d 109 (Okla. 1962)

Piscataway Township Board of Education v. Taxman, 91 F.3d 1547 (3rd Cir. 1996) cert dismissed 118 S.Ct. 595 (1997)

Rock Island Improvement Company v. Helmerich & Payne, Inc., 698 F.2d 1075, 1078–1079 (10th Cir. 1983)

Seacoast Anti-Pollution League v. Costle, 572 F.2d 872 (1st Cir.) cert. den. 439 U.S. 824 (1978)

Wells Fargo Bank v. Goldzband, 53 Cal. App. 4th 596, 61 Cal. Rptr. 2d 826 (Cal. App. 5 Dist. 1997)

Willard v. First Church of Christ, Scientist, 7 Cal.3d 473, 102 Cal. Rptr. 739, 498 P.2d 987 (1972)

7

Federalism and the Environment

Jonathan R. Macey and Henry N. Butler

The term *federalism* has different meanings in different contexts. In particular, the idea of federalist principles often is used to connote the value judgment that the general quality of policy making would improve if more decisions currently made centrally by the federal government were made by the states. In this chapter, federalism is a system in which there is more than one level of government, and each level of government has been allocated some independent realm of power and authority. Federalism describes the allocation of power among various levels of government within a particular jurisdiction. Federalism thus has the potential to introduce a degree of competition among governments, an important part of the common law system as discussed elsewhere in this volume.

The purpose of this chapter is to articulate a general theory of federalism and to apply that theory to the allocation of power over decision making regarding environmental issues among the various levels of government, particularly between state authorities and federal authorities. In order to clarify the relevant issues, the first part of this chapter describes the origins of the confusion over the meaning of the term federalism. The second part of the chapter describes the theory, and the third part relates the theory to the environment.

THE MEANING OF FEDERALISM

If the term *federalism* is to have a coherent meaning, the term must mean that states are truly sovereign in the sense that there is some limit on the regulatory jurisdiction of the federal government. In other words, federalism reflects the concept of dual sovereignty (*Garcia v. San Antonio Metropolitan Transit Authority* 1985).

One obvious implication of the simple point that federalism means dual sovereignty is that where the states only are allowed to regulate where the federal government voluntarily abdicates what it considers to be its right to regulate in a particular area, true federalism is not being practiced. Thus, when Republicans in the U.S. Senate or House of Representatives advocate what they call the "devolution" of power to the states, such a devolution does not reflect truly federalist principles. Rather, such rhetoric reflects the view that the states are rather like administrative agencies to which Congress can delegate power when and to the extent it chooses to do so.

Another, more subtle implication of the idea that states must be allowed to have their own, distinct, and independent policy space in order to regulate is that the states must be free to decline to regulate entirely. Thus a system in which the states are *required* to regulate to a certain extent to meet "federal" (national) standards, but are allowed to regulate even more, is not a truly federal system.

Perhaps the most difficult conceptual aspect of the conception of federalism developed here involves the question of the level of government that is responsible for maintaining the constitutionally prescribed balance between the states and the federal government. Commentators often erroneously presume that the U.S. Supreme Court is the natural forum to decide disputes about the proper allocation of power between the states and the federal government. But this is clearly not the case. Despite its independence under Article III of the U.S. Constitution, the Supreme Court, like the other federal courts, is a branch of the federal government. And giving one sovereign (the national government) the power to define the contours of the responsibility of another sovereign is inconsistent with the simple definition of federalism offered here, which envisions independence for each level of government within the system.

Of course the idea that the Supreme Court's authority to decide, as between a state and the federal government, which has regulatory authority in a particular context presents an analytical problem. After all, if the Supreme Court cannot properly decide, it is far from obvious who could. The point here is not to resolve this issue of constitutional procedure. Indeed, it may well be the case that the problem of designing a properly functioning federal system is intractable. Be that as it may, policy questions remain. The purpose of this chapter is simply to explain how *federalism* should properly be defined and to suggest how difficult it is to construct an operational federalist system in practice.

In the first section of the chapter we consider the issue of whether federalism matters. Specifically, to motivate a chapter on federalism and the environment, one must address the question of whether changes in the allocation of decision-making authority between the states and the federal government will make a difference in the quality of the policies that are generated by government action.

A THEORY OF FEDERALISM

The issue of whether environmental decision making can be improved by invoking principles of federalism can only be answered by developing a theory of how the allocation of power between the states and the national government would be allocated in a world in which public policy was developed from a purely public interest perspective, that is, in a world without rent seeking.

Here the theory of federalism we offer is the one we have articulated in earlier joint work (Butler and Macey 1996, 23). We call this theory the Matching Principle. The principle serves as a guide to determining the most efficient governmental level for regulation of different types of environmental concerns.[1] The Matching Principle suggests that, in general, the size of the geographic area affected by a specific pollution source should determine the appropriate governmental level for responding to the pollution. There is no need for the regulating jurisdiction to be larger than the regulated activity. In other words, when a particular polluting activity is limited to a particular locality or state, there is very little justification for federal environmental regulation. When a federal government response is justified, it should be the most limited response possible.

Although the Matching Principle may seem radical to some environmentalists, this idea has a long history in American constitutional law and theory. As James Wilson explained at the Pennsylvania ratifying convention, "Whatever object of government is confined in its operation and effect, *within the bounds* of a particular State, should be considered as belonging to the government of that State" (J. Elliot 1836, 424). As we will show, many important environmental problems are problems of purely local concern and should be regulated at the state and local level. In particular, most of the sites targeted by Superfund are contained within a single state. The cleanup of these sites presents issues of purely local concern, and the economic theory of federalism articulated here, which is consistent with the Framers' design, would confine authority over these issues to local regulators. Under our Matching Principle, if the federal government wants to intrude on local decision-making authority over the cleanup of local sites, it should confine itself to lending expertise and providing funding. It should refrain from imposing substantive standards or imposing legal liability.

The Matching Principle suggests that determining the efficient level of regulatory authority within a federal system is not very complicated. In general, regulatory authority should go to the political jurisdiction that comes closest to matching the geographic area affected by a particular externality. Traditional federalism theory tells us that local government reflects the environmental quality preferences of the affected parties and allows for jurisdictional competition and diversity. Thus, primarily local externalities should be regulated by local governments.

FEDERALISM AND THE ENVIRONMENT

The area of environmental law and policy has been hit particularly hard by the expansion of federal powers. As Jonathan Adler has observed:

> The current federal-state environmental framework developed in the 1970s as environmental protection became a national political concern. Prior to that time, environmental protection was largely the responsibility of state and local governments, occasionally augmented by federal common law. Although federal funding of environmental research and state-level pollution control efforts began in the late 1940s, such efforts were relatively minor. The federal regulations of that era dealt with federal agencies or uniquely federal concerns, such as keeping navigable waterways free from obstructions.
>
> The federal presence in environmental policy exploded in the 1970s. Beginning in 1969, Congress enacted a series of sweeping federal statutes to regulate environmental quality at the national level, including the National Environmental Policy Act (1969), the Clean Air Act (1970), the Clean Water Act (1972), the Endangered Species Act (1973), the Safe Drinking Water Act (1974), the Federal Insecticide, Fungicide, and Rodenticide Act (1975), the Resource Conservation and Recovery Act (1976), and the Toxic Substances Control Act (1976), among others. (Adler 1998, 575–76)

Most federal environmental laws either empower federal agencies to regulate environmental impacts directly or require or "entice" the states to implement the program along federal requirements (Adler 1998). This pattern of state implementation has been described as "federalism" or "cooperative federalism," but, as suggested earlier, these descriptions are inaccurate.

The experience of thirty years of intensive federal regulation of environmental risks has demonstrated the severe drawbacks of centralized environmental policy. The "command-and-control" regulatory strategy that dominates environmental policy has proven to be inadequate: It has not set intelligent priorities, it has squandered resources devoted to environmental quality, it has discouraged environmentally superior technologies, and it has imposed unnecessary penalties on innovation and investment (Ackerman and Stewart 1985). As Richard Stewart (1988, 154) has observed, "the system [of federal control over environmental policy] has grown to the point where it amounts to nothing less than a massive effort at Soviet-style planning of the economy to achieve environmental goals."

Of course, there are numerous trade-offs in the allocation of environmental regulatory authority within a federal system. For example, different levels of interest in environmental quality across states lead to the development of a hodgepodge of state regulations, which creates confusion and inefficiencies in production and marketing strategies. The strict California air pollution regulations are but one of the many examples of this confusion. Thus, it is not surprising that there has been a substantial discussion among business groups about whether they are better off with state or with federal environmental regulations. In general, large producers favor federal preemption of the hodgepodge of state regulations.

On the other hand, there are problems with federal preemption of state environmental regulations. First, federal preemption may reduce the ability and the incentives of state regulators to experiment with creative solutions to local environmental problems. Second, federal preemption centralizes many environmental decisions in Washington, where interest groups dominate decision making and where economic consequences, particularly at the local level, often are ignored. Third is a problem with federal preemption related to this insensitivity to economic consequences: it fails to provide sufficient funding for required local actions. Our analysis suggests that the current problem with environmental regulation derives from an imbalance in the allocation of governmental functions.

We begin with an introduction to externalities and the economic justification for environmental regulation. This is followed by a survey of the economics of federalism, which focuses on the conditions under which competition between jurisdictions will tend to produce optimal environmental laws and regulations. We then consider a variety of situations in which the federalism conditions are satisfied to differing degrees. Our analysis supports the Matching Principle as a benchmark for determining which level of government should be granted regulatory authority to deal with different types of externalities.

Externalities and the Economics of Pollution Control

The economic goal of government regulation of pollution is to force polluters to bear the full costs of their activities. In economic jargon, the regulatory goal should be to force the internalization of externalities. *Externalities* are costs and benefits that are not directly priced by the market system. Because individuals in a market system respond only to the benefits and the costs that they actually receive and pay for, the market system may be inadequate to deal with externalities. The market failure that results when market participants do not internalize the external costs of their activities causes resources to be misallocated. Thus, the negative externalities—or spillover costs—associated with pollution are an economic problem because they lead to an inefficient allocation of resources. Externalities in the use of resources generally arise where property rights are either nonexistent or poorly specified, as is the case with resources such as the atmosphere. From the perspective of users, such resources are free. Those who manufacture products creating externalities do not pay the full costs of the resources consumed by the production of such goods. Because producers will manufacture the quantity of goods that reflects their private costs of production, externalities lead to overproduction, which means an inefficient overallocation of resources to the production of that good. This is the standard economic justification for government regulation of pollution. This rationale for government intervention must be tempered by at least five caveats.

1.   Not all pollution creates an externality. If a property owner bears all the costs of polluting his or her property, then there is no externality and no justification for government regulation.

2.   Externalities that affect a small number of economic actors (so that transaction costs are low) can be internalized by Coasian bargaining. In this situation, the proper role of government intervention is the clear assignment and enforcement of property rights.

3.   Government regulation is not costless and is not perfect. Thus, the benefits of regulating the externality must be greater than the costs of the regulation. This implies that social welfare is maximized by a government policy that does not attempt to deal with all externalities.

4.   The economics of pollution control demonstrate that it would be undesirable to prevent all externalities because many externalities are the result of socially desirable economic activity (Buchanan and Stubblebine 1962). Even if all negative externalities are internalized and the private cost of production equals the social cost of production, pollution will not be eliminated. Instead, the result of internalization will be that those causing pollution will be required to pay the full social costs associated with their activities. Pollution is a necessary by-product of our modern lifestyle. Getting rid of waste is not free in terms of either monetary costs or the productive capacity of the nation. One of the costs of producing more man-made goods is sacrificing some environmental quality. Similarly, the cost of a cleaner environment is sacrificing some man-made goods. These observations represent the basic economic problem of scarcity—our resources simply are not sufficient to satisfy all of our demands. Thus, we are forced to make trade-offs. For example, only the most devout environmentalists would give up the personal freedom associated with the use of an automobile because of the fact that use of the automobile causes air pollution. The economic goal of pollution-control regulation should not be to reduce the level of pollution to zero. The goal of regulation should be to set the level of pollution produced to the level it would be if producers bore all of the costs created by their pollution. In this regard, it is important to recognize that the facts of small externalities and non-trivial costs of government intervention suggest that many externalities cannot be internalized.

5.   It is unclear that the presence of an externality is sufficient to justify government intervention. In reality, *externality* is a slippery concept, used more often to achieve the categorization of an event as a "problem" than to justify government intervention to solve the problem. Put another way, virtually everything that anybody does is an externality when viewed from some perspective or

other (Boudreaux and Meiners 1998). An example is an externality argument in favor of federal regulation that concerns a type of psychological externality that arguably arises even when pollution does not physically cross state lines. This argument is based on the notion that all citizens of the United States may justifiably be concerned about environmental quality throughout the nation, although they are not physically exposed to local externalities in other localities. For example, devoted environmentalists in Oregon may be deeply concerned about the local environmental effects of chemical plants and oil refineries in Louisiana. They may argue that Louisiana's environmental laws do not adequately address the local environmental risks and therefore should be preempted by more-stringent federal regulations. According to this "externality" argument, federal regulation to require more-stringent local environmental regulations may be justified on the efficiency ground that purely local pollution (local in its physical damage) actually imposes additional costs in other states where citizens have stronger preferences for environmental purity. These costs can take the form of lost utility by environmentalists in states with more-stringent regulations as well as the exiting of polluting industries to less restrictive states.

Although the existence of such "interdependencies" raises provocative questions about the demand for regulations and who should bear the burden of their implementation, there are several problems with this argument for federal intervention. The major problem with this argument is that the local residents in Louisiana, not the Oregon environmentalists, would bear the costs of reducing pollution. The Louisiana political process would have already indicated that the local residents believe the costs of a cleaner Louisiana to be greater than the benefits. It is tempting to assert that we are simply dealing with different sets of preferences about environmental quality and that the national consensus is for greater environmental quality than that preferred in Louisiana. No doubt the citizens of Louisiana would be happy with even higher environmental quality if they did not have to pay for it with reduced economic opportunities. In a similar way, it is not surprising that the people who do not pay for higher environmental quality are in favor of more-stringent standards than the local citizens who must bear the costs. Allocation of regulatory authority over local externalities to local governments allows decisions to be made by the representatives of the citizens who benefit the most from and pay the most for higher environmental quality. This analysis supports the Matching Principle that we described earlier.

Jurisdictional Competition and Environmental Quality

In most areas of economic activity, competition tends to produce the efficient or optimal allocation of resources. It is plausible that competition among states for environmental quality may generate the optimal mix of environmental regulations across the country (Revesz 1992, 1233–44). Competition among political jurisdictions is likely to generate optimal laws if four conditions are fulfilled: (1) the economic entities affected by the law must be able to move to alternative jurisdictions at a relatively low cost; (2) all of the consequences of a particular jurisdiction's laws must be felt within that jurisdiction; (3) lawmakers must be forced to respond to adverse events (such as a decrease in population or falling real estate prices, market share or revenue) and to other manifestations of voter discontent that result from inefficient regulations; and (4) jurisdictions must be able to select any set of laws they desire (Tiebout 1956; Romano 1993; Easterbrook 1983). Of course, in the real world there are no purely local externalities, no perfect markets, and no perfect governments. As a consequence, failure to achieve all four conditions is not a mandate for federal government intervention, but rather an indication that local regulation may be imperfect.

The *first federalism condition* requires that the economic entities affected by the law must be able to move to alternative jurisdictions at a relatively low cost. With respect to environmental protection laws and regulations, this condition applies to two types of economic entities: (1) the parties adversely affected by the pollution, such as individuals and households, as well as businesses that must pay higher wages to attract workers to a polluted area; and (2) polluters adversely affected by the high cost of compliance with the jurisdiction's environmental laws and regulations. Most economic entities are mobile, at least in the long run, and both types always will contain a substantial portion of marginal entities that are very mobile. However, regulators at both the state and the national levels will be aware that some firms are more mobile than others. Firms lacking mobility are particularly vulnerable targets for governmental regulation that threatens to expropriate investments in immobile capital. In determining how regulatory authority should be allocated between state and federal authorities, we should be concerned about the ability of governmental actors to expropriate fixed investments.

Government expropriation of fixed investments can take a variety of forms. For example, an industry might spend considerable resources simply learning the details of a particular state's environmental law prior to entering that state to do business. The firm's investment in learning that law is a fixed investment that would be expropriated if the law changed or was preempted by Congress. Hence, beneficiaries of a particular regulatory regime might prefer to keep an existing regulatory structure in place even where a marginally superior alternative exists if the benefits of the new regulations are outweighed by the costs of learning how to cope with the new regime.

Similarly, a firm might make a considerable investment in configuring its plant and equipment in reliance on the assumption that a particular set of environmental laws will remain in place for a certain period of time. The ability of politicians to change—or to threaten to change—the applicable environmental laws reduces the incentives of firms to make investments in capital assets. Thus, a sensible environmental policy seeks to allocate authority among state and federal regulators to reduce the possibility of expropriation of fixed capital investments by industry. This can only be done by establishing clear spheres of authority between state and federal actors and by limiting the incidence of overlapping regulatory authority. In general, however, if a state is able to expropriate capital because of the inability of a firm to leave the state, then the federal government is in an even more advantageous position because it is usually more difficult to leave the country than to leave the state.

Although the discussion of the mobility condition tends to focus on exit from unfavorable jurisdictions, the entry of mobile economic entities into more favorable jurisdictions also is a significant factor. It is important to note that the two types of economic entities identified here may have conflicting preferences. For example, individuals affected by pollution are likely to favor strict environmental laws, whereas polluters are likely to favor lax environmental laws. The federalism model is designed to find the optimal balance between these conflicting preferences at the local level.

The *second federalism condition* requires that all of the consequences of one jurisdiction's laws must be felt within that jurisdiction. Some types of local externalities involve the location of a stationary pollution source, such as a factory, within the local jurisdiction. Where this is the case, the local political decision makers take the costs imposed on the factory into account when devising local environmental policy.

This condition is violated when a state has lax environmental regulation and pollution spills over from one jurisdiction to another. As discussed earlier, this interstate externality is a strong justification for some form of federal intervention. If the pollution allowed by one state's lax regulation crosses the relevant political boundaries and if there is reason to believe that the out-of-state victims are not represented in the polluting state's decision-making processes, then there will be a political market failure, regardless of whether the regulation is passed in the name of economic development. Local governments can be prevented from playing this game by state regulations or policies, and states can be prevented by federal regulations or policies. The extent of the response could be fairly minimal when compared to today's command-and-control regulation. For example, states or even individuals could be given the right to sue neighboring states that fail to meet minimum federal standards. Alternatively, the federal government could arbitrate claims between states involving interstate pollution.

The *third federalism condition* requires that the political process be sufficiently competitive that lawmakers must be forced to respond to adverse events, such as a decrease in population or falling real estate prices, market share, or revenue. The basic federalism model is based on the belief that lawmakers enact laws that reflect local preferences as expressed through the political process. Thus, constituents who are not on the margin with respect to mobility or exit can still exert considerable influence by exercising their voice option in the political process.

State and local environmental regulation often is claimed to be inadequate because states and localities are under pressure to relax environmental controls in order to attract industry. To the extent that such pressures influence environmental policy, many of the costs (negative externalities) and benefits (economic growth) are borne locally. If the pollution is purely local in all respects, then competition among states can be viewed as beneficial because it forces politicians to consider the costs as well as the benefits of environmental regulations:

> [S]ome may object that state and local governments will compete for industries by offering lax environmental standards. We suspect that this is a very real possibility and welcome its effects. In particular, state and local governments will balance voters' interests in economic activity and environmental quality more closely than the federal government will. Therefore, a few states may offer themselves as sinks and servers, but that will save the rest of the nation from these depredations. Similarly, many states may have residents who want a much higher environmental quality than federal regulations now mandate. This higher quality is more likely to prevail under local control. (Aranson 1982, 383–84)

Allowing for local decision making at least leaves the choice for whether there should be a given level of pollution with the people most likely to be affected by it.

The *fourth federalism condition* is that jurisdictions must be able to select any set of laws they desire. If the first three federalism conditions are met, then the economics of federalism suggest that local governments should retain discretion in selecting the level of environmental quality they prefer as well as the regulatory policies used to achieve those goals. Granting local jurisdictions this authority should generate benefits from several sources:

> First, public policy toward environmental policy would more accurately reflect the preferences of those affected. Second, where serious divergences from individual preferences do occur, people have the option of moving to more favorable locations. Thus, a real interpolity competition in public policy toward the environment would emerge, as would productive experimentation with governmental alternatives. A veritable marketplace of governments would give the citizen, the consumer of public services, a choice among the competing units. Fourth, decentralization would also generate competition in the use of externality-abatement techniques. Fifth, decentralization would help to ensure that resources flow to their highest-valued use, because those who would receive the benefits of an improved environment would also have to pay the cost. Finally, by reducing substantially the number of people involved with particular environmental problems, decentralization would markedly diminish transactions costs, which, in turn, would allow for the use of market-like abatement policies. We should not deceive ourselves that state and local governors

are better than EPA officials. However, decentralization allows other people to visit on legislators and regulators the content of their preferences and the rigors of the marketplace. (Aranson 1982, 384)

Thus, decentralization would encourage the adoption of the optimal pollution-abatement policies.

Although jurisdictional competition in environmental regulation is not perfect, it must be compared with the relevant alternative: federal preemption of state regulation with centralized, monopoly regulation. In fact, one of the primary benefits of federalism—the ability of states to experiment with new policies—is all but eliminated by centralization. Moreover, the political accountability that drives jurisdictional competition is replaced by the necessary delegation of major legislative decisions to federal bureaucracies. The result is an excessively litigious system combined with a decision-making process in which "[c]hoices about environmental protection priorities and goals are buried in thousands of highly technical standard-setting decisions made by agencies and reviewed by courts" (Stewart 1988, 158). This observation reinforces the lesson of the economics of federalism that there should always be a presumption in favor of local solutions to local externalities. In the final analysis, and consistent with the Matching Principle, purely local externalities can best be dealt with locally.

Minimal Federal Regulation of Interstate Environmental Externalities

The presence of interstate externalities means that the political and regulatory processes of states with pollution sources will not take all costs into account when formulating their environmental policies. The optimal state regulation, which controls pollution up to the point where marginal benefit equals marginal cost, will tend to allow more pollution than would be optimal if all costs were internalized in the state's political process. The neighboring state or states must bear the costs of pollution coming from outside their state. This situation is analogous to the primary justification of all environmental regulation—forcing decision makers to bear, or internalize, the full costs of their decisions.

The excessive pollution generated by interstate environmental externalities is the consequence of poorly defined property rights in the political marketplace. This property rights perspective suggests that the basis for co-internalization could be found through a productive, minimal role for the federal government—the assignment to states of either the property right to clean air (no pollution from neighboring states) or the property right to pollute across state lines. For example, when only a very small number of states are involved, the federal government's intervention could be limited to the assignment and the enforcement of property rights among the states. However, when the number of states involved is too large for effective bargaining among the states or when states evince a proclivity for acting strategically to obtain payoffs from out-of-state interests, a more interventionist role might be justified. The key to our position is that local governments ought to be allowed to make judgments about their own interests, even if those judgments turn out to be misguided, as long as the costs of these decisions are fully internalized by the particular communities served by the local government.

Assignment and Exchange of Property Rights

Assume two neighboring states, A and B, where industrial air pollution from state A lowers the quality of air in state B. There are two possible allocations of property rights. First, if state A were assigned the right to pollute, state B could still obtain an improvement in its environmental air quality by paying state A to enact and to enforce more-stringent air-quality laws. Citizens in state B would be taxed to pay for their cleaner air. Obviously, this would involve tremendous political battles, but it would force the politicians to assess the actual costs of their actions, a necessary first step for better government. If state B is unwilling to raise the necessary funds to induce A to agree to stop or reduce pollution across the state boundary, then state A would continue to pollute. The opportunity cost to state A of polluting would be the amount that state B is willing to pay for A to stop. Thus, state A's decision to pollute is not free, and political competition in state A is likely to inform constituents of the costs associated with continued pollution.

Second, and the choice that is more likely in today's political environment, state B might be assigned the legal right to be free of pollution coming from state A. This right could be enforced by either a property rule (through an injunction) or a liability rule (through a suit for damages against state A). Either rule would force the internalization of pollution externalities in state A. A property rule would allow state A to negotiate with state B for the right to pollute state B. One can envision state B holding out for progressively higher prices in return for accepting more pollution in the form of lower pollution standards in state A. State A could raise revenues for this right through the taxing of its polluting industries or, if the state is concerned about adverse consequences on state industries, through the use of general fund tax revenues. Taxing the polluting industry on the basis of the pollution emitted would give some polluters the incentive to reduce pollution. On the other hand, state B's right to clean air could be protected by a liability rule under which state A would be forced to compensate state B for damages resulting from excessive pollution from state A. A liability rule raises problems because of the measurement of damages, which in many cases is subjective. Bargaining under a property rule appears to be the preferred allocation of rights because it requires that all exchanges be mutually beneficial. A liability rule allows for taking with compensation for objective damages, but not subjective costs.

Although state B might be assigned the legal right to be free from pollution coming from state A, it is certainly possible that pollution sources in state B also will lower the air quality in state B. The use of Coasian bargaining to protect or to compensate state B for pollution emanating from state A is complicated by the combined impact in state B of pollution sources located in both states. For example, when a liability rule to protect state B is assigned, Coasian bargaining will not be possible until there is some objective way to separate and to measure the pollution costs imposed from state A from the pollution costs generated in state B. The federal government or federal courts could be called on to determine responsibility.

Although the Coasian framework predicts that bargaining will result in the optimal level of pollution regardless of the initial allocation of property rights, an important normative policy issue concerns the initial allocation of property rights. Transaction costs can be reduced if the initial allocation is to the party or the state with the highest valuation of the resources, but this determination is a difficult one. Moreover, basic conceptions of private property suggest that the initial allocation of rights should include the right to exclude others from using one's resources. Thus, this analysis supports a rule requiring the polluting state to obtain permission from the recipient state before allowing harmful pollution to cross its border into the neighboring state.[2] Such a property-rights allocation probably would be popular in today's political environment, but it must be stressed that the determination of the politically feasible rule would depend to a large extent on preexisting pollution patterns across state boundaries. An alternative reasonable initial bargaining position would be that the recipient state could force the pollution-exporting state to reduce its pollution to the level that the polluting state would produce if it had the same pollution standards as the recipient state; that is, the recipient state would not be able to hold its neighboring states to a standard higher than that to which it holds polluters in its own backyard.

The potential benefits of such a Coasian system in forcing the internalization of pollution costs across a small number of jurisdictions are substantial. Of course, such a system would have problems. Bargaining costs, in particular, might be high due to political grandstanding. After all, even if the property rights are assigned, the individuals in charge of enforcing them are politicians who do not personally own the property rights. Political competition could force politicians representing states to the bargaining table.

A potential objection to such a Coasian scheme might be the inability of poor states to purchase the right to pollute in rich neighboring states. A clean environment typically becomes more important after basic necessities are met. A related objection might be that rich states would be able to continue to pollute if they paid poor states to accept their pollution. Similarly, bargaining problems faced by poor states are exacerbated by allocating all pollution control to the federal government, where larger and wealthier states are likely to have greater influence over policies.

Stewart also has considered the possibility of bargaining among states as a solution to interstate externalities (spillovers). Stewart rejected the use of bargaining on the following grounds:

> Bargaining among the states to minimize the losses occasioned by such spillovers is costly (particularly given the complexity and wide dispersion of many forms of environmental degradation), and may do little to improve the lot of states in a weak position (such as those in a downwind or downstream position). These states are likely to favor federal intervention to eliminate the more damaging forms of spillover. (Stewart 1977, 1216)

The problem with this analysis is that Stewart fails to take the crucial first step, the assignment of property rights, probably to the "weak" states (making them "strong") and necessarily by the federal government (a very limited form of federal intervention).

Small, weak, and poor states are better off with the ability to trade pollution rights than they would be without this ability. Without the right to sell pollution rights, poor states would have "too little" pollution, in the sense that these states would be willing to accept a bit more pollution if, in turn, they also could get additional money. Depriving poor states of the ability to make these sorts of arrangements makes the residents of such states even worse off. And, of course, if the residents of poor states had a strong preference for high air quality, they could obtain such high air quality by electing officials who imposed tough local standards and refused to sell pollution rights to out-of-state polluters.

Regional Effects and Regional Responses

There are many situations in the United States in which several states have common environmental interests because they are part of the same regional environmental system, such as the Chesapeake Bay region and other watersheds. This is a classic commons problem in the sense that, first, the failure to define property rights means that each state's policies impact on the common resource and, second, that each state is hesitant to act independently. The federal government can play an important role as a catalyst for regional agreements, as the Clean Air Act Amendments of 1990 envisioned, and can also safeguard against certain regions forming alliances against other regions.

The assignment of enforceable property rights is also a potential solution to regional problems involving even a fairly large number of states. It is often assumed that when the pollution from a source in one state imposes costs on numerous other states, the assignment of property rights and the reliance on bargaining could not provide a practical solution to the externality problem. Transaction costs may be too high for meaningful bargaining among the states.

This inability to reach a contractual solution, coupled with the usual presumption in favor of the internalization of externalities, means that a response by the federal government may be justified. In contrast to these traditional assumptions about the limitations of contractual solutions, the federal government's role could be limited to the assignment of property rights and the facilitation of bargaining.

Experimental tests of the Coase theorem with large bargaining groups tend to support such a limited federal role in solving regional environmental problems. A study by Hoffman and Spitzer (1985, 1986) to reflect choices made on pollution levels in an externality problem demonstrated that the size of the bargaining group is less of a concern than perhaps traditionally thought.[3] The results indicated that 93 percent of the bargains among large groups were efficient and that no significant reduction occurred as the group got larger. In fact, bargaining efficiency may have improved as the group size increased. Such information is an affirmation of the potential of federalism to solve environmental problems. The role of the federal government in regional and even nationwide externality situations may be to provide a forum for large groups to organize and rules by which to bargain. The Coasian assumptions of enforceable contracts and assignment of property rights must also be a function of this limited federal intervention.

Nationwide Externalities and Federal Regulation

If Coasian solutions to interstate externalities do not appear workable, then the policy discussion turns to the precise nature of the federal regulation to be enacted. Such regulation can take a variety of forms, including: (1) centralized command-and-control regulation; (2) federally mandated pollution-based standards for environmental quality in states, where states are free to design their own regulatory apparatus; (3) federally mandated minimum standards for emissions with market-based incentives, where states play little, if any, role in implementation; (4) a system of Pigovian taxes, imposed by either the federal government or state governments; or (5) some combination of these and other strategies.

Although determining the optimal federal policy when federal regulation is appropriate is beyond the scope of this chapter, there can be little doubt that federal policy would be better informed if it could draw on the divergent experiences of states in dealing with other environmental problems. In this regard, governmental intervention on behalf of environmental protection can be viewed as a search for a policy that will produce the optimal amount of pollution. Our Matching Principle suggests that the most appropriate governmental level of environmental regulation is not necessarily the federal government—it may be the governmental unit most conterminous with the area subjected to the externalities. The economic model of federalism not only provides a way to analyze existing laws, it also prescribes, in the sense that it suggests that local laws should satisfy certain conditions. Obviously, all externalities are not national in scope. Thus, the idea of leaving some local control over local externalities seems logical. In fact, the economics of federalism provide strong theoretical arguments for allowing competition among state environmental regulators—such competition may be a source of future wisdom.

Interstate Externalities as an Excuse for National Regulation

As discussed earlier, one of the most convincing arguments for federal environmental regulation is the control of interstate externalities. If nontrivial external costs are imposed across political boundaries, then the issue should be addressed by a higher level of government. But the presence of interstate externalities does not imply that they must be corrected by federal regulation that usurps completely the role of local initiatives. Moreover, acceptance of the interstate externalities justification for federal environmental regulation does not necessarily lead one to support a specific type of regulatory response. The current regime of command-and-control regulations is no more justified under this analysis than alternative market-based approaches, such as the property-rights framework suggested earlier in this chapter or the creation of a market for environmental degradation credits (Revesz 1996). Rather than having federal regulators impose regulations on polluters, the interstate externalities problem can be addressed by reallocating environmental authority in a manner that would force states and state decision makers to bear the full costs of their decisions regarding the regulation of pollution.

Jurisdictional Competition: The Myth of the Race to the Bottom

A leading rationale for federal domination of environmental regulation is to prevent states from competing for economic growth opportunities by lowering their environmental standards in a so-called "race to the bottom" (Revesz 1992). The notion is that all states compete for economic growth by lowering environmental standards below the level they would select if they acted collectively at the national level.[4] What is individually rational for individual states is collectively irrational at the national level.[5] Stewart described the implication of this dynamic in concise terms:

> Given the mobility of industry and commerce, any individual state or community may rationally decline unilaterally to adopt high environmental standards that entail substantial costs for industry and obstacles to economic development for fear that the resulting environmental gains will be more than offset by movement of capital

to other areas with lower standards. If each locality reasons in the same way, all will adopt lower standards of environmental quality than they would prefer if there were some binding mechanism that enabled them simultaneously to enact high standards, thus eliminating the threatened loss of industry or development. (Stewart 1977, 1212)

According to this logic, federal regulation is necessary to correct a political-market failure at the state level. But there is a faulty link in the syllogism—*each locality does not reason in the same way*. Localities have different preferences for environmental quality, for a variety of economic and aesthetic reasons, and it is not at all clear that competition between jurisdictions would lead to a lower level of environmental quality than would a national median voter model (see also, Revesz 1992).

In fact, competition between jurisdictions may lead to improvements in environmental quality. It is often argued that environmental quality is a luxury good in the sense that individuals develop a greater concern for environmental issues as their incomes rise (Yandle 1993). If this is true, the key to increases in environmental quality may be found in higher incomes. This point has implications for the desirability of jurisdictional competition, as illustrated by the following example.

Assume that there is no national environmental regulation and that all environmental issues are the prerogative of the state and local governments. Firm X operates in New Jersey. As the incomes of those who live in New Jersey increase as a result of industrial growth provided by X, the citizens of New Jersey will place a higher emphasis on environmental quality. State and local government decision makers will respond to citizens' demands for better pollution control. Assume that X responds to the tougher pollution standards in New Jersey by moving to Missouri, where pollution control is not as stringent. Missouri's environmental laws could reflect Missourians' preferences, given their low relative incomes. Many people in Missouri welcome X's operations, even at the expense of some increase in pollution. As X's industrial production causes Missouri's economy to expand, the incomes of individuals will increase and so will their demand for a cleaner environment. The initial harmful levels of pollution may be a necessary first step toward increasing citizens' demands for a cleaner environment. The competition among different states may enhance economic growth and accelerate the evolution of more efficient pollution abatement equipment.

Finally, the race-to-the-bottom rationale for federal government domination of environmental regulation is based on the assumption that the federal government, in practice, can do a better job at regulating than the state governments can. There are strong reasons to believe that this assumption is wrong. The race-to-the-bottom justification for federal intervention, although critical of state political processes, ignores the problem of interest-group domination of the legislative process in Washington. The interest-group problem is more acute at the federal level.[6]

On the other hand, there are numerous reasons to believe that the Washington political market reflects its own regulatory common-pool problem with Congresspeople trading votes on environmental matters for votes on unrelated issues. Unfortunately, the race-to-the-bottom rationale underlies much of the federal environmental statutes (Revesz 1992, 1212).

Moreover, as Revesz has observed, federal environmental statutes often exacerbate rather than ameliorate the problem. For example, the Clean Air Act forces states to achieve particular levels of air quality:

> The federal ambient standards give states an incentive to encourage sources within their jurisdiction to use taller stacks. In this way, states can externalize not only the health and environmental effects of the pollution but also the regulatory costs of complying with the federal ambient standards. Thus, not surprisingly, the use of tall stacks expanded considerably after the passage of the Clean Air Act in 1970. In 1970, only two stacks in the United States were higher than 500 feet. By 1985, more than 180 stacks were higher than 500 feet and twenty-three were higher than 1000 feet. While this method of externalizing pollution is now less of a problem as a result of stack height regulations that followed the 1977 amendments to the Clean Air Act, tall stacks remain a means by which excessive pollution can be sent to downwind states. (Revesz 1997, 541–42)

Political Cost Externalization

State environmental regulations that impose financial costs on out-of-state producers are often cited as a justification for federal intervention (E. Elliot, Ackerman, and Millian 1985, 316). Some state environmental regulations restrict local consumption of products produced in other jurisdictions. The classic modern example of cost externalization is California's strict automobile emissions control requirements. But the concern here is that in enacting legislation, the local legislators tend to ignore the regulatory costs imposed on out-of-state automobile manufacturers who are unable to pass on all of the cost increase to consumers in the regulating state. In effect, it is alleged that political cost externalization is a political-market failure that requires federal regulatory interpretation.

Even if the cost-externalization analysis is correct, the implications of the analysis for the structure of federal regulation are not obvious. Historical experience suggests that caution is called for in responding to cost-externalization problems. Thus, the federal response should address the cost-externalization problems in the least restrictive manner. Federal regulations that preempt stringent local environmental regulations of local externalities may be justified on the grounds that the local regulations impose tremendous costs on businesses' national marketing strategies. However, there are several possible solutions to this economic problem that fall short of federal preemption and thus allow for the achievement of some of the benefits of federalism. First, the federal government could impose maximum limits on state regulations that affect products manufactured in one state but sold in another. States would be free to set environmental standards up to but not above this level. The perennial problem with this approach is that the larger states tend to adopt the maximum standard, and the maximum tends to become a minimum requirement. Second, the federal government could prohibit individual states from mandating design changes in products manufactured in other states. State responses should be limited to the least restrictive policy in terms of adverse consequences on national marketing strategies.

Take, for example, the Maine statute that prohibits the use of a particular type of fruit juice container because the container is not biodegradable or recyclable. An alternative policy that would result in less disruption of the fruit juice manufacturers' distribution systems would be a corrective tax on the containers. Such taxes would have to be structured so that the level charged corresponded to the level of local pollution caused by the product. Because a large portion of the tax would be borne by the local consumers, local politicians would face a greater constraint in setting the taxes than they do in setting pollution standards when they can externalize the political costs. Of course, the obvious problem with allowing federal regulations to restrain state activities is that it could result in a cure that is worse than the disease.

Furthermore, the presence of political cost externalization does not mean that there has been a political market failure. California's decision to require the installation of expensive antipollution equipment in all new cars sold in California adds to the marginal cost of producing the cars sold in California. As such, the increased marginal cost is analogous to a per car excise tax in terms of its impact on the selling price of automobiles in California. The incidence of the regulatory requirement is the same as the tax incidence of a per car excise tax. The marginal cost of the pollution equipment is shared by California consumers, who must pay more for cars, and by out-of-state manufacturers, who receive a lower after-regulation price because of the increased marginal costs. To the extent that California consumers observe that they must pay more for new cars than consumers in bordering states, the costs to California consumers are taken into account by California legislators.

Moreover, the costs imposed on out-of-state manufacturers cannot be ignored by state legislators because the out-of-state manufacturers will make political contributions, hire lobbyists and public relations firms, and otherwise attempt to prevent the passage of the legislation. It would be naive to expect out-of-state firms to passively accept the huge costs of the regulations. Finally, because the higher prices due to the regulations will result in fewer new car sales, new car dealers will have incentives to lobby California legislators to not adopt stringent regulations.

The fact that a particular cost-externalizing regulation is adopted does not mean that the adopting legislators ignored the out-of-state costs; it simply means that the legislators decided that the benefits to them were greater than the costs. This analysis suggests that the political cost-externalization justification for federal environment regulation is not a valid justification for federal intervention. There is no political-market failure. But even if there are some problems in the political market, they are likely to be small compared to the problems with the alternative of centralized federal regulation.

National Morals

Another argument in favor of federal regulation of even purely local externalities is that the federal government is the level of government best suited to reflect the moral obligation of United States citizens to one another as well as to future generations. The case for federal intervention to help realize moral ideals, such as protection of susceptible minorities or the opportunities of future generations, is only somewhat less strong than the spillover rationale. These ideals are valuable not merely for their own sake but also for the moral education fostered by their consideration. Environmental problems force us to face consequences of our immediate actions that we would prefer to disregard because of their disturbing impact of these actions on fellow citizens, on future generations, and on the nature of our society. Such a confrontation is indispensable to the collective moral growth of our society. Given the logic of the "politics of sacrifice," this form of collective education is likely to be attenuated if the crucial decisions are excessively noncentralized (Stewart 1977, 1264–65).

We strongly disagree with this argument, which favors centralized control of environmental policy making based on a morality rationale. The biggest problem with the moral ideals justification for centralization is that it is based on the flawed presumption that it is moral for the federal government to force people to pay for goods that they do not want.

There also are several practical problems with this argument for centralization. First, there is no reason to think that a centralized authority can deliver regulations that meet whatever moral ideals many of us share. For example, there are very powerful arguments and evidence that private property owners do a much better job of preserving and protecting large tracts of land than the government does (see Anderson and Leal 1997). Also, government-controlled land is more likely to be spoiled than privately held property because the bureaucrats who control public land do not bear the costs of overuse, whereas they do obtain political support from interest groups in exchange for allowing such overuse. Thus, even assuming that there is a strong public ideal that favors a cleaner environment, there is no reason to believe that centralized decision making is the best strategy for attaining that ideal.

An additional argument against the moral-ideals justification for centralization is that it is highly open ended and indeterminate. Anybody can argue that his or her version of a particular law is more legitimate than that of a rival on the grounds that the arguer's version is more consistent with the moral ideals of the nation. This is an argument impossible to refute or to prove. The most reliable guide for the moral ideals of a polity as diverse as the United States lies in the revealed preferences of its citizens, that is, in the willingness of its citizens to pay for environmental quality. Appeals to the moral ideals of the nation are often thinly disguised appeals to authority when more substantive policy justifications are lacking.

Whatever the benefits of centralization are said to be, centralizing authority over environmental policy has costs. Local preferences for varying levels of environmental quality are ignored, and the laboratory of the states is destroyed. Moreover, centralization makes it very difficult to identify and to correct the inevitable mistakes that are made by environmental policy makers. No one is prepared to argue that Congress is perfect or that the Environmental Protection Agency is above the influence of interest groups and partisan politics. Environmental policy may be too lenient or too strict, and implementation may be wasteful, but there is no corrective mechanism once policy making is centralized. In fact, the "iron triangle" of congressional committee, government bureaucracies, and industry and environmental lobbying groups is seen as conspiring to maintain the centralized status quo in the face of tremendous evidence that it is increasingly wasteful (Ackerman and Stewart 1988, 172) and in light of the political theory describing why centralization was excessively ambitious in the first place (E. Elliott, Ackerman, and Millian 1985).

CONCLUSION

The environmental policies that we actually observe are at odds with the Matching Principle theory of federalism articulated in this chapter. One of the most important attributes of a properly functioning federal system is the autonomy given to local governments to tailor regulatory solutions to local problems and concerns, leaving the federal government free to address multistate problems.

There are several reasons why state and local governments should be permitted to address environmental issues that have a primarily localized impact: First, different localities are likely to have different preferences and concerns. Decentralized government through a federalist system is far more responsive to local needs and concerns. Some communities might prefer to trade off environmental quality for more employment or greater revenue. Local control over environmental issues would permit this. Second, local control is beneficial because state and local governments will engage in healthy competition along a number of vectors.

They will compete to attract new business, for jobs and revenues, and to offer residents better environmental quality. By contrast, the centralized, monopolistic command-and-control apparatus of the federal government does not offer citizens the benefits of competition. Third, and finally, where local decision-making authority is replaced by federal regulators, rational local officials will compete at the national level to obtain wealth transfers from other localities. Every locality will consume resources by lobbying for environmental policies that produce local benefits, regardless of the consequences for the nation as a whole.

NOTES

1. For background, see Buchanan and Tullock (1962, 113–16).

2. In *Georgia v. Tennessee Copper Co.* (1915), the Supreme Court prohibited any damaging emissions. Such a rule would be much more strict than current environmental law, and it is not obvious that the litigation resulting from such a rule would be more efficient than the current regulatory scheme. The selection of the initial allocation of rights would be an important factor in determining the success of a property rights solution.

3. It has been suggested that a system of resource federations that allows the free transfer of property rights and enforceability of contracts among individuals would be the most efficient solution to environmental problems.

4. For a summary and repackaging of traditional arguments about why state regulation would result in an underprovision of environmental protection, see Swire (1996). All of Swire's concerns are addressed by Revesz (1992) or in this chapter. Moreover, Swire does not distinguish between different types of pollution and the extent of their impact across political boundaries. This distinction, of course, is the central point addressed by the Matching Principle.

5. This conclusion would hold even if there were no interstate externalities of the type described previously. The presence of interstate externalities and jurisdictional competition for economic growth is necessary for competition to degenerate into a tragedy of the commons, the common-pool problem. Such common-pool problems arise when a large number of firms, individuals, or other economic entities such as states all consume a single, finite, jointly owned resource at a rate faster than what it would be if the person owned the resource and when the resource is unable to replenish itself. Thus, for example, if one hundred people own one cow each, and if all one hundred cows graze unrestrictedly in a single jointly owned field, the field's grass will be exhausted far more quickly than it would be if the field had a single owner because, unlike a single owner, none of the one hundred cow owners has any incentive to conserve or to replenish the field's resources. In this regard, the environment can be viewed as a common pool that is "overgrazed" by states competing for economic growth. The tragedy of the commons requires two distinct conditions: (1) interstate externalities and (2) jurisdictional competition. Both interstate externalities and jurisdictional competition have been used as separate arguments in support of federal regulation. Hence, they are treated here as separate arguments. Other commentators have tended to combine the two arguments into a single tragedy of the commons jus-

tification for federal intervention. For example, Stewart (1977, 1212) has stated that the "characteristic insistence of federal environmental legislation upon geographically uniform standards and controls strongly suggests that escape from the Tragedy of the Commons by reduction of transaction costs . . . has been an important reason for such legislation." Most of Stewart's tragedy-of-the-commons argument is really a race-to-the-bottom argument that does not depend on the existence of interstate externalities. In fact, Revesz (1992, 1210) cites Stewart's argument as a race-to-the-bottom rationale.

6. Stewart was well aware of the influence of interest-group politics on environmental policies. In fact, one of the items he listed as a possible rationale for centralization of environmental regulation was that environmental groups are likely to have relatively greater influence in Washington than in the states (Stewart 1977, 1213). Although this may have been true at some point, it may not always be true. See E. Elliott, Ackerman, and Millian (1985, 316). Moreover, it is not clear that greater influence for self-styled environmentalists is the best policy for the environment.

REFERENCES

Ackerman, Bruce A., and Richard B. Stewart. 1985. Reforming Environmental Law. *Stanford Law Review* 37: 1333–65.

———. 1988. Reforming Environmental Law: The Democratic Case for Market Incentives. *Columbia Journal of Environmental Law* 13: 171–99.

Adler, Jonathan. 1998. The Green Aspects of Printz. *George Mason Law Review* 6: 573–633.

Anderson, Terry L., and Donald R. Leal. 1997. *Enviro-Capitalists: Doing Good While Doing Well.* Lanham, MD: Rowman & Littlefield.

Aranson, Peter H. 1982. Pollution Control without Politics. In *Instead of Regulation: Alternatives to Federal Regulatory Agencies*, ed. Robert W. Poole, Jr. Lexington, MA: Lexington Press, 339–93.

Boudreaux, Donald, and Roger Meiners. 1998. Existence Value and Other of Life's Ills. In *Who Owns the Environment?* ed. Peter J. Hill and Roger E. Meiners. Lanham, MD: Rowman & Littlefield, 153–85.

Buchanan, James M., and William C. Stubblebine. 1962. Externality. *Economica* 29: 371–84.

Buchanan, James M., and Gordon Tullock. 1962. *The Calculus of Consent: Logical Foundations of Constitutional Government.* Ann Arbor: University of Michigan Press.

Butler, Henry N., and Jonathan R. Macey. 1996. Externalities and the Matching Principle: The Case for Reallocating Environmental Regulatory Authority. *Yale Law and Policy Review* 14: 23–66.

Easterbrook, Frank H. 1983. Antitrust and the Economics of Federalism. *Journal of Law and Economics* 26: 23–50.

Elliot, Jonathan, ed. [1836] 1941. *Debates in the Several State Conventions on the Adoption of the Federal Constitution.* 2d ed. Reprint, Charlottesville, VA: Michie Co.

Elliott, E. Donald, Bruce A. Ackerman, and John C. Millian. 1985. Toward a Theory of Statutory Evolution: The Federalization of Environmental Law. *Journal of Law, Economics, and Organization* 1(2): 313–40.

Hoffman, Elizabeth, and Matthew Spitzer. 1985. Experimental Law and Economics. *Columbia Law Review* 85: 991–1036.

———. 1986. Experimental Tests of the Coase Theorem with Large Bargaining Groups. *Journal of Legal Studies* 15: 149–71.

Revesz, Richard L. 1992. Rehabilitating Interstate Competition: Rethinking the "Race-to-the-Bottom" Rationale for Federal Environmental Regulation. *New York University Law Review* 67: 1210–54.

———. 1996. Federalism and Interstate Environmental Externalities. *University of Pennsylvania Law Review* 144: 2341–416.

———. 1997. The Race to the Bottom and Federal Environmental Regulation: A Response to Critics. *Minnesota Law Review* 82: 535–64.

Romano, Roberta. 1993. *The Genius of American Corporate Law.* Washington, DC: AEI Press.

Stewart, Richard B. 1977. Pyramids of Sacrifice? Problems of Federalism in Mandating State Implementation of National Environmental Policy. *Yale Law Review* 86: 1196–272.

———. 1988 Controlling Environmental Risks through Economic Incentives. *Columbia Journal of Environmental Law* 13: 153–69.

Swire, Peter P. 1996. The Race to Laxity and the Race to Undesirability: Explaining Failures in Competition among Jurisdictions in Environmental Law. *Yale Journal on Regulation* 14: 67–108.

Tiebout, Charles M. 1956. A Pure Theory of Local Expenditures. *Journal of Political Economy* 64: 416–24.

Yandle, Bruce. 1993. Is Free Trade an Enemy of Environmental Quality? In *NAFTA and the Environment,* ed. Terry L. Anderson. San Francisco: Pacific Research Institute for Public Policy, 1–11.

CASES CITED

Garcia v. San Antonio Metropolitan Transit Authority, 469 U.S. 528, 557 (1985)

Georgia v. Tennessee Copper Co., 237 U.S. 474 (1915)

Part IV

Perspectives on the Shift away from the Common Law

8

Industry and Environmental Lobbyists: Enemies or Allies?

Todd J. Zywicki

The inefficiencies of the current environmental regulation regime are widely recognized (Spence 1995, 175–76; Tietenberg 1992, 402–405). Law journals and economics journals are filled with articles bemoaning the costs, the perverse effects, and the inefficiencies of the regulatory monolith that have arisen in the twentieth century. With the fall of the Soviet Union, the current environmental regulatory structure in the United States has been characterized as one of the largest centralized, command-and-control planning structures still in existence (Stewart 1988). Moreover, experience in recent years has led to the recognition that more-flexible and decentralized institutions are available that can deliver comparable (or even superior) environmental protection at lower cost than the current regime. Some of these, such as tradable pollution permits or emission taxes, are of relatively recent vintage. Others, such as renewed reliance on markets and the common law, are of ancient vintage (Meiners, Thomas, and Yandle 2000; Yandle 1997; Meiners and Yandle 1993; Zywicki 1996, 961). Regardless of differences in age, however, these institutions share a common fate: that of remaining largely academic curiosities with little real-world impact.

Despite the widespread recognition of the failures of the current regime and of the availability of superior alternatives, the current system remains largely impervious to change. Although small and limited exceptions can be identified, such as limited use of tradable pollution permits, these remain anomalous, notable for their rareness (Joskow and Schmalensee 1998, 37–38). The dominant approach remains a centralized, command-and-control system headquartered in Washington, D.C., and resistant to rationalization and improvement.

Why does such a manifestly failed system continue to persevere in the face of its own failures and the failures of similar command-and-control bureaucracies around the world? This chapter attempts to answer this question by examining special interests usually thought to be in conflict when it comes to environmental regulation: industry and environmental interest groups. These two groups traditionally have been modeled as being diametrically opposed to each other in the regulatory process. But closer inspection shows that industry (or at least some identifiable subset of industry) and environmental interest groups benefit from the current inefficient system of environmental regulation and share a commitment to preservation of the status quo.

THE DYNAMICS OF ENVIRONMENTAL REGULATION

The process of environmental regulation is conventionally modeled as a zero-sum conflict between regulated "industry" on one hand and environmental activists and "the public" on the other (Swire 1996, 101). In this view of the political process, regulation is all about imposing costs on industries and about the attempt by industries to avoid these costs. The battle is between polluters on one side and pollutees on the other.

It is argued that in this regulatory game the deck is stacked in favor of industry. The reasoning is seductively simple: regulation imposes costs on discrete producers, whereas the benefits of clean air are distributed among the public at large. "Individual citizens who wish to breathe clean air are a classic example of a large, disorganized population seeking a collective good which will benefit each individual by only a small amount" (Elliott, Ackerman, and Millian 1985, 322). "The costs of environmental regulation, on the other hand, tend to fall heavily on a relatively small number of companies, which are already reasonably well-organized and thus presumably less subject to free-rider problems. According to most popular theories of political influence, well-organized industries would be systematically overrepresented and diffuse environmentalists systematically underrepresented in formulating policy" (Swire 1996, 101–103).

This view is based on a flawed understanding of the regulatory process and does not explain the actual pattern of environmental regulation in the economy. To understand how environmental regulation is carried out, it is necessary to pierce the myth that the system is driven by a zero-sum conflict between environmentalists, business, and regulators. Rather, the current regulatory regime reflects the truism, "Where gains to trade exist, they will usually be identified and captured." As this chapter demonstrates, there are ample gains from trade available so that industry and environmental activists can benefit.

Who loses? The primary losers in this process are those who lack the incentive or the ability to influence the political process—the dispersed, powerless public that is forced to pay higher prices for the goods they consume, to subsidize the preferences of environmental interest groups, to bear the burden of complex regulations and litigation that enriches lawyers, and to support politicians and regulators. Regrettably, the environment itself often suffers as a result of the current system, thereby harming those who genuinely care about the environment. The public also suffers from the impact of environmental regulation that stifles competition and entrepreneurship.

Well-organized interest groups can use the regulatory process to transfer wealth to themselves at the expense of the dispersed public. Thus, even if commentators are correct that environmental organizations have more difficulty getting organized relative to industry, environmental groups still have a huge comparative advantage relative to the mass of unorganized consumers who suffer from inefficient regulation. The collective action problems of environmental lobbying groups are trivial in comparison to those of the public. The relevant comparison for predicting the outcome of the regulatory struggle is not industry against environmental groups. At a minimum, regulation is a three-way struggle among industry, environmental interest groups, and dispersed consumers and taxpayers. Among these three groups, industry and environmental interest groups will find fertile ground to ally against the unrepresented interests of the public, especially when their interests mirror the preferences of politicians and regulators.

The modus operandi of modern environmental law scholarship is to identify a purported environmental externality that cannot or will not be resolved by the market and to call for political regulation to correct this externality. Nonetheless, these same scholars rarely acknowledge the externalities of the political process. The analysis is identical, regardless of whether the party imposing the externality is a private actor imposing the cost or private actors using the political process to impose the cost. As Buchanan and Tullock (1962, 89–90) have observed,

> the discussion about externality in the literature of welfare economics has been centered on the external costs expected to result from *private* action of individuals or firms. To our knowledge little or nothing has been said about the *external costs* imposed on the individual by *collective* action. Yet the existence of such external costs is inherent in the operation of any collective decision-making rule other than that of unanimity. Indeed, the essence of the collective-choice process under majority voting rules is the fact that the minority of voters are forced to accede to actions which they cannot prevent and for which they *cannot* claim compensation for damages resulting. Note that this is precisely the definition previously given for externality.

Political externalities are inherent in any collective decision made according to any non-unanimous voting rule. Non-unanimous voting rules make it possible for some people to obtain goods and services without being forced to bear their full costs. Those in the majority can defray their costs by forcing those in the minority to subsidize their preferences (Buchanan 1973, 583–87; Pritchard and Zywicki 1998). As Epstein (1987, 40) has explained, democratic politics in effect give a politician "a spigot that allows him to tap into other people's property, money, and liberty. The legislator that casts a vote on an appropriations bill is spending not only his own wealth, but everyone else's." Under majority voting rules, political externalities are routine.

Finally, in a perverted way the current system of environmental regulation is consistent with Demsetz's (1967) model of the rise of private property. The demand for environmental purity fits his model of the evolution from a free good to a scarce good. It has been only recently that a widespread demand for environmental purity has developed. This is for two reasons: First, environmental purity is a luxury good, and only recently have large numbers of people reached a stage of sufficient wealth that they have been willing to forego economic development in exchange for greater environmental purity. Early environmental efforts were aimed at the eradication of life-threatening health risks, such as the control of malaria and typhus. Similarly, the rise in demand for control of less severe health discomforts from pollution and for the widespread use of environmental amenities as a consumption good is a recent phenomenon. Second, technological improvements have made it increasingly possible to control pollution in a cost-effective manner (Goklany 2000). The combination of these demand-and-supply factors has given rise to incompatible uses of environmental goods: productive use that pollutes the environment on one hand versus consumptive uses of clean air and water on the other. In short, we have seen an evolution of environmental inputs from an essentially free good to a scarce good marked by incompatible uses. As Demsetz noted, where a free good becomes a scarce good, common-use arrangements will tend to break down and will be replaced by private-property arrangements.

But unlike other areas in which property rights developed, environmental resources have not been privatized for the benefit of private individuals. Instead, politicians and the regulators they manage have expropriated environmental resources for their own benefit, and the politicians distribute these valuable rights according to their preferences and in exchange for campaign contributions and other benefits. In some cases these benefits are little more than the opportunity for an EPA administrator to indulge his or her personal preference as to whether certain land will be used for backpacking or for paper production. Again, the regulator gains a private benefit for which the public pays—not the regulator. Other recreational users also benefit by getting to use the land without paying for it. A backpacker who uses the political process to avoid paying the opportunity cost for using the land as desired is imposing an externality on the public in the same way as a paper plant that does not have to pay the full value of the resources it uses (Buchanan 1987).

The current regime can be understood as an implicit collusion of several well-organized, discrete, and powerful interests that conspire to act in ways that use the political process to impose externalities on the public through the political process and to transfer wealth to themselves. This chapter focuses on two such groups: industry and environmental interest groups. As will become evident, the traditional view of industry opposition to regulation and a purported conflict between these groups has been misunderstood. Instead, these groups share many common goals, and their large overall gains explain why they generally support the current system of complex, centralized, command-and-control regulation. Thus, although there are conflicts among these groups at the margins, they share a commitment to the general approach of the current regime.

Industry Beneficiaries: Regulation and Rent Creation

The classic model of environmental regulation pits proregulatory forces (such as the public, so-called public-interest lawyers and environmental lobbyists, and government regulators) against antiregulatory forces (such as polluting industry). In this model, the final amount and type of regulation results from a compromise among these clashing interests.

But this classical model of regulation ignores two important complexities: First, it ignores that *industry* is not a homogeneous term. Some industries may be injured by regulation; but other industries, in fact, benefit from regulation, at least relatively, and thus will support regulatory initiatives. The latter can be called the "directly benefited" industries. Second, it ignores that government will have at its disposal alternative mechanisms for regulating the offensive conduct. Although some forms of regulation may be opposed by regulated industries, other forms of regulation may actually be beneficial to the regulated industry, or at least to some identifiable set of firms within that industry. And if a regulation transfers wealth to a given industry or to certain firms within that industry, the regulation will be favored by those parties, not opposed. We can call these "indirectly benefited" industries or firms.

Directly Benefited Industries

Industries that are directly benefited by regulation are those that directly and foreseeably benefit from the imposition of the regulation. Regulation can directly benefit an industry either by increasing demand for the industry's product or by restricting the entry of competitors into that industry, thereby increasing the profits of incumbent firms. Two obvious and well-documented direct beneficiaries of environmental regulation are the ethanol industry and the waste industry. The size of the wealth transfers to these industries during the era of federal environmental regulation is quite staggering.

Consider the ethanol industry. For many years, the government has encouraged ethanol use through a 5.4 cent per gallon tax subsidy, a subsidy that was recently extended through the year 2007. The 1990 amendments to the Clean Air Act added additional government preferences designed to support the ethanol industry. Given that ethanol is far more expensive than ordinary gasoline, the very existence of an ethanol industry attests to the size of the direct transfers to particular industries through environmental regulation. According to Adler (1992, 19–23), without subsidies, ethanol would cost at least a dollar more than gasoline for the same energy equivalent. Likewise, gasohol would cost ten to twenty cents more for the same energy equivalent. Indeed, some estimates conclude that producing ethanol uses more energy than the final product generates. These calculations do not even include the increase in food prices that consumers have to pay to compensate for the diversion of grain from food to fuel production (Anderson, Lareau, and Wollstadt 1988, 48).

Perhaps the billions of dollars in subsidies would be justified if increased use of ethanol actually increased environmental quality. But ethanol is not a "cleaner" fuel than gasoline. Increased use of ethanol injects different but equally dangerous pollutants, such as carcinogenic aldehydes, into the air we breathe. Presented as a proenvironment program, the ethanol subsidies mostly benefit politicians currying favor with corn farmers.

The waste industry is another direct beneficiary of the current scheme of environmental regulation. Superfund, which was ostensibly designed to clean up toxic waste, illustrates the point. From the beginning, Superfund's primary mission seems to have been to enrich the hazardous waste industry and environmental lawyers. As the initial Superfund statute worked its way through Congress, votes for tougher provisions were reflected in statistically significant gains in the value of waste-treatment company stocks (Dalton, Riggs, and Yandle 1996, 79–86). As the statute became tougher, the waste treatment industry became richer. Companies engaged in the treatment of hazardous waste have grown at phenomenal rates since the creation of Superfund in 1980. One small company grew into a 160-person firm in just four years; "[m]ost of this growth is attributable to stringent environmental regulations, and to Superfund in particular" (Landy and Hague 1992, 78).

The influence of the hazardous-waste-treatment lobby is manifest in Superfund's design. Superfund is primarily concerned with the cleanup of hazardous waste sites, not with containment or disposal of hazardous waste. If hazardous waste is reduced or contained, of course, then there is less to clean up and fewer hazards. As a result, the hazardous-waste-treatment lobby has consistently obstructed efforts to limit the amount of hazardous waste produced, such as by encouraging conservation by taxing the amount of waste produced or by recycling certain substances used in industrial production. Similarly, the hazardous-waste-treatment lobby has also sought to expand the number of sites designated as Superfund sites requiring cleanup and has sought to ensure that the most expensive forms of cleanup be required. A former Environmental Protection Agency (EPA) counsel summarized the waste industry's strategy: "They're interested in having a lot of waste designated as hazardous so they can get rid of it" (Carbonara 1990, 44).

The joint and several liability provisions of Superfund also provide a disincentive for containment procedures. Joint and several liability imposes cleanup costs on all parties regardless of their contribution to the problem. Thus, whereas a corporation bears the full cost of containment efforts, it will likely bear only a fraction of the cost for cleanup, externalizing the remaining costs on others (Epstein 1995, 296–97).

By increasing demand for the services of the ethanol and toxic waste industries, ethanol subsidies and Superfund policies transfer wealth directly to those industries. Moreover, these policies have limited (if any) beneficial impact for the environment. In the case of Superfund, the lobbying pressures of the waste industry have helped to perpetuate an inefficient obsession with postspillage cleanup, rather than reduction in overall waste levels through taxes and recycling. There are other examples of interests lobbying for environmental regulations that will directly benefit them (Adler 1996, 26–27).

Indirectly Benefited Industries

Much environmental regulation does not appear to benefit certain industries directly. Is it possible that environmental regulation could actually benefit the industry regulated? Not only is it possible, but it happens. A desire to benefit the industry, or parts of the industry, that is the subject of regulation helps to explain the structure of environmental regulation, and especially its reliance on centralized, command-and-control regulations, as opposed to decentralized market, common law, and incentive-based forms of pollution control.

Regulation as Cartel-Creation. Buchanan and Tullock's (1975) unjustly neglected article on the political economy of environmental regulation provides insight into the ways in which certain types of environmental regulation can be used to enrich the regulated industries. Given the level of neglect that legal scholars have shown toward the article, it is worth discussing Buchanan and Tullock's thesis here.[1] Once it is understood how environmental regulation can operate to transfer wealth to those regulated, it will become more evident why regulatory initiatives generally follow inefficient centralized, command-and-control approaches, rather than more decentralized and flexible approaches, such as taxes or tradable pollution permits. The paradox is striking: Whereas economists stress taxes and emissions fees, regulators generally prefer direct restrictions on pollution emissions or the imposition of technological requirements.

Part of the reason for the prominence of direct regulation is that the regulated industry may actually prefer direct regulation. Where firms are charged a tax in proportion to the amount of pollution they create or are required to buy the right to pollute through purchase of tradable pollution permits, the cost of doing business will increase. The polluter previously was entitled to use the environmental resource for free; now the polluter must pay for each unit of waste it creates. After this reallocation of property rights, firms will minimize their use of these inputs (the input being the right to pollute), just as they do with any other resource that they must purchase, whether it be labor, capital, or any other rights. Although costs will increase, there will be a tendency toward an equilibrium that will fully reflect the cost of this input when used in connection with other inputs. Firms that fail to use their pollution rights efficiently will be driven from the market by firms that do. Pollution rights will tend to flow toward the firms and industries that can use them most efficiently (Coase 1960). Costs will be higher and output lower; but a competitive outcome will be achieved, and all remaining producers will earn normal returns.

Direct controls, however, will reduce overall industry output, thereby raising prices. If the marginal price increase that results from the output restriction exceeds the marginal cost increase from regulation, especially if it makes the firm's supply curve more inelastic, then the regulated industry will be more profitable after the imposition of the regulation than before. In short, the regulation will effectively cartelize the industry by artificially restricting output and thereby raising prices (Pritchard and Zywicki 1998). This is not to say that all firms in a given industry will benefit or will benefit equally, because the increase in cost may be larger for some firms than for others; and the increase may even drive some firms from the market, especially where there are no limitations on entry. This potential for greater profitability does suggest, however, that at least some firms within the industry will benefit from this cartelizing effect.

Empirical support for Buchanan and Tullock's thesis is provided by Maloney and McCormick's (1982) study of the Occupational Safety and Health Administration's (OSHA's) promulgation of cotton-dust standards for textile mills and the Supreme Court's decision upholding copper smelting regulations that effectively limited entry of new smelting plants. In both situations, tough regulations increased costs and thereby reduced output. Despite this increase in costs, the stock values of incumbent firms in those industries increased, implying increased profits and price increases that exceeded the increased costs. Similar forces may also account for the otherwise puzzling decision of some automobile producers to support even stricter miles-per-gallon standards than Congress eventually adopted (Yandle 1980, 300). Presumably, for these manufacturers, the relative benefits of regulation in raising prices outweighed the direct compliance costs.

Of course, it will also be necessary to restrict entry into the industry so as to prevent the dissipation of these rents, but such entry restrictions are routine. Environmental regulations commonly impose stricter pollution control requirements on new firms than on existing firms. For example, the 1970 Clean Air Act and its amendments imposed standards on existing pollution sources as a function of the ambient air quality, whereas new firms had to meet the strictest standards regardless of local air quality (Hahn and Noll 1983, 64). The law "heap[s]" requirements on those seeking permits that "can only be described as baroque," while remaining silent about existing sources (Crandall 1983, 126). In short, "[e]ntry restrictions seem to pervade every aspect of this regulatory process" (Maloney and McCormick 1982, 101). Not only does this quash entry by new firms, but it also discourages existing firms from replacing older, heavier polluting plants with new, cleaner plants, thereby harming the environment in the process.

Some barriers to entry are de facto instead of de jure. Large up-front investments in pollution-abatement equipment raise the minimal capital demands of doing business. Increasing capital requirements tends to fall hardest on start-up businesses, thereby choking off entrepreneurship and entry by new firms (Dean and Brown 1995, 299). This dampening of the entrepreneurial market process harms consumers.

These barriers to entry in a given industry are compounded by the application of different rules to different regions of the country. Under Prevention of Significant Deterioration (PSD) rules, established, heavily polluted regions of the country are held to a lower standard of ambient air quality than less-developed regions of the country that lack both industry and accompanying pollution. It would seem that cleaner but poorer regions of the country would be those most interested in attracting industrial development, and would have the greatest room to allow some amount of pollution in exchange for economic growth (Quinn and Yandle 1986). But these are the regions of the country that were held to the highest standards of air quality and, thus, were disadvantaged in attracting new industry from dirtier industrial areas. Indeed, Pashigian's (1984) study of this phenomenon in the 1977 Clear Air Act revealed that politicians were driven more by the desire to protect home-state special interests from competition from less-developed areas of the country than by environmental concerns. Crandall has also noticed that industrial interests in northern states have deliberately used strict environmental regulations to restrict the migration of industry to the southern and western parts of the country (Crandall 1983). As one scholar has commented, "[c]ommon sense suggests that dirtier regions would have to clean up more. The statute required just the reverse" (Yandle 1997, 71).

Intra-Industry Wealth Transfers. The costs of complying with environmental regulations do not fall equally on all producers in a given industry. The cost of command-and-control regulations, such as those requiring the installation of smoke scrubbers or other fixed-capital investments, is approximately the same regardless of the size of the firm complying with the regulation. Because the cost of this investment is fixed, it falls harder on small businesses than on large businesses (Pashigian 1984; Pittman 1981). Because most regulatory compliance measures impose relatively constant costs, they also fall harder on small firms and dampen competition (Adler 1996). Large firms can more easily absorb the costs of the numerous lawyers needed to weave their way through the regulatory and litigation thicket (Pashigian 1982). Thus, large firms may benefit twice: they are more able than small firms to absorb these costs, and they do not have as much competition when the small firms are eliminated from the industry.

Various studies of the coal industry have illustrated the intra-industry impact of regulation. Limitations on strip mining, for instance, raise the relative costs of surface mining, thereby resulting in a wealth transfer from surface mining interests to underground mining interests. Thus, underground mining interests traditionally have been strong supporters of strip mining regulations (Kalt 1983). Ackerman and Hassler's (1981) classic study of the Clean Air Act, *Clean Coal, Dirty Air*, reveals a similar intra-industry tension. They document the alliance between eastern-based coal producers and United Mine Workers to protect the high-sulfur eastern coal industry. The alliance of eastern industry, eastern labor, and eastern politicians forced through a requirement that all plants install expensive scrubbers—regardless of whether a plant was burning "clean" western coal for which scrubbers would have been unnecessary or "dirty" eastern coal. Not only did this regulation impose large and unnecessary costs on coal-burning facilities; but, as evidence indicates, the regulation actually harmed the environment.

Dividing the Spoils: Labor Union Beneficiaries of Regulation. The beneficiaries of this rent-seeking legislation are not limited solely to industry. Whereas environmental legislation can create economic rents for various companies, the distribution of rents within the company is up for grabs. Thus, there is some evidence that organized labor shares some of these rents with the benefited corporations: "If labor is organized in the polluting industries, unions may bargain for higher wages to be paid from rents generated by regulatory-derived output restrictions. . . . Union leaders would support stricter enforcement of standards so long as the gain in worker wages and total dues was greater than the additional cost of bargaining" (Yandle 1983, 107). But because rents are created by restrictions on output, this windfall for organized labor comes at the expense of other workers who lose their jobs or who are never hired.

Labor unions have an interest in improving the working conditions of their members. One way to do this is to reduce the air pollution to which their members are exposed. Under normal circumstances, however, the acquisition of a benefit, such as improved working conditions, would come only at the expense of reductions in salary or other benefits, resulting in these workers having to internalize the cost of pollution reductions. If unions can help force all taxpayers to subsidize certain pollution-control devices, such as publicly owned treatment plants, they can externalize some of the costs of improved working conditions on the public. Empirical tests suggest that union members can indeed use the public fisc to acquire private benefits of superior working conditions and to externalize the costs on the public (Yandle 1985, 431–33).

Labor unions share with industry a desire to prevent entry and to fight regulatory reform. As noted earlier, businesses in the established industrial areas of the country favor strict and unequal environmental standards so as to prevent movement of industry to the growing southern and western areas of the country. The older, industrialized areas of the country tend to be the areas with the greatest union activity, so unions share the desire to use federal law as a mechanism to limit the movement of jobs to the south and west, where labor costs tend to be lower. State regulation will not accomplish this end because, by definition, it requires the imposition of costs on other areas of the country: "The fact that environmental control eventually migrated from the state-local level to the federal level suggests that some potential gainers or losers were not satisfied with the mid-1960 result [prior to federal regulation]. Firms could relocate and escape the control net. Unions could lose members. . . . By imposing uniform standards and levels of enforcement across space, most of the principal rent-seeking groups could gain" (Yandle 1983, 108–9).

Organized labor also will favor command-and-control systems of regulation. First, as with industry beneficiaries of the cartel-like effects of command-and-control regulation, economic rents can be generated only through output-restricting forms of regulation. Taxes on pollution would not have that effect, so there would be no economic rents to be shared among the various constituencies. Second, command-and-control regulations usually mandate certain capital investments. More particularly, technology-based command-and-control regulations require the installation of nonproductive capital, in that it adds no value to the production process. In essence, command-and-control regulations act like a tax on capital, inducing firms to substitute labor for capital at the margin. Market-based mechanisms will not have the same effect of inducing a substitution of labor for capital. The labor-substitution effect helps to explain the prevalence of command-and-control regulation instead of market-based mechanisms because investments in pollution-control technology tend to be higher in areas of high union membership.

Implications of Political Externalities. The failure to recognize the existence of political externalities plagues legal scholarship on environmental law. Consider Esty's article (1996) arguing for continued centralization of environmental regulation. Esty correctly recognized that some pollution problems overlap jurisdictions; thus, arbitrary political boundaries will not match up with the scale of the externality to be regulated. As a result, he concluded, "centralized" action is necessary to cope with these problems.

But this conclusion does not necessarily follow from the premise. Although Esty recognized the problems of interjurisdictional spillover of pollution, he ignored the interjurisdictional spillover of regulation—namely, the application of inefficient regulation to those who do not need it or want it. Federal political boundaries do not match up any better with the scope of the externality than local and state boundaries do and may match significantly worse (Macey and Butler 2000). Thus, "political boundaries may be both more inclusive and more exclusive than the group affected by the externality" (Zywicki 1996, 986). Given that most pollution problems are local or regional, not national problems, the prevalence of national regulation suggests that interest-group dynamics, not efficiency, are driving the choice of which jurisdiction has regulatory authority.

Like many other legal scholars, Esty appears to be unaware of the abundant literature briefly discussed earlier that demonstrates the ways in which regulation is used to punish or to deter potential competitors of well-established firms. Centralized political control means that many people who are not directly affected by pollution that occurs elsewhere can impose their preferences. This suggests that the inefficiencies caused by underrepresentation of third parties in the case of environmental externalities, the central concern of Esty and others, is replaced by political externalities. Moreover, elevating the question to the national level will not necessarily lead to the inclusion of "more" voices than are present at the local level; it may simply lead to domination by different voices (Zywicki 1994). As I wrote several years ago:

> With respect to large-number externalities such as pollution, severing the costs from the benefits of collective action suggests that one type of inefficiency simply may replace another. Separating influence over results from the costs of those results means that the original underrepresentation of third parties to the externality is replaced by an ability of those only tangentially linked to the matter to dominate the decision process. For example, third parties may vote for stricter pollution regulation when they are hardly affected by the pollution source in question, but feel none of the costs of the action, such as the loss of jobs. (Zywicki 1996, 986)

Given this failure of traditional environmental law scholarship to consider the problem of political externalities, it should not be surprising that in the end many scholars propose that it would be appropriate to concentrate authority in even more centralized bodies—those with an international scope. In so doing, these scholars fail to realize that exactly the same problems of political externalities arise again on the international stage, only this time the gains to special interests from capturing the levers of power to transfer wealth to themselves are potentially even greater because it becomes impossible for competitors to escape the grasp of inefficient regulation.

For example, it is estimated that the phase-out of production of chloroflourocarbons (CFCs) mandated by the Montreal Protocol on Substances That Deplete the Ozone Layer has cartel-like effects will create a windfall profit of $1.8 billion to $7.2 billion to American producers. American producers are also the likely beneficiaries of a move toward CFC replacements because these producers hold most of the world's patents on CFC substitutes and had a substantial head start on research for replacements. Among these firms, the largest producers of CFCs (DuPont and Imperial Chemical Industries) benefit to a disproportionate degree because they are also the frontrunners in the race to develop CFC substitutes. Thus, it is not surprising that DuPont favors the treaty.

DuPont's favorable response to CFC regulation suggests another fruitful area for the strategic use of regulation. Firms can create new compliance technologies before the enactment of domestic or international legislation and then can proceed to encourage regulations that employ the developed technology to create entry barriers. This strategy will often meet with great success. As one commentator observed, "[c]ompanies that spot what society wants have an opportunity for innovation. . . . Once they have done so, government is likely to raise standards. . . . When this happens, the innovative company acquires a protected market, hedged in by environmental standards that it can meet, but its competitors cannot" (Cairncross 1992, 16). This leverage is even greater because once new technology is created, the "best available technology" (BAT) requirement of environmental law creates a built-in ratchet that makes it easy to raise the standards to the new level.

The recent Kyoto Protocol reflects many of the same interest-group pressures. In particular, the Kyoto Protocol would transfer wealth from coal-dependent industries and countries to those that have adopted alternative energy sources. Thus, it is not surprising that producers of alternative fuels have endorsed the Kyoto Protocol (Yandle 1998).

Two additional examples will help explain how regulation can be used strategically. The first example relates to the 1970 Clean Air Act amendments that required that automobiles reduce pollution emissions by 90 percent within five years. It turns out that Ford had a technological lead in developing pollution-control technology and thus was able to reach the goals much easier than other companies (*International Harvester Co. v. Ruckelshaus* 1973). As a result, Ford benefited by the new regulation at the expense of other manufacturers.

The second example shows that the use of technology-inducing regulation is not uniquely American. Consider Henkel, a German detergent manufacturer. Henkel informed the German government that it had developed a detergent ingredient that reduced phosphates by 50 percent, and then it built a plant to produce the new ingredient. The government responded by requiring that all detergent phosphates be reduced by 50 percent, providing a windfall to Henkel, which had created the production capacity to meet the new regulations. In short, international lawmaking confronts problems of interest-group pressure that are similar to those that domestic lawmaking confronts.

A Story of Spotted Owls. Even enforcement of the Endangered Species Act can be used to dampen competition and to raise prices for those in a regulated industry (Yandle 1997, 74). Weyerhaeuser hired wildlife biologists to look for spotted owls—on non-Weyerhaeuser-owned federal lands. Laws protecting spotted owl habitat had forced Weyerhaeuser to curtail logging on 320,000 acres of land. So Weyerhaeuser was pleased to assist in the effort that resulted in over five million acres of federal land being made off-limits to other loggers as well. As expected, taking that much forestland out of circulation caused lumber prices to jump up. The *Wall Street Journal* (June 24, 1992) summarized the benefit to Weyerhaeuser of spotted owl protections: "[o]wl-driven profits enabled the company to earn $86.6 million in the first quarter [of 1992], up 81% from a year earlier." Thus, even though Weyerhaeuser was unable to log on 320,000 acres of its own land, this sacrifice was more than offset by the overall effect of the logging restrictions on the market as a whole.[2] By 1995, the reduction of supply in the timber market caused by federal protection of spotted owls had reduced the supply of timber to the point where industry profits were up 43 percent—essentially doubling the value of the positive effect on timber. The impact on industry profits was not uniform, however. Many large corporations were enriched while smaller, independent mills were bankrupted. Of course, consumers also lost because these logging restrictions drove up the prices of new homes.

In short, the assumption of a "conflict" between industry and the public is often fictional. Industry, or at least some members of industry, are often the beneficiaries of the proposed regulation. This helps to explain the seeming perversities of the current environmental regulatory environment.

ENVIRONMENTAL INTEREST GROUPS

Environmental interest groups also are both direct and indirect beneficiaries of the current command-and-control regime. They benefit directly by the prominent role that they play in the current regulatory and litigation-based system of environmental protection, a role that would be reduced by a movement to more decentralized market-based forms of control. They benefit indirectly by the opportunity to share in the rents created for industry by command-and-control regulatory systems. Thus, rather than being unbiased advocates of the public interest, environmental interest groups are riven with conflicts of interest that lead them unerringly to support centralized, command-and-control methods of pollution control. They stand by this orientation even when it has negative consequences to the environment when compared to more efficient and environment-friendly regulatory mechanisms.

Direct Benefits of Command-and-Control Regulation

The current command-and-control system of environmental regulation gives environmental lobbyists significant input into the creation, implementation, and enforcement of environmental laws and regulation. The lobbyists maintain almost a complete stranglehold on the flow of information to politicians and regulators. They also play an important role in generating legislative proposals and in drafting statutory language. Given their inherent tendency to favor command-and-control strategies over decentralized, incentive-based strategies, this control over legislation effectively allows them to block alternative forms of regulation. Indeed, in at least some cases, they have the power to stop regulatory reform from reaching the floor of Congress (Adler 1995). Through their ruthless enforcement of their party line, they play a pronounced role in making or breaking the careers of individual politicians.

This disproportionate control over the legislative process is backed up by an equally prominent role in the enforcement process, which generates direct revenues for these nonprofit groups. As Farber noted (1992, 73), environmental activists play a crucial part in enforcing environmental laws.

Since early in the emergence of modern environmental law, these groups have been the major sources of litigation on behalf of environmental quality. The major national groups, most notably the Sierra Club and [the] Natural Resources Defense Council, have participated in scores of major suits against EPA and other government agencies such as the Interior Department. Even a cursory study of environmental law reveals their pivotal role in shaping judicial decisions. They have also made effective use of litigation and other procedural delays to stall adverse agency action. Congress allowed them to pursue private enforcement actions as a substitute for agency enforcement.

Furthermore, many members of the Clinton administration's environmental policy team were lifted from the leadership ranks of environmental interest groups, thereby strengthening the grip of environmental lobbyists on the environmental regulation process (Adler 1995, 65–70).

Given the obvious conflicts of interest that environmental lobbyists face in deciding when to litigate, Farber is remarkably sanguine (and seemingly enthusiastic) about the vast powers given to unaccountable environmental activists to enforce command-and-control regulations. Ironically, Farber's greatest concern is not that environmental groups have too much power over the implementation of environmental law, but that recent Supreme Court decisions have limited the standing of environmental interest groups to bring suits to enforce environmental laws and regulations, thereby reducing their influence.

There is little benefit to environmental organizations from accepting proposals endorsed by some economists to impose an emission rights scheme or to tax the amount of pollution created. Such regimes are largely self-executing and self-enforcing, resting on decentralized, market-based, decision-making processes. As a result, these regulatory schemes would reduce the prominence of environmental groups in controlling information, punishing politicians, writing legislation, and enforcing regulations through litigation: "A self-enforcing regulatory system that mimicked market incentives would make advocacy groups superfluous, at least with respect to the enforcement process; a coercive and litigious regulatory system makes them essential. This may help explain why environmental groups have been so slow and reluctant to endorse more flexible regulatory schemes even when such schemes would demonstrably result in greater environmental gains" (Greve 1992a, 8).

The conflicts of interest of environmental interest groups are evident in their continued enthusiasm for command-and-control forms of regulation, even where the schemes conflict with environmental goals. Thus, they have favored higher restrictions on new sources of pollution, even where this deters the replacement of old, polluting plants with new, cleaner plants. They have supported smokestack scrubbers for coal-burning plants, reducing incentives to shift to cleaner-burning, low-sulfur coal. They have supported continued subsidies for recreational use of public lands, despite the environmental damage caused by these uses. The priorities of environmental activists and their attitude toward more efficient and effective pollution-control mechanisms were further illustrated by their opposition to "waste-end" taxes in the 1986 Superfund amendments debate. One proposal raised at that time was to tax the actual amount of waste produced, thereby creating an incentive to produce less waste. Environmental activists opposed this recommendation—precisely because it would lead to less waste! Less waste would mean less revenue for the fund that pays for Superfund cleanup. It is striking that they were willing to sacrifice an opportunity to encourage source reduction for the much less clear benefit of spending more federal money on abandoned sites. Similarly, environmental groups have strenuously objected to the use of containment strategies at abandoned toxic-waste sites instead of cleanup, even where containment would have a large positive marginal impact by allowing more sites to be addressed. Needless to say, the adherence of environmentalists to a firm cleanup position found them fighting side by side with the waste treatment industry.

Environmentalists also favor the current regime that centralizes power in Washington. Keeping the locus of regulation at the national level does not increase the number of voices that are heard and considered in policy making. It simply changes the voices that are dominant (Zywicki 1994). Most professional environmental groups have a weak grassroots foundation, but they are highly active and influential inside the Beltway. As a result, they favor the national focus, which makes good use of their sophisticated lobbying apparatuses in Washington. Indeed, it was the failure of earlier environmentalists to build localized, grassroot support for their programs that led them to use the federal government as a mechanism to end-run the process of local consensus building. Needless to say, Washington politicians and regulators provide receptive ears for this Washington-centered approach.

But it is not just politicians who pay the price when they cross the dominant national environmental interest groups. Consider the fate of the Quincy Library Group, an informal group formed by local environmentalists in Quincy, California, a northern California logging area (Fitzgerald 1998). After a fractious fifteen-year debate over logging in the area, all of the interested parties reached a mutually agreeable compromise, only to see it vetoed by national interest groups. The national groups attempted to strong-arm the local group to make changes to their plan before the national environmental groups would support it. When members of the Quincy Library Group proposed legislation to implement their agreement, the national groups attacked and were successful in killing the legislation.

These conflicts of interest in the legislative and regulatory processes are exacerbated by similar conflicts of interest in the enforcement process of current law. The enforcement process rests heavily on litigation, where the law provides substantial monetary incentives for environmental groups to bring suit to enforce regulations. Most federal environmental statutes contain a so-called "citizen suit" provision allowing "any citizen" to sue private parties for noncompliance with the statute. Under these statutes, no harm to any particular plaintiff needs to be shown. All that is necessary is to show a technical violation of the statute. This allows private parties to step into the government's shoes and to act as "private attorneys general," unconstrained by the usual restraints of balancing competing priorities in enforcement (Greve 1992b, 105–6).

Although the claim is that these provisions allow grassroots "citizen suits," in practice these suits are brought almost exclusively by professional environmental groups, such as the Sierra Club Legal Defense Fund or the Natural Resources Defense Council. Indeed, through strategic use of citizen suit provisions, environmental groups have been able to establish an ongoing program of litigation, using the attorneys' fees recovered in one case to bankroll operations with surpluses available to fund other operations. Moreover, evidence suggests that the decision by these groups regarding the allocation of their litigation resources is driven more by the cost of the action, the ease of victory, and the likely payoff, rather than by the severity of the harm or an absence of public enforcement:

> The fact that transfer payments to environmental organizations constitute the overwhelming portion of settlements of Clean Water Act citizen suits might lead one to suspect that the pattern and scope of private enforcement are determined *not*, as intended, by its expected public benefits, but rather by the enforcers' expected rewards or, more precisely, the "spread" between the costs and the benefits of enforcement *to the enforcer*. A closer examination of the Clean Water Act enforcement campaign shows this suspicion to be correct. (Greve 1992b, 110–11)

As a result of these economic incentives, professional environmental litigants have focused on litigation under the Clean Water Act, which contains the desired criteria. Clean Water Act suits are usually settled, with the plaintiff-group recovering attorneys' fees. Rather than receiving only *actual* attorney's fees, however, environmental groups are usually compensated according to the going rates of private attorneys, rather than their actual costs *(Blum v. Stenson* 1984, 892–96). As a result, they routinely recover significantly more than their actual costs, meaning that "litigation is potentially a profit-making activity" (Farber 1992, 74). Moreover, most settlements provide for the payment of certain "credits" or "mitigation" programs, such as the establishment of environmental education programs. Unsurprisingly, environmental groups are usually the recipients of many of these payments, some of which have exceeded $1 million per case. This combination of easy victory, overcompensatory attorneys fees, and windfall "credit" program payments has created a potent revenue source for environmental organizations.

The fee-seeking nature of suits brought by activist environmental groups is illustrated by the suits' almost complete focus on private defendants. Although municipalities violate their permits with greater frequency than private parties, between 1984 and 1988, environmental activist groups filed more than six times as many notices to sue against private industry than against governmental entities. By contrast, individuals and nonprofessional environmental groups sued governmental entities with the same frequency as private defendants. In short, many actions simply redistributed wealth from private defendants to groups blessed with nonprofit status, which used that money to fund similar suits against other private defendants, in an endless cycle of litigation that produces few, if any, environmental benefits.

Indirect Benefits of Command-and-Control: Rent Sharing

No doubt, most environmental groups are animated at least in part by a sense of protecting the environment (Schoenbrod 2000). But in order to do this effectively and to sustain the large number of people on the payrolls of environmental organizations, the organizations need money. They seek to maximize their donor base to increase their political clout and to enhance their prestige in the policy arena. Often a compromise is reached in which environmental activists form an alliance with various industries to support their projects, thereby furthering both parties' goals simultaneously. In other cases, however, such compromise is not available, and environmental activists' desire for environmental protection will clash with their desire for funds, prestige, and policy influence. In either case, it is evident that the notion of environmental interest groups as "public interest" groups is naive; environmental activists represent the interests of themselves and their members, and it is serendipitous if their private interests overlap with those of the public generally.

A key variable for understanding the methods of environmental interest groups is that, like private firms, they produce certain outputs. Their "output" is cleaner air and water.[3] The means available to secure this output are quite flexible. Moreover, they bear virtually none of the costs associated with providing this output—it is borne by the industries regulated. As a result, environmentalist lobbyists can pursue environmental purity without having to worry about the offsetting economic costs of their agenda. In short, through the political process they are able to externalize onto producers and the public the entire amount of the production of the goods they desire. There is no incentive for them to consider the costs that they are imposing on other parties because they bear practically none of those costs.

Because they do not bear the costs, environmentalists should be indifferent in choosing among different competing means to accomplish the ends of environmental purity. Given a goal of reducing air pollution by, say, 10 percent, environmentalists will be indifferent between realizing this goal through efficient means (such as tradable pollution permits) or inefficient means (such as command-and-control mandates). Because the costs of the inefficient form of regulation are spread across all consumers in the economy, individual environmentalists bear a trivial amount of the costs of choosing inefficient means instead of efficient ones. This indifference as to means gives environmental groups great flexibility in choosing political coalition partners with other interest groups that benefit from environmental regulation.

But industry will not be indifferent among means. As discussed earlier, command-and-control regulation raises the prospect of creating economic rents in an industry through a cartelization effect or by directly enriching some industries. Tradable permits, by contrast, will simply raise costs of all current and potential competitors. The command-and-control scheme and the economic rents that the scheme makes possible raise the possibility of gains to trade between the benefited industry and environmental groups. Given the indifference of environmental groups between the alternative regulatory schemes, it is a simple application of economic logic to predict that the industry can buy the support of environmentalists for the command-and-control scheme. By sharing with environmentalists some of the gains generated by the command-and-control regime, the benefited corporations can garner the political support of environmental groups and the public relations benefits of the green cloak. Under this scheme, both industry and environmental groups win. Under a permit system, by contrast, no clearly identifiable economic gains are generated, thus there is no "surplus" to be shared between industry and environmental lobbyists.

The gains to trade between environmental lobbyists and industry interest groups are even more striking when one considers the ways in which federal environmental law is used to redistribute wealth across the country. Incumbent industries in the more polluted areas of the country agree with environmentalists that less-developed areas of the country should be subject to more-stringent regulations. Environmentalists want to preserve the environmental purity of these areas, and established industry wants to prevent the migration of competitors to those areas of the country. Similarly, environmental lobbyists, the waste-treatment industry, and lawyers will often find common ground in pushing for increased cleanup of Superfund sites.

The presence of these gains to trade politics may explain the otherwise puzzling financial support of industry for environmental interest groups (Adler 1995, 97). Members of the waste treatment industry have pumped hundreds of thousands of dollars into the coffers of various environmental advocacy groups, including the National Audubon Society and the National Wildlife Federation. Oil companies including Atlantic Richfield and Chevron contribute to environmental groups such as the National Audubon Society, which lobbies to restrict opening new areas for drilling, thereby keeping new supplies off the market. As these examples illustrate, there are ample gains to trade between environmentalists and polluting industries, and they are usually exploited.

Backpackers and Recreational Cost Externalization

Finally, environmental lobbyists personally benefit by the massive subsidy created by the current regime for environmental recreation and tourism. Charging below-market rates for recreational uses results in a subsidy of millions of dollars per year to these users. The Bureau of Land Management (BLM) estimated in 1988 that recreational users, who pay less than $2 million in user charges on BLM land, cost the BLM $125 million (Oesterle 1996, 548). Forest Service losses on timbering activities, although large, are dwarfed by its losses on recreational activities (Burnett 1998). This massive subsidy for recreational users has resulted in overuse of public lands by recreational users, thereby creating new problems of pollution and environmental damage.

Moreover, recreational users tend to be primarily wealthy and upper-middle class users; thus, this subsidy goes to those who need it least (Tucker 1982, 48). "The caricatures of environmentalists as well-educated and wealthy, and [of] outdoor recreationalists as Winnebago owners and back-to-the-earth college-aged offspring of well-to-do families are inaccurate, but not terribly so" (Kalt 1983, 909). Moving to a market-based system would likely force environmentalists to pay market rates for their use of these valuable resources. Little wonder that they favor expanding the current system of environmental regulation.

CONCLUSION

Business is quite cognizant that environmental regulation can be used as a tool to raise competitors' costs and to effectively cartelize a given industry. Writing in *Business Strategy Review*, a journal aimed at educating businesspeople, economist Scott Barrett (1991, 1) provided the following advice:

Today, business leaders are taking a more positive attitude to new [environmental] regulation. This is not just because they are concerned citizens; there is now also the recognition that environmental controls—such as those which compel all firms in an industry to meet some minimum standard of emissions—do not generally reduce competitiveness across the board. . . . [S]ome regulations can even benefit firms . . . directly, possibly by restricting entry to their industry, or by limiting output in a way that raises prices. So the business response to the imposition of regulations should not be to argue for easier standards. . . . The challenge for business is to identify how regulation will affect them, and then to influence the shape of regulation that is imposed accordingly. At least some firms will find that they can influence the form of the regulations that are introduced in such a way to enhance their competitive advantage and also to improve the environment.

It is doubtful that Barrett and other scholars who are providing similar advice (Dean and Brown 1995) are telling industry something new. Weyerhaeuser did not need to be informed that finding spotted owls on public land would increase the value of Weyerhaeuser's own lumber. DuPont did not need to be told that international regulation through the Montreal Protocol would both increase the value of DuPont's existing CFC stock by reducing CFC supply, while simultaneously increasing demand for DuPont's new CFC substitutes. Nor did the waste treatment industry need to be informed that Superfund would be a boon for them. Indeed, logic suggests that the firms that have survived and prospered under the current regime have acted in a manner consistent with this advice, even if unconsciously (Alchian 1950). In fact, even express coalitions between industry and environmental activist groups appear to be routine (Adler 1995, 72–76). It seems that it is primarily law professors who remain reluctant to accept the self-serving behavior that underlies the current inefficient structure of environmental regulation.

This suggests that those seeking to move the environmental regulatory process to a more efficient and decentralized system must account for the distributive consequences of reforms. Politically and financially powerful interest groups benefit greatly from the current regulatory system and are unwilling to consent to a destruction of their influence without a compensating benefit. The current environmental regulatory regime creates large economic benefits to many wealthy and politically powerful interests. Does this mean that deregulation or decentralization of the environmental regime is impossible?

We might learn a lesson from a rare exception where incentive-based regulation was installed—tradable emission permits under the 1990 Clean Air Act. There, the initial allocation of emission rights was established by a grandfathering approach, where rights were allocated according to the amount of pollution emitted prior to the new market-based regime. As a practical matter, this created a profit opportunity for incumbent polluters, which they could use themselves or sell to highest-valued users (Dewees 1983, 59). Put more directly, the drafters of the Clean Air Act "bought off" the opposition of industry to the implementation of the tradable permit scheme. The loss suffered by polluters due to the new regulation was compensated by a one-time lump-sum payment in the form of valuable pollution rights.

Further light is shed on this by Paul Joskow and Richard Schmalensee's (1998) article on the allocation of tradable permits. Joskow and Schmalensee found that the most significant variable in determining the amount of emissions rights that a state received was the political clout of that state, specifically large states that were swing states in the 1988 presidential election, states with competitive gubernatorial campaigns in 1990, or states that had representatives in the House Energy and Commerce Committee leadership. This suggests that key politicians must share in the gains from moving to a more efficient regulatory system.

Deregulation or devolution to the state, local, and individual levels may come about only if the distributive consequences to entrenched interest groups and politicians are large enough to offset the losses they must incur. As Buchanan and Tullock advised in 1975 (147), "For economists who continue to support [market-based regulations and taxes], the analysis suggests that they [should] begin to search out and invent institutional arrangements that will make the [market-based regulations and taxes] acceptable to those who are primarily affected." Similarly, politicians may be induced to deregulate if their gains from doing so exceed their losses. Effective reform, however, requires a proper understanding of the status quo.

NOTES

1. I say that their article is "neglected" because a recent Westlaw search of law journals and periodicals revealed that Buchanan and Tullock's (1975) article has only been cited a total of thirteen times in legal literature (two of which were in previous articles of mine). Ignorance of Buchanan and Tullock's insight may help to account for the continued perception that regulated industries have nothing to gain and much to lose from the imposition of environmental regulation. Professor Daniel Farber, for instance, said that the model rested on "dubious economics." It is not clear whether he was actually aware of Buchanan and Tullock's article at the time, as he did not cite it. Nor did he cite Maloney and McCormick's (1982) later restatement of the thesis. As a result, Farber apparently remains trapped in the mindset that environmental regulations impose costs on regulated firms with no offsetting benefits.

2. President Clinton's "timber summit," which was conducted shortly after he took office, led to further restrictions on lumber harvesting. Far from dealing a blow to the lumber industry, as some papers reported, financial markets responded by driving up the stock values of paper companies and lumber companies in anticipation of lower harvests and, thus, higher lumber and paper prices (Yandle 1997, 74).

3. This may be an unduly favorable characterization of the "outputs" of environmental lobbying groups. In practice, an output such as "clean air" may be too intangible to measure, especially for donors. Thus, their real output actually may be rules and regula-

tions as ends in themselves, as evidence of influence and success. Moreover, environmental interest groups rarely celebrate good environmental news. If the true output is indeed rules and regulations, this will exacerbate the problems identified in the text.

REFERENCES

Ackerman, Bruce A., and William T. Hassler. 1981. *Clean Coal, Dirty Air.* New Haven, CT: Yale University Press.

Adler, Jonathan H. 1995. *Environmentalism at the Crossroads: Green Activism in America.* Washington, DC: Capital Research Center.

———. 1996. Rent Seeking behind the Green Curtain. *Regulation: The CATO Review of Business and Government* 4: 26–34.

———. 1992. Clean Fuels, Dirty Air. In *Environmental Politics: Public Costs, Private Rewards*, ed. Michael S. Greve and Fred L. Smith, Jr. New York: Praeger, 19–23.

Alchian, Armen A. 1950. Uncertainty, Evolution and Economic Theory. *Journal of Political Economy* 58: 211–21.

Anderson, Robert C., Thomas Lareau, and Roger Wollstadt. 1988. The Economics of Gasoline Ethanol Blends. *Research Study* 45. Washington, DC: American Petroleum Institute.

Barrett, Scott. 1991. Environmental Regulation for Competitive Advantage. *Business Strategy Review* 2(1): 1–15.

Buchanan, James M. 1973. The Coase Theorem and the Theory of the State. *Natural Resources Journal* 13(October): 579–94.

———. 1987. Rights, Efficiency, and Exchange: The Irrelevance of Transaction Costs. In *Economics: Between Predictive Science and Moral Philosophy*, ed. Robert D. Tollison and Viktor J. Vanberg. College Station: Texas A&M University Press, 153–68.

Buchanan, James M., and Gordon Tullock. 1962. *The Calculus of Consent: Logical Foundations of a Constitutional Democracy.* Ann Arbor: University of Michigan Press.

———1975. Polluters' Profits and Political Response: Direct Control Versus Taxes. *American Economic Review* 65(March): 139–47.

Burnett, H. Sterling. 1998. States Save Trees and Make a Profit. *Investor's Business Daily*, August 13, A28.

Cairncross, Frances. 1992. UNCED: Environmentalism and Beyond. *Columbia Journal of World Business* 27(Fall/Winter): 12–17.

Carbonara, Peter. 1990. The Greening of Waste Management. *American Lawyer* 12: 42–45.

Coase, Ronald H. 1960. The Problem of Social Cost. *Journal of Law and Economics* 3(1): 1–44.

Crandall, Robert W. 1983. *Controlling Industrial Pollution: The Economics and Politics of Clean Air.* Washington, DC: Brookings Institution.

Dalton, Brett A., David Riggs, and Bruce Yandle. 1996. The Political Production of Superfund: Some Financial Market Results. *Eastern Economic Journal* 22(Winter): 75–88.

Dean, Thomas J., and Robert L. Brown. 1995. Pollution Regulation as a Barrier to New Firm Entry: Initial Evidence and Implications for Future Research. *Academic Management* 38(1): 288–303.

Demsetz, Harold. 1967. Toward a Theory of Property Rights. *American Economics Review* 57(May): 347–59.

Dewees, Donald N. 1983. Instrument Choice in Environmental Policy. *Economic Inquiry* 21: 53–71.

Elliott, E. Donald, Bruce A. Ackerman, and John C. Millian. 1985. Toward a Theory of Statutory Evolution: The Federalization of Environmental Law. *Journal of Law, Economics, and Organization* 1(2): 313–40.

Epstein, Richard. 1995. *Simple Rules for a Complex World*. Cambridge, MA: Harvard University Press.

———. 1987. Judicial Review: Reckoning on Two Kinds of Error. In *Economic Liberties and the Judiciary*, ed. James A. Dorn and Henry G. Manne. Fairfax, VA: George Mason University, 39–46.

Esty, Daniel C. 1996. Revitalizing Environmental Federalism. *Michigan Law Review* 95(December): 570–653.

Farber, Daniel A. 1992. Politics and Procedure in Environmental Law. *Journal of Law Economics and Organization* 8(1): 59–81.

Fitzgerald, Tim. 1998. The Quincy Library Affair. *PERC Reports* 16(1): 3–5.

Goklany, Indur M. 2000. Empirical Evidence Regarding the Role of Nationalization in Improving U.S. Air Quality, this volume.

Greve, Michael S. 1992a. Introduction: Environmental Politics without Romance. In *Environmental Politics: Public Costs, Private Rewards*, ed. Michael S. Greve and Fred L. Smith, Jr. New York: Praeger, 1–18.

———. 1992b. Private Enforcement, Private Rewards: How Environmental Citizen Suits Became an Entitlement Program. In *Environmental Politics: Public Costs, Private Rewards*, ed. Michael S. Greve and Fred L. Smith, Jr. New York: Praeger, 105–28.

Hahn, Robert W., and Roger G. Noll. 1983. Barriers to Implementing Tradable Air Pollution Permits: Problems of Regulatory Interactions. *Yale Journal of Regulation* 1: 63–91.

Joskow, Paul L., and Richard Schmalensee. 1998. The Political Economy of Market-Based Environmental Policy: The U.S. Acid Rain Program. *Journal of Law and Economics* 41(2): 37–83.

Kalt, Joseph P. 1983. The Costs and Benefits of Federal Regulation of Coal Strip Mining. *Natural Resources Journal* 23(October): 893–915.

Landy, Marc K., and Mary Hague. 1992. The Coalition for Waste: Private Interests and Superfund. In *Environmental Politics: Public Costs, Private Rewards*, ed. Michael S. Greve and Fred Smith, Jr. New York: Praeger, 67–88.

Macey, Jonathan R., and Henry N. Butler. 2000. Federalism and the Environment, this volume.

Maloney, Michael T., and Robert E. McCormick. 1982. A Positive Theory of Environmental Quality Regulation. *Journal of Law and Economics* 25(April): 99–123.

Meiners, Roger E., Stacie Thomas, and Bruce Yandle. 2000. Burning Rivers, Common Law, and Institutional Choice for Water Quality, this volume.

Meiners, Roger E., and Bruce Yandle. 1993. Clean Water Legislation: Reauthorize or Repeal? In *Taking the Environment Seriously*, ed. Roger E. Meiners and Bruce Yandle. Lanham, MD: Rowman & Littlefield, 73–101.

Oesterle, Dale A. 1996. Public Land: How Much Is Enough? *Ecology Law Quarterly* 23: 521–75.

Pashigian, B. Peter. 1982. A Theory of Prevention and Legal Defense with an Application to the Legal Costs of Companies. *Journal of Law and Economics* 25(October): 247–70.

———. 1984. The Effect of Environmental Regulation on Optimal Plant Size and Factor Shares. *Journal of Law and Economics* 27(April): 1–28.

Pittman, Russell W. 1981. Issue in Pollution Control: Interplant Cost Differences and Economies of Scale, *Land Economics* 57(1): 1–17.

Pritchard, A. C., and Todd J. Zywicki. 1998. Finding the Constitution: An Economic Analysis of Tradition's Role in Constitutional Interpretation. *North Carolina Law Review* 77: 409–521.

Quinn, Robert, and Bruce Yandle. 1986. Expenditures on Air Pollution Control under Federal Regulation. *Review of Regional Studies* 16(3): 11–16.

Schoenbrod, David. 2000. Protecting the Environment in the Spirit of the Common Law, this volume.

Spence, David B. 1995. Paradox Lost: Logic, Morality, and the Foundations of Environmental Law in the 21st Century. *Columbia Journal Environmental Law* 20: 145–82.

Stewart, Richard B. 1988. Controlling Environmental Risks through Economic Incentives. *Columbia Journal Environmental Law* 13: 153–69.

Swire, Peter P. 1996. The Race to Laxity and the Race to Undesirability: Explaining Failures in Competition among Jurisdictions in Environmental Law. *Yale Journal on Regulation* 14: 67–109.

Tietenberg, Thomas H. 1992. *Environmental and Natural Resource Economics*. 3d ed. New York: HarperCollins.

Tucker, William. 1982. *Progress and Privilege: American in the Age of Environmentalism*. Garden City, NY: Anchor Press/Doubleday.

Yandle, Bruce. 1980. Fuel Efficiency by Government Mandate: A Cost-Benefit Analysis. *Policy Analysis* 6: 291–301.

———. 1983. Economic Agents and the Level of Pollution Control. *Public Choice* 40: 105–9.

———. 1985. Unions and Environmental Regulation. *Journal of Labor Research* 6(4): 429–36.

———. 1997. *Common Sense and Common Law for the Environment: Creating Wealth in Hummingbird Economies.* Lanham, MD: Rowman & Littlefield.

———. 1998. Bootleggers, Baptists, and Global Warming. *PERC Policy Series* PS-14. Bozeman, MT: Political Economy Research Center, November.

Zywicki, Todd J. 1994. Senators and Special Interests: A Public Choice Analysis of the Seventeenth Amendment. *Oregon Law Review* 73: 1007–55.

———. 1996. A Unanimity-Reinforcing Model of Efficiency in the Common Law: An Institutional Comparison of Common Law and Legislative Solutions to Large-Number Externality Problems. *Case Western Reserve Law Review* 46(4): 961–1031.

CASES CITED

Blum v. Stenson, 465 U.S. 886 (1984)

International Harvester Co. v. Ruckelshaus, 478 F.2d 615 (D.C. Cir. 1973)

9

On the Commons and the Common Law

Jason Scott Johnston

The notion that the failure to assign property rights in environmental resources subjects those resources to overuse and degradation as free-access or unowned resources has become commonplace. However, very few aspects of the external environment were ever actually subject to free and uncontrolled access. Human groups have occupied and used even the most remote areas of the earth. These groups have established customary norms regarding resource use. The norms have been enforced through extralegal, collective sanctions and have remained stable for centuries. The great episodes of environmental change, and, arguably, destruction, have come at those historical points when customary rights in environmental resources have come under pressure from new uses and new user groups. Norms, which rely for their effectiveness on exclusion of some uses and users, cannot manage these transitions in use. It is at such points that the law, and particularly the common law, has been most important, for the decision by common law judges regarding the assignment of legally enforceable rights in common resources shapes private incentives in contesting transitions in the use of those resources. Common law judges have generally not simply followed the economists' prescription by making a definite assignment of private rights in previously common resources. Instead, in areas ranging from nuisance law to the law of riparian rights, the judges have attempted to balance competing claims to common resources, using the rubric of "reasonable use" as a means of permitting competing but simultaneous use of the commons.

Such reasonableness tests are inherently uncertain and indefinite. In this chapter, I generate a positive theory of how private incentives in contesting common resources will be shaped by such indefinite common law rules. My theory rests on the recognition that under majoritarian government, there are two ways of acquiring rights in the commons: through private acquisition or through legislative reassignment of rights. Rather than buying off existing users, a new user may simply seek to persuade legislators to extinguish the existing right. However, whether there is any right in the first place is a matter determined not by the legislature, but by the courts. At times of major transitions in the use of common resources, "whether there is any right in the first place" is precisely the question that courts must decide. On my theory, the common law choice between a clear, general answer (assigning the right to either the old user group or the new) and an uncertain, highly particularistic answer (balancing the harm to old users against the value to new users, location by location) will strongly influence whether the competing user groups seek a legislative reassignment of rights. When courts attempt to make general, definite assignments, the effect is to cause interest groups to coalesce to seek legislative reversal. Conversely, when courts adopt particularistic balancing tests, they tend to weaken the viability of interest group lobbying for legislative change. Under particularistic balancing, courts end up defining entitlements; when courts attempt instead to make general allocations of entitlements, they merely shift the contest to the legislature.

In the final part of this chapter, I test this theory against historical evidence drawn from two great late-nineteenth-century American contests over the commons: the battle between hydraulic miners and farmers in California's Sacramento Valley and the conflict between the great new industrial polluters (coal, railroads, iron, and steel) and existing residential users in Pennsylvania. Before discussing these case studies, which I believe strongly confirm my theory of the commons and the common law, I discuss the evolution of limits on collective norms in common resources and set forth the theory of contests over transitional rights in such resources.

THE COMMONS AND CUSTOM

It is no exaggeration to say that an entire school of contemporary political economy has been built on a body of empirical work showing that the "tragedy of the commons" is often overcome by local collective action.[1] The "tragedy" of the commons arises when a commonly owned resource, such as a fishery or timbered forest, is managed on an open-access basis, leading to overexploitation of the resource.[2] There is now a very large and still growing body of empirical literature detailing cases in which local commons have been managed efficiently, so as to prevent overexploitation.[3] In some cases, such collective action has quite clearly been extralegal. For instance, the Maine lobstermen studied by Acheson (1988) set up a system of exclusive territories, backed by credible (albeit illegal) enforcement strategies (destroying the equipment of outsiders who violated the exclusive territories), that maintained the catch at long-term sustainable levels. Similarly, for many centuries, coastal fishing in Japan was managed under a complex system of local village rights; and in Nepal, the *shingo naua* (forest guards) effectively managed the near-tree-line forests (McNeely 1991). In England and Wales, common lands have existed for centuries (Hoskins and Stamp 1963). Comprising woodland, moor, and marsh, the English common lands are private lands subject to ancient common rights, typically held by some (not necessarily all) members of nearby villages. Of the various common rights, the right of common pasture—the right to graze one's animals over the "wastes," or uncultivated fields—was perhaps most well known, but there were also common rights to gather wood for fuel, to dig turf for fuel or for roofing, to fish in common waters, and to cut bracken for fuel or for bedding (Hoskins and Stamp 1963, 4). In the fens (wetland regions), for instance, each villager had an exclusive right to use land adjacent to saltwater marshes which was made arable by dikes; and villagers also had rights to use common peatlands for pasture, fishing, fowling, and reed gathering (Bosselman 1996, 279). The right of common pasture was crucial to the medieval peasant economy; and as population and pressure on the local common pastures increased, a rationing system known as "stinting" was introduced (Hoskins and Stamp 1963, 37). By the thirteenth century, village bylaws limiting the number of animals that might be pastured on the common or on the open fields after the harvest had been promulgated. As pressure on the commons increased even further during the sixteenth century, stints were reduced; indeed, it has been argued that records of manorial court orders indicate that the commons were managed with "extreme care" through detailed regulations that showed keen appreciation for the sustainable use of local common resources (Hoskins and Stamp 1963, 49).[4]

Even when customary norms regarding the use of common resources have been codified in local legal regulations, it is typically the case that the formal, legal sanctions for their violation are low relative to the potential benefit from norm violation.[5] For this reason, local regulation of common property resources is likely to be effective if and only if a system of extralegal sanctions is both credible and effective at deterring resource overuse or overexploitation.

The analytical objective is to identify the structural preconditions under which such a cooperation-inducing extralegal enforcement mechanism might arise and be maintained even without formal legal intervention. One possibility is to employ the theory of repeated games to identify equilibrium outcomes. As emphasized by Sethi and Somanathan (1996), however, one problem with the theory of two-person repeated games is that so many outcomes are sustainable as equilibria that the theory does not really help to identify the empirical conditions under which cooperation is likely to be observed.

Even greater problems are revealed when one considers that most commons problems involve not repeat interactions between two users, but rather between $N > 2$ users. Suppose that the commons problem is a kind of Prisoner's Dilemma, in which if all members of the community graze lots of animals, then the commons will become degraded and all will be worse off in the next period. By grazing only a moderate number of animals, the value of the commons is preserved over both periods. Table 9.1 depicts the payoffs to a particular member of the commons and to other N–1 members of the commons as a function of their choices between high and moderate numbers of animals. If $\delta<1$ denotes the rate at which all members of the community discount future payoffs, then it is clear from table 9.1 that for sufficiently high δ, the total two-period value of the grazing commons will be maximized if all N members of the collective graze a moderate number of animals. It is equally clear, however, that the payoff to the Nth user will maximize that user's payoff by grazing a large number of animals, no matter what the others do.

This problem—the divergence between the interest of the individual and the interest of the group—would be solved were the group able to credibly punish members who deviated from the group optimum. The option of having all the N–1 cooperative members of the group graze a large number of animals is, however, not credible, for in so doing they would each receive a lower payoff than if they acquiesced in the noncooperator's overgrazing. It might well be that some number m ($m < N$) could overgraze and actually increase their own payoffs; but with identically productive animals, it could not then be true that the payoff to the noncooperator had been lowered.

What table 9.1 clarifies, and what is often misunderstood by legal commentators in particular, is that strategies that may constitute (subgame perfect)[6] equilibria in repeated games between two players (even when the players are randomly drawn from a large population) will generally not be equilibria in N-player versions of the same game. When members of a community are randomly drawn to play a single round of a two-player Prisoner's Dilemma type game, there exist (subgame perfect) equilibria in which any player who cheats (by grazing a large number of animals) will forever after be cheated by his or her opponents.[7] As table 9.1 shows, this will generally not be true when all N members of the com-

Table 9.1   The Multiperiod Commons Game

$(0 < \delta < 1)$

		N–1 Users	
	Period 1	*High*	*Moderate*
Nth User	High	50,1000	50,800
	Moderate	40,1000	40,800

	If N – 1 Chose Moderate		*If N – 1 Chose High*	
Period 2	*High*	*Moderate*	*High*	*Moderate*
High	50,1000	50,800	25,500	25,400
Moderate	40,1000	40,800	20,500	20,400

munity play the same game each period. In order to effectively punish a noncooperator by playing within the game, so many others would have to emulate the noncooperator's behavior that all would be worse off, destroying the credibility (subgame perfection) of the punishment strategy.

This problem arises whenever there is a common-pool resource subject to threshold effects—whenever harm to the commons occurs if and only if the level of overuse exceeds a threshold. In such a situation, intentional overuse by some subgroup of the collectivity is ineffective as a punishment for overuse when it is less than or equal to threshold, whereas overuse above that threshold would be an effective punishment but is incredible because of the harm it would cause to those who inflict the punishment. It is for this reason that norms regarding common-pool resource use are enforced not by mutually destructive communal overuse, but rather by direct punishments. Monetary fines are not viable as primary sanctions themselves, for whether fines are effective depends on what happens if the violator doesn't pay the fine. Primary sanctions involve coercive force. Primary extralegal sanctions for violations of norms regarding use of a commons invariably involve excluding the cheater from access to the collective resource. The credibility of these sanctions depends on their being proportional to the level of the offense. For instance, Maine lobstermen begin by warning violators of territorial boundaries (for such a violation might be accidental). Continued violations lead to destruction of the transgressor's traps and eventually escalate to the ultimate sanction—the destruction of the transgressor's boat. These direct punishments are targeted precisely at those who violate group norms, and they appear to be fundamental to the collective resolution of commons problems.[8]

Punishment involving exclusion systematically reduces the number of resource users. In the absence of economies of joint effort, therefore, there exists an incentive for competition among subgroups within the collective to label others as cheaters, to trigger the exclusion punishment strategy, and thereby to obtain a greater share of the collective resource. Such an incentive may be weak when the resource is still available in great abundance (when the cod are so numerous, as it was once said, that one can walk across the fishing banks on their backs),[9] but whenever there really is a potential Prisoner's Dilemma, and overuse is a real problem, creating an incentive for honest enforcement of group norms becomes necessary to the group's survival. It is therefore crucial that the existence of the violation—overgrazing, for instance—be verifiable to other members of the collective and that the incentive for fraudulent enforcement effort be controlled. Only with such safeguards can group members distinguish between enforcement and expropriation.

The need for such safeguards may be one justification for apparently wasteful acts such as the destruction of equipment or animals. As Ellickson (1991, 215–17) observed, destruction, as opposed to confiscation, cuts the enforcer's incentive to trigger enforcement merely for self- or group enrichment. In addition, norms must be such that violations are verifiable by other members of the group. For this reason, such collective norms are likely to take the form of easily observable rules regarding use—such as what equipment may be used, when, and where—rather than output or catch rules (for what if a fisherman simply happens to be very lucky?). If violations are infrequent, then resource users may take turns acting as enforcers. However, as the frequency of noncooperative behavior increases, it may be necessary to create a special enforcement class in order to effectively enforce group norms.

In more general terms, for norms regarding exploitation of a collective resource to survive, the penalty for violating collective norms must be great relative to the cost of imposing it. If there are three types within the population—cooperators, overexploiters, and enforcers—then a norm against overexploitation will be most costly when the population consists primarily of overexploiters. Indeed, it is likely that there exists a threshold population proportion of overexploiters such that if the proportion ever exceeds this threshold, then enforcement becomes so costly that overexploiters always do better than either cooperators or enforcers do, and the community is doomed to ruin the commons.[10] On the other hand, once the proportion of overexploiters is below such a threshold, then both cooperators and enforcers will (for sufficiently effective punishment) enjoy higher payoffs; and on any evolutionary dynamic in which relative success increases relative population frequency, such types will flourish and come to dominate the community.

Shocks such as the introduction of a new technology increasing the productivity of overexploitation or an increase in demand for the products produced with or from the resource will cause a discontinuous increase in the return to overexploitation (Sethi and Somanathan 1996). If such an increase is sufficiently large, then for any given penalty, the cooperative equilibrium may be destabilized, in that the return to overexploitation will exceed the return to cooperation and enforcement. To preserve the cooperative state, it will be necessary to increase the punishment. However, the factors that increase the return to overexploitation—increasing market demand and technological change—are precisely those factors that mark the integration of once-isolated local communities and their commons into national and international industrial economies. Such integration makes threatened ostracism or expulsion from the community far less severe a punishment (Sethi and Somanathan 1996). Thus even as the return from overexploitation increases, so does the effectiveness of collective, extralegal punishment weaken.

This story rests on an implicit presumption that technological change and increasing market demand increase the return to overexploitation of the commons, but that it remains inefficient overexploitation. This is, of course, not necessarily the case. In table 9.1, for instance, if Techie Tom were to employ the other $N-1$ members of the community as laborers farming what were once common pastures, using Tom's marvelous new technology to grow and harvest wheat, then the total return to the N members of the community might increase. It may well be the case that whichever $N-1$ laborers Tom employs, he will generate the new, higher return by enclosing and farming the commons with this new technology. In that event, there is no need for any of the return from the introduction of the new technology to go to the existing users of the common. Of course, depending on the distribution of the return from this new use, the payout to existing users may fall. Tom may be proposing a new use that increases the total value of his land plus the value of the commons, but it may be that the effect of this new use on the commonly held air or water resources will be to directly reduce their value to the existing users.

The social problem is to distinguish new uses that actually enhance the value of the existing resource base by developing them more efficiently from those that may indeed be characterized as overexploitation, in that they reduce the discounted total value of the resource. The real need for social norms regarding resource use comes precisely at this stage—when supply and demand conditions change, prompting calls for a rearrangement of existing norms regarding resource use to permit new and more efficient exploitation of the resource. But collective norms regarding resource use are not reliable in managing such transitions, for the issue raised by such transitions is whether previously excluded, new uses are to be permitted. Norms themselves may change, and yet the mere fact that a subgroup is able to coalesce in support of a new use does not ensure the efficiency of that new use. It may be that the subgroup has formed simply to expropriate the benefits of prior efficient collective action. Exclusion is the primary means by which collective norms regarding common resources are enforced. When exclusion breaks down, the limit of norms has been reached.

LEGAL RIGHTS AND EFFICIENT TRANSITIONS

As the foregoing suggests, the great danger in the transition from norm-governed collective use of common resources to more formal systems of allocation is that once exclusion breaks down, the common resource becomes a free-access good. It is true that the free-access problem arises as a consequence of the failure to grant legal rights in the common. For this reason, one might argue that the remedy is simply to grant legal rights in the common to the existing traditional users. With such rights, one might argue, any transition in use must be purchased. If Tom has bought out all the existing commoners, then his new use is surely more valuable than his old use. Indeed, on the approach pioneered by Coase (1960), it would not matter whether a property right was given to Tom to despoil the common or to the commoners to keep it from being despoiled. In either event, were the cost of transacting sufficiently low, one would expect that rights would be exchanged so as to allow the resource to be put to its value-maximizing use.

One difficulty with this way out of the problem is that the process of acquiring individual rights in common resources is likely to face very high transaction costs. Consistent with the evolutionary story told earlier, Libecap (1989, 16–19) has argued that pressure to change existing property rights comes when there has been a shock that increases relative prices and/or decreases costs of development so that the rents from resource development increase, thus increasing competition for access to the resource. But even when there are clear gains from consolidating existing rights to permit a more efficient use of the resource—as in the case of unitization of oil-field extraction rights—asymmetric information regarding the value of existing rights (leases in the oil field, for example) may impede contractual reallocation of existing rights (Wiggins and Libecap 1985). Here, imperfect and asymmetric information is the "transaction cost" that obstructs efficient reallocation. Such information asymmetries are an especially severe impediment to the consolidation of private rights in common resources, for in order to privatize the resource, each holder's right must be purchased. As the number of users increases, the strategic or "hold-out" obstacles to rights consolidation become insuperable (Mailath and Postlewaite 1990; Rob 1989). Indeed, even without informational problems, the need to acquire the rights of all members of the common greatly increases the cost of consolidating rights in the common into private property. With large numbers, the rights-acquisition process is beset by a negative strategic externality: the smaller each existing rights holder is, the smaller is his or her effect on the probability that the consolidation succeeds, and so the stronger is his or her incentive to hold out for a high price. In theory, allowing the existing rights holders to collude via an association with formal enforcement authority may actually improve matters, for the association internalizes the effect of its bargaining stance in determining whether efficient consolidation proceeds, and if all existing rights holders are included, then the rights should eventually (perhaps with some delay) be sold if it is ex post (full information) efficient to do so (see Eckart 1985).

This might seem to imply that especially when the new use requires large-scale consolidation of existing communal rights, the rights consolidator should be happy to see communal rights holders organize and negotiate collectively. The problem with such an association is that although it does facilitate bargaining to acquire common law rights, it also facilitates collective action for legislative intervention. There are, after all, two ways of acquiring existing individual rights in common resources: market acquisition and legislative nullification. A rational acquirer ought to choose the least-cost method of rights acquisition. The cost of acquiring rights from the existing individual holders is equal to the value of the rights to those users plus whatever informational rents the users are able to obtain. The formation of an association of existing rights users will increase the expected informational rent earned by rights holders as a group in bargaining with the acquirer. Legislative nullification or modification of existing rights will take place through the intervention of a third party, the legislature. The formation of an effective joint association will enable existing rights holders to overcome the holdout problem in bargaining with the potential acquirer, but it also allows them to overcome the free-rider problem in lobbying the legislature.

Leaving the common law aside for the moment, the conflict between old users and new users may thus be resolved either through costly bargaining or through costly attempts to secure favorable legislation. These two alternatives are in fact closely related and are likely to be strategic complements. In general, unless the exercise of bargaining power is constrained—unless the parties are compelled to accept a "reasonable" offer ex post—one of them (the weaker party ex post) will be unwilling to incur the cost of bargaining.[11] But this makes the success of bargaining to effect changes in resource use itself contingent on the existence of effective legal or extralegal norms regarding the division of the gains from such changes. By hypothesis, the old and the new user groups are distinct, and hence there are no effective means by which extralegal norms may be established to govern their interaction. This then makes the success of private bargaining contingent on the existence of a legal norm regarding the division of the gains from bargaining.

The struggle for legislative modification of existing rights may itself generate such a division of the gains from transitions in use. For instance, if (as occurred with the English Enclosure Acts of the eighteenth and early nineteenth centuries) new users are able to persuade the legislature to simply declare that existing communal users have no legal right to continue to use the commons, then new users obtain the right without paying anything to existing users. This is equivalent to giving all the gains from the transition in use to the new users. There are other alternative divisions. The legislature may hit on a compromise that allows the new use but mandates various benefits to old users. In this way, existing users may functionally be bought out. But as a general matter, legislation is a way of bypassing the need to get the consent of existing users.

This is not to say that legislation is free. In representative democracies, legislation involves an implicit price paid to persuade representatives that median voter sentiment favors the proposed legislation. The price is not paid to existing users but to lobbyists employed to persuade legislators and, more indirectly, to constituents who receive benefits exchanged for their representative's support of the successful initiative.

Reference to the implicit price of legislation should not obscure the fact that the "price" of obtaining legislation differs fundamentally from the price paid to obtain consent via bargaining. The legislative game involves persuading one's representative that his or her constituents (more precisely, the median constituent) favor(s) the legislation. One very effective way of doing this is by having constituents spend their own time in communicating and lobbying their representatives. Such citizen lobbying is costly but does not involve any sort of valuable transfer (other than the transfer of information) to representatives.

This distinction is especially important in understanding legislative contests between old users and new users of the environmental commons. Bargaining requires a direct transfer from members of one group to members of the other. The transfer need not be monetary, but some valuable consideration must be exchanged (or else there would be legally enforceable agreement). When one group, say the old users, derive their income from the very use of the commons that is being challenged and have few other sources of income or wealth, they will have little to exchange other than a contingent claim on the returns they will get if they are allowed to continue their use of the commons. In other words, in the capital market, they would be borrowing against the future returns they will earn if they succeed in buying off the conflicting use. Capital market frictions may well prevent such transactions from occurring. When they do, private bargaining between old and new user groups may fail. Capital market imperfections do not, however, affect the ability of the old users to lobby and petition their representatives for a legislative settlement of the conflict. It is important to note that the cost of such efforts is actually likely to be lower during periods of conflicting use of the commons, for such use lowers the value of these directly productive uses and thus lowers the marginal cost of lobbying for legislative intervention.[12]

The actual struggle for legislation is a contest in which the relative expenditures in lobbying and other efforts to persuade determine the outcome of the contest. Especially when lobbying efforts are complements (meaning more effort by one side must be matched by more effort from the other), there will be a tendency for such contests to escalate and for legislative modification to be much more costly than acquisition by bargaining. This might seem to imply that both old and new users will be better off bargaining over consensual exchange rather than fighting legislative contests for redefinition of rights. This would indeed be the case were the parties forced to make a binding choice between the two alternative means of acquisition. But of course both options may be pursued, in whatever sequence the parties wish. In particular, the credible threat to initiate a legislative contest if the right is not obtained by bargaining may significantly alter the bargaining environment.

To see how the altering may occur, suppose that the new user makes a credible threat to initiate a legislative contest if the old users reject their offer. Such a threat will be credible provided that the expected return to the new user from a legislative contest exceeds the new user's opportunity cost. For a sufficiently serious threat—one that is likely to succeed in persuading the legislature to nullify existing rights—the old users will be willing to sell whatever rights they believe they have for a very low price. In effect, the credible threat to contest and to nullify the old users' rights if they don't sell out changes their willingness to bargain for a sellout. The threatened legislative contest may induce users to bargain when they would not otherwise do so—because bargaining is too costly in terms of its opportunity cost—and to agree to offers that they would otherwise reject—because if they reject, the legislature will nullify their right. This makes possible ex post inefficient consensual exchanges, but it also may induce bargaining toward efficient use that would not otherwise occur. This latter happy prospect is unlikely to result because the credibility of a threat to engage in a costly contest increases as the new user's opportunity cost falls. It is precisely those new users who have little better to do with their time but engage in costly lobbying who are the most serious threat to existing rights. In this sense, the alternative of fighting over existing rights may be a serious impediment to efficient bargaining over their reallocation (Rajan and Zingales 1995).

THE COMMON LAW AND TRANSITIONAL EFFICIENCY

The preceding argument shows that when contests over entitlements are an alternative to bargaining over their exchange, there is reason to be concerned about inefficient transitions from the commons, even when the commons is owned. But ownership is a common law concept. Thus the question prior to the issue of transition is how the common law adjudicates competing claims to the commons, and how this may affect transitional incentives.

History establishes the priority of common law ownership to all such transitional disputes. Beginning with the earliest Enclosure Acts in England, the first question confronting holders of customary use rights in common resources has been whether they hold any rights at all that are enforceable as a matter of the common law (see Thompson 1991). There are examples of "comedic," or (from the point of view of the commoners) happy, resolution of such questions (Rose 1986). But many of these involve very short term common rights with little impact (such as the right to hold annual maypole festivals on the village commons) or rights that only indirectly relate to the economic value of natural resources (such as the right to unobstructed passage on highways that cross through private lands) (Rose 1986). Perhaps the best-known instance of common law recognition of customary use-based rights is the California Supreme Court's mid-nineteenth-century adoption of the miners' norms regarding claim ownership and water rights (McCurdy 1975). There are, on the other hand, plenty of instances in which common law courts refused to enforce customary rights in common resources. In the eighteenth century, English courts upheld the power of manorial lords to enclose previously common lands, effectively abrogating any rights in landless cottagers or copyholders who had made common use of the enclosed lands (Thompson 1991). In the nineteenth-century United States, the courts of Pennsylvania often found that the harm to existing landowners from industrial pollution of air and water did not justify injunctive relief (Rosen 1993). During roughly the same period, the courts of California slowly reached the conclusion that uncontrolled discharge of mine tailings into major navigable rivers constituted an actionable nuisance to downstream farmers, even though the miners had been the prior users of the rivers (Kelley 1959).

The basic Coasean prescription calls for common law rights to be created and allocated in a definite way ex ante so that private bargaining can take place. Indeed, formal models of bargaining implicitly assume that the parties know which of them has the right and which of them does not, thus knowing who is the seller and who is the buyer. During periods of major transitions in the use of common resources, the issue confronting common law courts has been precisely which of the parties to the conflict has the right and which does not. Properly speaking, when the parties bargain prior to a common law determination of whether an old user versus a new user has the right, the parties are not bargaining over the exchange of an entitlement, but rather choosing to bargain rather than to initiate a legal contest to determine who has the entitlement (see Johnston 1995).

From the perspective of old users and new users, common law adjudication to determine their relative rights to the commons is just as much a contest as is the struggle for legislative determination. In both arenas, much expense may be incurred in hiring professionals in the arts of persuasion—lawyers and lobbyists. Unlike legal contests, however, where the dimensionality is limited, (the court must decide somewhere, albeit perhaps fuzzily, between the conflicting claims of the two parties), legislative contests over one issue may easily spill over into other issues. A common law judge's remedial powers do not include the power to allow the defendant to continue to cause a nuisance by polluting upstream from the plaintiff's riparian lands in exchange for the defendant's promise to contribute funds for the local public school. Yet there is nothing to prevent the legislature from simultaneously authorizing both actions.

What is most noteworthy about how common law judges have responded to conflicts involving relative rights during periods of major transitions in the use of common resources is their unwillingness to declare clear victors. Judges have employed balancing tests hinging on the notion of "reasonable use" to determine the relative rights of different users of the commons. Under such a balancing process, common law courts have only slowly recognized new individual rights in common resources. Common law judges have time and again refused to adopt simple and general ex ante rights assignments. Instead, they have preferred very fact specific, uncertain tests for the allocation of rights. Essentially, when confronted with a conflict between an old, established use of the commons and a new use, common law judges have tried to balance the rights of old users and new users.

This is not the only approach the courts have taken, they have at times opted for simple, definite, and general assignments of entitlements, the kind that result under a strict liability regime, for instance. One issue that might be explored is the efficiency of the way courts have adjusted the mix of general versus fact-specific rights assignments. Rose (1990), for instance, argued that common law water rights in the eastern United States efficiently evolved from a general first appropriator system to a more particularistic "reasonable use" standard. She explained that unlike the western United States, where water was fundamentally a private good, making the general assignment of rights to the first appropriator efficient, eastern water conflicts gradually came to involve a single upstream polluter or appropriator (such as a mill) and a large number of downstream users. Such conflicts, Rose argued, were over water flow as a public good and, hence, posed holdout or free-rider problems that would have doomed private bargaining. The common law decision to resolve such disputes by giving all riparians on a particular stream correlative and roughly equal rights to reasonable use was therefore the value-maximizing alternative (Rose 1990, 285).

While Rose's normative analysis is interesting and provocative, my interest here is positive. One positive question involves what might motivate judges to adopt general versus fact-specific rights assignments. I leave that question aside and focus instead on another issue, the analysis of which turns out to be very suggestive regarding judicial behavior. Whatever one thinks judges are attempting to accomplish by opting for a particular form of rights assignment (blurry and particularistic balancing versus a determinate and general assignment), there remains the question of how these alternative types of rights assignments affect the behavior of the groups who are fighting over old uses and new uses of the commons. It is this question to which I now turn, setting forth (informally) a testable model of how the form of common law rights in common resources is likely to affect the behavior of the individuals and groups contesting for private rights in common resources.

Litigation versus Legislation

Suppose, as in the mid-nineteenth-century conflict between miners and farmers in California's Sacramento Valley, that old users (hydraulic miners) are confronted by a new use (valley farming). And, suppose that the old use lowers the value of the common resource (the river) as an input in the new user's production process; that is, if the old use were terminated, then the value of the new use would increase. Assume that both old users and new users are a heterogeneous lot, with some having low-value production and others having high-value production. Suppose that the conflict between miners and farmers has arisen in many different river valleys in the region. In the initial state of affairs, there has been no legal determination of whether the discharge of mining waste (tailings) into the river constitutes an infringement of the farmers' rights or whether, conversely, the miners have a right to discharge into the river. Consider the decision by a group of farmers who are suffering harm from tailings being discharged into the river. Suppose that the amount of anticipated harm increases with the value of the farming operation. Consider two alternative common law regimes: one that definitely assigns the right to either the farmers or to the miners as a group and one that employs a case-by-case balancing test under which individual conflicts between particular farmers and miners are decided by giving the right to whichever party is believed by the court to have the higher value use of the commons. However determined, the holder of the right shall be supposed to have the right to enjoin the conflicting use (but the injunction may, as is commonly supposed in the law and economics literature [Calabresi and Melamed 1972] be alienated). Suppose finally that lobbying to overturn a court decision is always possible. If, for example, the farmers lost in court, then they might appeal to the legislature to enact a statute holding that the mining operation must either stop dumping tailings into the river or else cease operation. Lobbying for legislation is possible not only in response to a common law decision but also as an alternative or supplement to common law decision.[13]

Suppose that the farmers become fed up with the harm caused by mining debris being dumped into the river and bring an action at common law seeking a determination of their rights relative to the miners'. Now consider the incentives facing miners and farmers if the court opts for a simple and general ex ante assignment of the right. The right might, on a principled basis, be granted either to the miners or to the farmers: to the miners on the ground that they were the first, or prior, appropriators of the commons; to the farmers on the ground that no one may use the commons so as to harm the value of that commons to other users. For concreteness, suppose that on the basis of the latter principle, the court awards the right to be free from pollution to farmers injured by the upstream activities of several mines.

On Coase's theory, if the value of these particular mines is greater than that of the harm caused to the farmers involved in this particular suit, then the miners ought to buy out the farmers. Thus if the court made a mistake in assigning the right, it wouldn't matter to the efficiency of the final (post-exchange) assignment. There are two primary obstacles to such a bargain around the injunction. The first obstacle is the strategic cost of collective action by the two groups. The larger and the more heterogeneous the groups, the bigger this cost. Farmers as a group would accept any per capita amount equal to their average harm, but a payment equal to average harm will make the high-value farmers worse off. And yet every farmer has an incentive to pretend to be a high-value farmer, especially as the number of farmers in the group increases (by the argument made previously). Similarly, if the average mine value exceeds average farm harm, then the miners as a group would be made better off if they made some offer somewhat less than their average per capita harm. But some miners may have lower value mines, and they will refuse to be taxed at such a high rate; miners who really do have high value and could afford the tax will have an incentive to pretend to be lower value in order to reduce their tax, failing to take account of the reduction in the chance of agreement caused by this behavior. It might well be that the number of miners and farmers is so small that these costs of collective action do not present a great obstacle to bargaining. Yet even if there is only a single mine injuring a single farmer, the parties will retain an incentive to bluff and to delay as they haggle over the terms of the deal.

There is an additional problem with bargaining around the injunction. Because by assumption the court has adjudicated this particular dispute by invoking the general principle that a miner may not in operating his mine cause harm to downstream farmers by dumping tailings and debris into upstream tributaries, the court has effectively put all mines within the jurisdiction at risk. Any farmer can cheaply and quickly invoke this precedent to shut down any mine within the jurisdiction. And to the extent that farmers actually enforce their newly created general right, they will lower the wealth of miners and hence reduce their willingness to pay to get the right back. Were capital markets perfect, so that miners could borrow against their contingent future operations to finance a buyout of the effected farmers, this effect would be lessened. But it would be exceedingly difficult for lenders to determine how much to lend. The greater the amount borrowed, the greater is the potential offer that the borrower miners might make to the farmers. But the more that the miners pay to the farmers to get their consent to their continuing operation, the lower the present value of the miners' holdings and the more uncertain is their ability to pay back the loan. Lending to finance a buyout without which operations cannot continue is fraught with moral hazard problems for the lender. When this problem is coupled with the general adverse selection phenomenon in credit markets—a borrower's willingness to pay a high interest rate may simply indicate that it does not expect to be able to pay what is due anyway (Stiglitz and Weiss 1981)—it is very unlikely that capital markets would provide much assistance in enabling the miners to buy out farmers as Coase envisioned. Owners of very high-value mines would undoubtedly self-finance deals with small and lower value farmers. But this leaves a large number of potentially inefficient injunctions stuck in place.

This problem is likely to be especially severe when the generalized injunction is threatened at an early stage in the development of the new use. The newer the use, the more difficult it may be to convince investors that the new use will be profitable and, hence, the more difficult it may be to raise money to bargain around the law. More directly, the larger the number and the greater the dispersal of old users, the more difficult it will be for new users to bargain around the law. Indeed, when virtually any old user can obtain an injunction—regardless of the magnitude of injury—and the old use is ubiquitous (an entire valley of downstream farms using stream water for irrigation), then it will be virtually impossible for new users to know whether they have indeed bought off all the existing rights holders.[14]

Bargaining around the generalized injunction is not the only alternative open to the miners. By the argument made earlier, the miners will almost surely be better off when they at least threaten to seek legislative redress than when they simply offer to buy the farmers' right. Moreover, because the court has made a general rather than a circumstance-specific determination and has ruled that, on general principle, the mines may not use the commons in a way that injures other farmers, miners now share a common interest in lobbying the legislature for redress, just as all farmers now share a common interest in lobbying the legislature to codify the common law rule giving them a right to be free of harm. By adopting a clear and absolute assignment of the right, the court has created political interest groups that have strong economic incentives to pursue legislative conflict. As argued earlier, an important distinction between legislative versus judicial conflict is that legislators count votes as well as dollars. Even if many miners are capital constrained and will not contribute financially to a collective offer to the farmers, they may well contribute their time and effort in personally lobbying their representatives. Miners' ability to make side payments to farmers falls when the farmers enforce their newly declared right; conversely, the more farmers who actually enforce their newly declared right by enjoining upstream mines, the lower is the opportunity cost to miners of lobbying instead of mining (which would put them in contempt and subject to potential criminal sanctions). Thus the more effective is the newly declared right in halting mining, the greater is the miners' incentive to engage in political action.

It remains true that the newer the mining activity and the fewer the miners, the lower will be the miners' power in a political or a legislative conflict. Mining, however, is likely to be geographically concentrated. Although new, it may be the most important and promising development activity in the mountainous upstream regions of the state. Hence if legislative districts are not too large, they may well be cut so as to make the miners' votes very important within these districts. Thus even a new, capital-constrained industry might have significant power in a legislative conflict.

The general point that emerges from this discussion is that an abstract and general common law determination of the rights of new users versus old users tends to weaken the ability of the parties to bargain around the legal rule, while lowering the opportunity cost of taking political action to get the legislature to alter the common law determination of rights. This is especially so when the legal remedy is an injunction; for under a general assignment of rights, if one mine is enjoined, then all others employing a similar technology (and causing similar harms) are also subject to injunction. Operation of a mine in violation of an injunction will constitute contempt. The injunction thus attaches an extreme sanction (potential fines and imprisonment) to productive activity (operating the mine) and thereby dramatically increases the miners' marginal net benefit of legislative conflict versus economic production. In the most simple terms, because under the injunction productive activity is illegal, it is conflict rather than production that is likely to have the highest expected return.[15]

On this model, a general, definite assignment of the right by any one court tends to crystallize interest groups and to trigger costly legislative struggle to overturn the court's assignment. Consider, by contrast, the likely chain of events if the first court to decide the matter had adopted a balancing test under which it attempted to assess and weigh the harm done to the farmers against the value generated by the upstream miners in that particular valley. Under such a test, the court would enjoin the operation of the mines if and only if it found that the value of the farmers' harm was greater than the value of the mines. Suppose that the court found that the harm value was greater than the mines' value and enjoined the continued operation of the mines in that valley. Although the miners in this particular valley may be unhappy with the result, the legal decision itself has not created any general entitlement whatsoever. It simply represents a (possibly erroneous) determination by one legal-decision maker that in one particular location, the harm suffered by the farmers was greater than the value of the mines whose operation was enjoined. Only if all valleys were identical in terms of the value of the upstream mines and the harm suffered by downstream farmers would this particular decision be taken as putting all miners at risk. More generally, high-value mines would be confident that they would prevail under the particularistic balancing approach. Even with imperfect information about the value of different mines, farmers might well have some notion that the really large mines would almost surely prevail under the balancing test. Hence these mines would rationally expect a very low probability of ever being sued at all. The same would be true of high-value farmers. They would readily sue under the particularistic balancing regime and would expect to win. The very prospect of such a suit might force many lower value mines to close up shop and to move to other locations where mining would cause less harm to downstream farmers.

Under the particularistic balancing regime, it remains true that general legislation establishing a general entitlement in miners would be of value to all miners. But under the particularistic balancing regime, legislation would be of greatest value to the lowest value miners, who stood the highest risk of losing out in case-by-case, particularistic adjudication under the balancing test. Legislation embedding the court's decision in a more general entitlement to farmers would be of similar value to all farmers, but it would be of only marginal value to high-value farmers who expected to win under the particularistic balancing regime. For high-value miners and farmers, particularistic balancing cuts the comparative value of lobbying for legislative reassignment versus the value of private bargaining for reassignment, and thus the higher value types on both sides of the conflict will tend to eschew legislative conflict. Lower value farmers and miners have a high risk of losing under particularistic balancing. Still, some low-value miners will win (because the farms they harm are few and small), and some low-value farms will win (because the upstream mines are small and do not provide big benefits). As the determination of rights is particularistic and relative—comparing the harm to farmers in a particular valley against the value of the mines upstream of that valley—it will be difficult for low-value miners and low-value farmers to recognize their common interests and, hence, difficult for them to organize to lobby for legislative action.

There are two caveats to this conclusion. The first is that in the story I have told, the harms are not reciprocal. Upstream mining activities directly lower the productivity of downstream farms. Downstream farming has no effect on the productivity of upstream mines. This asymmetry means that regardless of how the common law goes about making the entitlement assignment—via a general versus a particularistic approach—it is the farmers who will have to bear the cost of bringing suit. For this reason, even under a particularistic regime, high-value farmers may have reason for seeking legislative redress. They may realize economies of scale by getting a single general bill passed rather than by litigating the same issue individually. In addition, if mining causes harm that cannot be easily measured and compensated ex post, the farmers may seek legislative intervention before the harm occurs. This is especially true when instances of harm (due, say, to flooding caused by unusually heavy rainfall) are unpredictable and catastrophic in scope.

The second caveat is that the effectiveness of particularistic balancing as a way of displacing pressure for legislative assignment (or reassignment) of rights may depend strongly on the accuracy of the particularistic regime. If courts are very prone to err in estimating the harm to farmers and the value of mining, then high-value farmers and miners will perceive a large risk of actually losing in a common law conflict. Such a highly uncertain and error-prone particularistic balancing regime is actually the worst of both worlds: like a threatened general assignment, it puts all farmers and miners at risk, but the uncertainty it creates can only be resolved on a case-by-case basis. Hence, if a particularistic regime is too prone to error, it may enhance rather than reduce the incentive for legislative action.

With these caveats, the model that I have outlined here generates the following general prediction: as between the alternative common law approaches to assigning rights in public resources, particularized balancing forces particularized litigation and particularized bargaining, whereas general and abstract ex ante rights assignment triggers general legislative rights conflicts. A final set of points go to the likely evolution of judicial balancing tests. Balancing is flexible intertemporally, so that if structural conditions change, then judicial outcomes can change with them. The adoption by courts of general, abstract ex ante rights assignments cannot be easily modified. Because the legal justification for assigning such simple ex ante rights assignments is stability, the initial justification itself tends to argue against later modifications. In a somewhat similar way, legislative reversal is much more costly when entitlements have been generally and abstractly defined than when they are determined on the basis of case-by-case balancing. The constitutional requirement to pay just compensation for the legislative taking of private property applies most clearly when the property has been abstractly and broadly defined by common law courts. Under a balancing regime, by contrast, the scope of any private property right is relative: some uses may not be included within the scope of the right because of the harm those uses cause to other private-property-owner users of the shared commons. When put together with the takings doctrine, the conclusion of the preceding analysis must be modified slightly: under particularistic balancing, legislative conflict is less costly to common law losers, but there are fewer (and less wealthy) common law losers; under a general and abstract common law determination of rights, losers have a greater incentive to organize and seek legislative redress, but such legislation will be costlier to obtain.

Case Studies

Although the predictions of this model are testable econometrically, here I present two historical case studies. In each of these, attempts by common law courts to make a general assignment of the property right—an assignment that did not depend on case-by-case inquiry into the relative values of the conflicting uses in a particular location—catalyzed the losers to effectively pursue collective action in seeking legislative reversal of the common law rights determination.

The Conflict between Hydraulic Mining and Farming in California

Robert Kelley's (1959) wonderfully detailed account of the mid-nineteenth-century dispute between miners and farmers competing over rights in tributaries of the Sacramento River strongly confirms my positive theory of the command law and conflict over the commons. As the brief but colorful era of placer mining in the Sierra Nevada foothills ended during the 1850s, new technologies permitted the rapid expansion of hydraulic mining,[16] a process of gold mining. In hydraulic mining, tremendous streams of water were discharged at very high pressure from cannonlike devices called monitors against hills, banks, and other areas where gold-bearing gravel was believed to lie. In this way, entire hillsides were reduced to streams of gravel, sand, and stones and boulders that were then carried through flumes, sluices, and other conduits where the gold was separated out. This process generated massive quantities of debris; indeed, the main technical problem in hydraulic mining (once sufficiently powerful water guns had been designed) was to drain off the waste water containing mine tailings. By the mid-1860s, so many creeks had become completely clogged by tailings that the cost of draining became extremely high—the only solution being to bypass the mountain creeks and discharge directly into the deep canyons of major tributaries of the Sacramento, such as the Bear, Feather and Yuba rivers. Such deep drainage was enormously costly to construct; but by 1870, with vastly improved drilling and water-blasting technology, and statutory authorization of fee-simple patents of mining lands, large quantities of foreign (primarily English) capital were attracted to the hydraulic mining interest. By the mid-1870s, enormous hydraulic mining operations were drawing water from the High Sierra and dumping it as waste water directly into the deep canyons of Sacramento tributaries such as the Yuba. Indeed, by 1879, nine ditch companies owned almost 900 miles of ditches in Nevada County alone (Kelley 1959, 54).

When the mining companies began dumping tailings directly into the river canyons, the downstream farmers and town dwellers were inundated. One of the hydraulic mines that vastly expanded during the period 1870–72 was the Spring Valley mine along the upper reaches of Dry Creek. The mine had a hundred miles of ditches and operated around the clock with the latest equipment. In 1872, a flood of debris from the mine spread downstream, covering farms and orchards as it went, eventually reaching the orchard of Jacob Crum, 8 miles downstream. Crum and some nearby farmers pooled their assets and sued the mining company; but in 1873, the jury found (according to contemporary newspaper accounts) that because so many companies had worked the upstream area (as many as fifty), it was impossible to say which mining company had caused the harm, while "a single day's yield [from the mine] probably amounted to more than the value of every farm damaged by debris" (Kelley 1959, 63). The jury quite clearly engaged in a limited, fact-specific balancing inquiry.

When heavy rains brought even more debris down the river in the winter of 1874, another group of farmers threatened to get a more definite, judicial ruling on their relative rights. Even though he had come out the victor when the balancing test was applied, the president of the Spring Valley Mining Company responded immediately to the threat of renewed litigation by buying up all the land that had been injured by debris and by building a vast and expensive ditch to carry debris to waste lagoons he established on some 21,000 acres that the company purchased in the Sacramento delta. This, according to Kelley, ended the conflict in Butte County, and the Spring Valley mine was not a player in any of the further conflict between miners and farmers (Kelley 1959, 64).

This is precisely the sort of behavior that my model predicts would occur under a particularistic balancing regime: even after one adjudication of relative rights, the threat to initiate another such determination created a strong incentive for private bargaining. The bargaining occurred in the shadow of what might have happened the next time around (rather than being precipitated by a loss the first time). This is precisely what game-theoretic models of bargaining predict will occur in the shadow of an uncertain balancing regime (Johnston, 1995).

Farmers in nearby Yuba and Sutter counties were aware of the success of the

Crum lawsuit. There were a large number of mines operating on the three rivers (the Bear, the Feather, and the Yuba) that converged in those counties; and as the beds of these rivers rose above the surrounding farmlands due to the accumulation of mining debris, farmers spent thousands on levees, channels, and sloughs, and many farmers simply gave up and relocated. It was not, however, until great floods of the Yuba completely inundated the downstream town of Marysville during the winters of both 1875 and 1876 that the downstream farmers took collective action. As my model predicts, when prompted by catastrophic harm, the farmers who convened in Yuba City in 1876 to take action against the mines found litigation to be far too slow and instead opted to petition the state legislature for laws "which would solve the problem in its entirety" (Kelley 1959, 71). Later that year, the legislature discussed two strongly competing reports. One, from the Mining Committee, reported that although $1.1 billion in gold had been mined from the Sierra foothills (over $900,000,000 from hydraulic mines), total damages to farms were not more than $3,000,000; the other, from the Agriculture Committee, couched the question in very general terms, as involving the simple question of whether any man should be allowed to use his own property to injure another (81). Although the farmers won the vote on which report to accept, their legislative proposal (to impose a moratorium on new mines and to require damage payments) was narrowly defeated. Couching the issue again in very general terms—as involving a simple question of whether hydraulic mining would be allowed to operate and injure farmers in the Sacramento—a group of Bear River farmers soon thereafter began a careful and collective effort to get an injunction and damages against nineteen mining and ditch companies in the Bear River basin. This in turn prompted the miners from all over the northern Sierra to form the Hydraulic Miners' Association, to pool information and funds to defend the industry against both legislative and legal action. The lawsuit *Keyes v. Little York Gold Washing & Water Co.* was tried in July 1878. It was widely viewed as a great event—as implicating the general future of the hydraulic mining industry. Lawyers for the mines argued not only that mining generated job and profits and had been responsible for the creation of entire communities, but that the miners had a prior and therefore superior right to dump tailings into the river (108–9). Lawyers for the farmers argued simply that law and custom had to change, that farming was the more profitable activity and should be given the right, to the exclusion of the miners' use.

Unsurprisingly, even before the trial court ruled in *Keyes,* the stark and general formulation of the issues in that case and the prospect of continued costly litigation and legislative conflict prompted the farmers to organize and to form the Anti-Debris Association of Sacramento Valley in August 1878, raising a not inconsiderable initial war chest of $170,000 (Kelley 1959, 116–17). Thus when the trial court ruled in favor of the farmers in March 1879—finding that the miners had no prescriptive right to dump debris into the river, that hydraulic mining was a nuisance and an obstruction to downstream users and subject to injunction because damages could not be ascertained—the prospects for a solution via private bargaining had all but ended. When the town of Marysville on the Yuba began preparations to sue in July 1879, the Hydraulic Miners' Association offered to pay $30,000 or up to half of the cost of work to be done on the city levee and would secure passage of a law that would compel the miners to impound tailings behind dams in the mountains; but the offer was rejected, and the town sued and obtained a permanent injunction (118–19). Having obtained a general common law declaration that the entitlement was theirs, the farmers had no incentive to bargain. By the same token, when later that year the Supreme Court of California reversed the lower court in *Keyes* and ruled that it was not proper to join a whole group of defendants without first showing who was actually responsible for causing the harm (121–22), the miners celebrated the decision as a general death knell to the farmers' litigation efforts, which involved an attack on hydraulic mining as an activity, rather than on particular practices of it. Whereas the prospect of further litigation under the balancing regime had actually spurred a negotiated resolution in the Spring Valley mine controversy, this perception of a general determination of the miners' continuing entitlement put an end to all such private negotiation and spurred further litigation and struggle for legislative resolution.

It was not until 1882 that the farmers finally succeeded against the mines, in the Gold Run case, where the trial judge found that the miners had no prescriptive right to dump into the rivers, that the mining customs did not apply outside the mining locality, and that the dumping was a public nuisance. The court enjoined the operation of the mines pending impoundment of the heavier debris, at which point they could resume operation, for the judge shrank from a consequence so "far-reaching" as to absolutely shut down the mines (Kelley 1959, 215). This victory spurred a number of new lawsuits during 1882, with the farmers continuing to press the issue as a general one involving simply whether hydraulic mining would be permitted to continue. Finally, in 1883, in the *Woodruff* lawsuit, the farmers obtained a judicial ruling that it was proper to join all the defendants who dumped into a particular river because "Defendants claim a common, though not joint, right . . . The final injury is a single one . . . and all defendants cooperate in fact in producing it" (234). With this important intermediate step, the farmers were in a position to obtain what they had so long sought, a final ruling in *Woodruff v. North Bloomfield Gravel Mining Co.* (1884) prohibiting Yuba River hydraulic mining until the company constructed reservoirs and impoundments that would contain the debris.

The defendant North Bloomfield Mining Company, one of the largest mining companies in the state, eventually constructed an impoundment system and began mining again.[17] Remarkably, it took almost ten years of litigation and legislative contest over the general question of whether hydraulic mining could legally operate in California for a method of minimizing harm to the commons to be worked out, the same basic method that had been achieved by private bargaining under threatened particularistic adjudication in the Spring Valley Mining case many years previously. At a time when the use of balancing tests in nuisance law was very controversial (see Bone 1986, 1178–79, 1178 n192), some contemporaneous commentators praised the California courts' refusal to "make a comparison of the value of the conflicting rights," in resolving the conflict between miners and farmers (Knight 1898, 386). However, the history of the conflict between hydraulic mining and farming in California's Sacramento Valley seems strongly at odds with a view that would predict that a general assignment of rights promotes bargaining. It is rather consistent with the central prediction generated by my model: that when contests between competing users of common resources are formulated as simple but very general questions of one-off rights, they trigger legislative conflict rather than promote bargained resolution.

New Industries and New Nuisances in Pennsylvania

Further evidence confirming the predictions of the model is provided by a somewhat better known historical instance in which judges employed balancing tests to resolve conflicting rights in common resources. This is the mid-to-late-nineteenth-century series of nuisance decisions by the Pennsylvania courts. At present, these cases shed only indirect light on the predictions from my model, for I have not yet completed historical research into the pattern of bargaining and legislative activity that took place in reaction to these decisions. The evidence now available is sufficient, however, to show how the theory set forth here promises to shed new light on late-nineteenth-century Pennsylvania nuisance law.

According to Rosen's examination of all reported nuisance decisions in New York, New Jersey, and Pennsylvania decided between 1840 and 1906, injunctions were granted in only 18 percent of the cases in which the courts applied a balancing test, versus 82 percent of the cases when they did not balance. Rosen found significant variation in how the balancing test was applied in her three-state sample: fully 85 percent of the Pennsylvania cases in which injunctions were denied relied on balancing, whereas only about 50 percent of the injunction denials in New York and New Jersey relied on a balancing justification (Rosen 1993, 323–25). Although New York and New Jersey courts came very close to applying a strict liability standard for any material damage, in Pennsylvania, the courts applied a strict standard only to nuisances per se, such as slaughterhouses and rendering plants (329). During the 1860s, 1870s, and 1880s, moreover, Pennsylvania courts limited actual damage to "narrowly defined economic costs, namely pecuniary damage to property and business, and excluded physical and emotional discomfort" (330). The effect of this rule is illustrated by the result in *Price v. Grantz*

(1888), where the court found the illnesses suffered by the plaintiff's family caused by lead and arsenic fumes from the defendant's shot factory to be a "mere trifling annoyance" and a "slight sacrifice" that had to be borne without compensation.

A variety of explanations have been set out for these trends in the late-nineteenth-century Pennsylvania nuisance law. One explanation is political, pointing to the Pennsylvania Republican political machine's close relationship with the big four polluting industries of coal, iron and steel, railroads, and oil and the machine's ability to control judicial elections (Rosen 1993, 359–60). In a somewhat similar explanation, economic models of incentives in litigation (Rubin 1983) have been employed to explain how the bigger stakes of repeat player business litigants may have generated inefficient legal rules when those businesses litigated against small, one-shot plaintiffs with far less at stake in the way that substantive common law rules developed in Pennsylvania. It is, on the other hand, possible to construct an argument for the efficiency of the approach taken by the Pennsylvania courts. For one thing, as economic development slowed, both the Pennsylvania and the New York high courts became more willing to enjoin industrial activities as creating common law nuisances.[18] Even Rosen (1993, 368–69) admits that the judicial shift to enhanced liability was not caused by some political upheaval in Pennsylvania, where the Republican machine was still in control of the judiciary, and the shift didn't mark any decline in the political power of the big polluting industries. It may well have been that as the harm from pollution increased[19] while the cost of abatement fell, common law judges became confident that there were efficient methods of abatement that simply were not being used.

My purpose here is not, in any event, to evaluate the efficiency of late-nineteenth-century Pennsylvania nuisance law, but instead to suggest that both the doctrinal and the positive political-economic significance of those decisions has been misunderstood. Consider, for instance, *Pennsylvania Coal Co. v. Sanderson* (1886), one of the most famous cases of the time, and one that is now viewed by many commentators as doctrinally significant because it introduced the natural use doctrine—under which there was liability for a natural use only if it was conducted negligently or maliciously—into Pennsylvania law (Bone 1986, 1164–65). The Pennsylvania Supreme Court's opinion introducing the natural use doctrine was in fact the fourth opinion by that court in the dispute between the Sandersons and the Pennsylvania Coal Company, a dispute that lasted over a decade. That dispute in fact provides additional evidence for my theory of the political effects of general and abstract versus particularized common law resolution of conflicts between old uses and new uses of the commons.

In 1868, the Sandersons bought a tract of land located within the city limits of Scranton. Meadow Brook ran through the Sanderson property, and it was undisputed that the purity of the brook was a major reason why the Sandersons chose that location. Mr. Sanderson had indeed traced the brook all the way to its source, up the slope of the Lackawana Valley; and by 1870, the Sandersons had finished construction of a home and had dammed the brook to create a fish and ice pond. By 1873, however, the water from the brook had become unfit for domestic use and was too acidic to support fish populations. This deterioration came about because in 1868, around the time the Sandersons were purchasing their land, the Pennsylvania Coal Company began tunnel and shaft mining for anthracite coal on 1,600 acres it owned about three miles above the valley from the Sandersons. As was conventional mining practice at the time,[20] the company pumped the groundwater that percolated into the mines (thereby becoming highly acidic) out into a surface ditch that ran directly into a stream, in this case Meadow Brook. As the scale of the mining operation increased, the quality of the brook declined. The Sandersons sued the company for nuisance, seeking damages.

In its first opinion in the case, the Pennsylvania Supreme Court found for the Sandersons, remanding to the trial court for a finding on damages (*Sanderson v. Pennsylvania Coal Co.* 1878). The defendants argued that the Sandersons' injury was but a "slight inconvenience" or "occasional annoyance," against which the court ought to balance the fact that there were more than one thousand coal mines in Pennsylvania that disposed of percolating water in precisely the same way. The court refused and based its decision on the general, abstract principle that one could not use one's own property so as to effect an "invasion of an established right" of a neighboring landowner without paying damages.

As my theory would predict, this opinion set off a firestorm of controversy. Indeed, after the case was finally ended, it was said that "no case ever arose in Pennsylvania of equal, or greater, importance to the material prosperity of the state" (Gest 1894, 7–8). It was clearly understood that the decision threatened coal mines throughout the state with liability. The second jury trial in the case resulted in a damage award for the Sandersons in the amount of $2,873, a very large figure for the time (Gest 1894, 7). Moreover, given that the Sandersons had since 1875 been relying on water supplied by the city waterworks (and made no claim of an injury to their health), the injury for which they recovered—stream contamination by acidic mine drainage—was one that virtually every riparian owner along every creek fouled by acid mine drainage could claim as well.

The Pennsylvania Coal Company continued to press its case and eventually claimed victory. This victory would probably not have happened at all were it not for a change in the composition of the court: the swing vote in the final decision for the company was provided by a justice who came from a major coal county (Rosen 1993, 364). Moreover, the decision to rehear the case was criticized by the dissenting justices as unnecessary and legally unjustified (see *Pennsylvania Coal Co. v. Sanderson* 1886).

Significantly, the final majority opinion finding for the company began by noting that 30 million tons of anthracite coal and 70 million tons of bituminous coal were mined in Pennsylvania and that whatever "remedy [Mrs. Sanderson] may have in this case, or in any other form, in law or in equity, is the right and remedy of . . . all other riparian owners throughout the Commonwealth" (*Pennsylvania Coal Co. v. Sanderson* 1886, 144–45). The majority clearly viewed the case as involving not a balancing of the Sandersons' harm and that particular mine's value, but as a general question of the rights to mine coal as then conducted against the generalized rights of downstream riparians. As the court reasoned, "if the responsibility of the operator of a mine is extended to injuries of the character complained of, the consequence must be that mining cannot be conducted, except by the *general consent of all the parties affected*" (145) (emphasis supplied). In the court's view, regardless of the remedy sought by the Sandersons (damages), a liability finding in their favor would threaten the operation of the mines.

   Given that the Sandersons had long since switched to city-supplied water for domestic use, the final damage award (of almost $3,000) in *Sanderson* (1886) may well have actually been more akin to the sort of punitive sanction imposed on a party violating an injunction than to a compensatory award. This is to say that the eventual majority may have been correct that a general riparian right to awards of this magnitude may have caused at least a temporary shutdown in coal mining operations. Given the general formulation of the riparian right (as a general right, which did not involve close inquiry into the actual harm suffered by any particular riparian), every affected riparian would have had a right to damages. On my theory, by putting all coal companies at risk in this way, the first *Sanderson* decision should have provoked coal companies to seek legislative reversal. Although the evidence I have found to date does not conclusively show that this did indeed occur, it does show a pattern of intense legislative activity by coal companies in Pennsylvania at just this period. In 1863, the Pennsylvania legislature passed a statute that permitted owners of swampy land to extend agricultural drains over the lands of their neighbors, provided they paid a set amount in compensation (Gest 1894, 12). Apparently during the 1870s, this act was extended to several coal-producing counties to authorize the "drainage and ventilating of coal and other mines." In addition, the Anthracite Coal Mine Act of 1885 (the Lackawana Valley is a source of anthracite coal) provided that a mine owner could make openings or outlets under, through, or upon adjoining lands for mine drainage and ventilation (12).

   Thus while the Pennsylvania Coal Company continued to litigate against the Sandersons, the coal industry in Pennsylvania was busily at work seeking legislative clarification of their rights to use the commonly held streams and creeks of the Commonwealth for mine drainage. The pattern in Pennsylvania—the judicial proclamation that one type of commons user (riparian owners) had a general common law right to be free of harm caused by another type of user (coal mines), followed by an immediate attempt to get legislative reversal of rights—parallels the pattern in California.

CONCLUSION

The immediately preceding case studies suggest that if I am right about the effects of generalized versus particularistic common law rights, then rational and strategically minded state court judges should take those effects into account in deciding how to cast the rights they create. If, for instance, judges wish to stay in the game, as it were, and avoid having their decisions become the focus of legislative conflict, then they ought to prefer the particularistic approach. Conversely, by making a general determination—for instance, that no right to be free of some widespread sort of harm exists—then judges would tend to throw the ball into the legislature's court.

I do not have the space here to fully develop and apply such a model. I do hope, however, that the model I have developed and applied here will go some way toward demonstrating the importance of putting the common law in a broader context in which legislation is an alternative to common law resolution. Only in this context can one understand why bargaining around a common law result often does not occur. Especially when the common law imposes a very general injunctive remedy and declares continued production illegal, it greatly increases the relative benefit of political conflict. This insight is central to understanding how the common law's treatment of rights in the environmental commons has shaped subsequent environmental legislation.

NOTES

1. See, generally, Anderson and Simmons (1993); Ostrom (1990); McCay and Acheson (1987).

2. In more formal terms, exploitation of any such resource occurs until the point where the average product from such use has been equated to the opportunity cost of exploitation, which with declining marginal product means that marginal product has been driven below marginal cost. This condition holds regardless of whether the resource is renewable. See Cheung (1987); Berck (1979).

3. A comprehensive though already somewhat dated bibliography of such studies is provided by Martin (1992). Some economists, see, for example, Johnson and Libecap (1982, 1007), are skeptical that local collectives are able to efficiently manage common resources. However, they invariably point to the failure to have complete contractual allocation of rights in the commons. But the relevant comparison is not with theoretically unobtainable complete contracts, but rather with alternative regulatory institutions, such as bureaucratic control or unregulated private ownership.

4. For a thorough description of the very detailed village bylaws, see Ault (1972).

5. As argued by Sethi and Somanathan (1996), citing Ostrom (1990).

6. The requirement that equilibria be subgame perfect rules out incredible strategies—

threatened punishment for deviation from cooperative play that are not themselves actually optimal to carry out when the time comes to punish. For a more formal definition of subgame perfection, see van Damme (1991, 106–117); Binmore (1992, 46–51).

7. Michihiro Kandori (1992) has shown that in large-population games where players are randomly drawn to play one round of the Prisoner's Dilemma Game, cooperation can be sustained as an equilibrium provided that the population is not too large, the players' information about past behavior is sufficiently good, and players are sufficiently patient.

8. See, for instance, Boehm (1997).

9. See the discussion in Kurlansky (1997).

10. A result that is established in Seth and Somanathan (1996).

11. For an elaboration on this point, see Anderlini and Felli (1997).

12. The obvious potential for multiple equilibria in games that involve such a choice between productive versus expropriative activity has been explored in a number of recent papers, such as Skaperdas (1992); Hirshleifer (1995); Grossman and Kim (1995); Rajan and Zingales (1995).

13. This is tacitly to assume that the court has not made a rights determination that might trigger the just compensation requirement.

14. This, of course, provides a rationale for the preclusive effect of class action lawsuits: the probability of a settlement with one group of plaintiffs is almost surely lower when there are others with an unknown number of similar claims waiting in the wings.

15. Buchanan and Faith (1981) likewise develop an argument for the potential inefficiency of the injunctive remedy, but their argument hinges on the assumption that entrepreneurs know more about the harm that their activity will cause and are more optimistic that it will be low than are victims of the harm, who are both ill informed and pessimistic about the magnitude of harm. It would seem much more plausible that new users are asymmetrically well informed and optimistic about the value of their activity, while old users are asymmetrically well informed about the harm they will suffer and they think it will be large. My theory does not rely on any such story of bargaining breakdown, but on the relative value of conflict versus production under an injunction.

16. I rely on Samuel Knight (1898) for this succinct description of hydraulic mining as it was then practiced.

17. And they even won a suit by the United States seeking to enjoin its operations on the ground that its operation continued to impair the navigability of the Yuba (*U.S. v. North Bloomfield Gravel Mining Co.* (1892).

18. *Sullivan v. Jones and Laughlin Steel Co.* (1904) and *Whalen v. The Union Bag and Paper Company* (1913). These cases have been understood as restoring a regime of strict liability, which then remained the rule in both states until replaced by balancing in *Waschak v. Moffat* (1954) and *Boomer v. Atlantic Cement Co.* (1970). As I discuss in the following text, it is not clear that these common characterizations of balancing versus strict liability and vice versa are functionally accurate.

19. According to Rosen (1993, 371–72), early-twentieth-century estimates put the annual harm in Pittsburgh at around $10 million.

20. Bone (1986, 1162). Moreover, as Bone (1165) notes, the final opinion in the case stressed that pumping was the only way to remove water, that removal of mine water was necessary to mine coal, and that its method of discharging water was the only economically viable way to mine coal.

REFERENCES

Acheson, James M. 1988. *The Lobster Gangs of Maine.* Hanover: University Press of New England.

Anderlini, Luca, and Leonardo Felli. 1997. Costly Coasian Contracts. *CARESS Working Paper* No. 97-11, University of Pennsylvania.

Anderson, Terry L., and Randy T. Simmons, eds. 1993. *The Political Economy of Customs and Culture: Informal Solutions to the Commons Problem.* Lanham, MD: Rowman & Littlefield.

Ault, W. O. 1972. *Open-Field Farming in Medieval England: A Study of Village By-Laws.* New York: Barnes and Noble.

Berck, Peter. 1979. Open Access and Extinction. *Econometrica* 47(4): 877–82.

Binmore, Ken. 1992. *Fun and Games: A Text on Game Theory.* Lexington, MA: D.C. Heath.

Boehm, Christopher. 1997. Impact of the Human Egalitarian Syndrome on Darwinian Selection Mechanics. *The American Naturalist* 150(Supplement): S100–S121.

Bone, Robert G. 1986. Normative Theory and Legal Doctrine in American Nuisance Law: 1850 to 1920. *Southern California Law Review* 59(6):1101–226.

Bosselman, Fred P. 1996. Limitations Inherent in the Title to Wetlands at Common Law. *Stanford Environmental Law Journal* 15(2): 247–337.

Buchanan, James M., and Roger L. Faith. 1981. Entrepreneurship and the Internalization of Externalities. *Journal of Law and Economics* 24(1): 95–120.

Calabresi, Guido, and A. Douglas Melamed. 1972. Property Rules, Liability Rules, and Inalienability: One View of the Cathedral. *Harvard Law Review* 85(6): 1089–129.

Cheung, Steven N.S. 1987. Common Property Rights. In *The New Palgrave: A Dictionary of Economics*, vol. 1, ed. John Eatwell, Murray Milgate, and Peter Newman. New York: Stockton Press.

Coase, Ronald H. 1960. The Problem of Social Cost. *Journal of Law and Economics* 3(1): 1–44.

Eckart, Wolfgang. 1985. On the Land Assembly Problem. *Journal of Urban Economics* 18(3): 364–79.

Ellickson, Robert C. 1991. *Order without Law.* Cambridge, MA: Harvard University Press.

Gest, John Marshall. 1894. The Natural Use of Land: Part I. *American Law Register* (New Series) 33: 1–18.

Grossman, Herschel I., and Minseong Kim. 1995. Swords or Plowshares? A Theory of Security of Claims to Property. *Journal of Political Economy* 103(6): 1275–88.

Hirshleifer, Jack. 1995. Anarchy and Its Breakdown. *Journal of Political Economy* 103(1): 26–52.

Hoskins, W. G., and L. Dudley Stamp. 1963. *The Common Lands of England and Wales*. London: Collins.

Johnson, Ronald N., and Gary D. Libecap. 1982. Contracting Problems and Regulation: The Case of the Fishery. *American Economic Review* 72(5): 1005–22.

Johnston, Jason Scott. 1995. Bargaining under Rules Versus Standards. *Journal of Law, Economics, and Organization* 11(2): 256–81.

Kandori, Michihiro. 1992. Social Norms and Community Enforcement. *Review of Economic Studies* 59(1): 63–80.

Kelley, Robert L. 1959. *Gold Versus Grain: The Hydraulic Mining Controversy in California's Sacramento Valley. A Chapter in the Decline of the Concept of Laissez Faire*. Glendale, CA: Arthur H. Clark.

Knight, Samuel. 1898. Federal Control of Hydraulic Mining. *Yale Law Journal* 7(9): 385–92.

Kurlansky, Mark. 1997. *Cod: A Biography of the Fish That Changed the World*. New York: Walker.

Libecap, Gary D. 1989. *Contracting for Property Rights*. New York: Cambridge University Press.

Mailath, George J., and Andrew Postlewaite. 1990. Asymmetric Information Bargaining Problems with Many Agents. *Review of Economic Studies* 57(3): 351–68.

Martin, Fenton. 1992. Common Pool Resources and Collective Action: A Bibliography. Workshop in Political Theory and Policy Analysis, Indiana University, Bloomington.

McCay, Bonnie J., and James M. Acheson, eds. 1987. *The Question of the Commons: The Culture and Ecology of Communal Resources*. Tucson: University of Arizona Press.

McCurdy, Charles W. 1975. Stephen J. Field and Public Land Law Development in California, 1850–1866: A Case Study of Judicial Resource Allocation in Nineteenth Century America. *Law and Society Review* 10(2): 235–66.

McNeely, Jeffrey A. 1991. Common Property Resource Management or Government Ownership: Improving the Conservation of Biological Resources. *International Relations* 10(3): 211–25.

Ostrom, Elinor. 1990. *Governing the Commons: The Evolution of Institutions for Collective Action*. New York: Cambridge University Press.

Rajan, Raghuram G., and Luigi Zingales. 1995. The Tyranny of the Inefficient: An Enquiry into the Adverse Consequences of Power Struggles. *NBER Working Paper* 5396. Cambridge, MA: National Bureau of Economic Research, December.

Rob, Rafael. 1989. Pollution Claim Settlements under Private Information. *Journal of Economic Theory* 47(2): 307–33.

Rose, Carol. 1986. The Comedy of the Commons: Custom, Commerce, and Inherently Public Property. *University of Chicago Law Review* 53(3): 711–87.

———. 1990. Energy and Efficiency in the Realignment of Common-Law Water Rights. *Journal of Legal Studies* 19(2): 261–97.

Rosen, Christine. 1993. Differing Perceptions of the Value of Pollution Abatement across Time and Place: Balancing Doctrine in Pollution Nuisance Law, 1840–1906. *Law and History Review* 11(2): 303–82.

Rubin, Paul H. 1983. *Business Firms and the Common Law: The Evolution of Efficient Rules.* New York: Praeger.

Sethi, Rajiv, and E. Somanathan. 1996. The Evolution of Social Norms in Common Property Resource Use. *American Economic Review* 86(4): 766–88.

Skaperdas, Stergios. 1992. Cooperation, Conflict, and Power in the Absence of Property Rights. *American Economic Review* 82(4): 720–39.

Stiglitz, Joseph, and Andrew Weiss. 1981. Credit Rationing with Imperfect Information. *American Economic Review* 71(2): 393–410.

Thompson, E. P. 1991. *Customs in Common.* London: Merlin Press.

van Damme, Eric. 1991. *Stability and Perfection of Nash Equilibria.* 2d. ed. Berlin: Springer-Verlag.

Wiggins, Steven N., and Gary D. Libecap. 1985. Oil Field Unitization: Contractual Failure in the Presence of Imperfect Information. *American Economic Review* 75(3): 368–85.

CASES CITED

Boomer v. Atlantic Cement Co., 26 N.Y. 2d 219, 257 N.E. 2d 870, 309 N.Y.S. 2d 312 (Ct. App. N.Y. 1970)

Keyes v. Little York Gold Washing & Water Co., 53 Cal. 724 (1879)

Pennsylvania Coal Co. v. Sanderson, 113 Pa. 126, 6 A. 453 (1886)

Price v. Grantz, 118 Pa. 402, 11 A. 794, 4 Am. St. Rep. 601 (1888)

Sanderson v. Pennsylvania Coal Co., 86 Pa. 401 (1878)

Sanderson v. Pennsylvania Coal Co., 102 Pa. 370 (1883)

Sullivan v. Jones and Laughlin Steel Co., 208 Pa. 540, 57 A. 1065 (1904)

United States v. North Bloomfield Gravel Mining Co., 53 F. 625 (1892)

Waschak v. Moffat, 379 Pa. 441, 109 A.2d 310 (1954)

Whalen v. The Union Bag and Paper Co., 208 N.Y. 1, 101 N.E. 805 (1913)

Woodruff v. North Bloomfield Gravel Mining Co., 18 F. 753 (1884)

10

On Being Regulated in Foresight versus Being Judged in Hindsight

Jeffrey J. Rachlinski

Where were industry's lobbyists? Between 1970 and 1976, Congress passed statutes regulating air pollution, pesticides, drinking water, toxic substances, and hazardous waste disposal (Percival et al. 1996). These statutes began imposing huge costs on industry; in fact, the current cost of complying with these statutes comprises over 2 percent of the gross national product (Stewart 1993). Despite these costs, Congressional support for passing environmental laws was strong and widespread. As public choice theory observes, concentrated interest groups, such as the industries targeted by environmental statutes, tend to win legislative battles over the diffuse interests of the general public (Farber and Frickey 1991). The tremendous Congressional support for these statutes is therefore difficult to explain (Farber 1992). Industry's lobbyists could not merely have been asleep at the switch; industry must have also supported, or at least acquiesced in, the creation of these statutes.

Somehow, industry in the early 1970s must have believed that it could profit from the creation of this expensive regulatory regime. A comparison of the two basic approaches to controlling pollution, regulatory systems and liability systems, suggests one key benefit that this new regulatory system might have provided for industry.[1] A *regulatory system* attempts to set and to enforce specific standards of conduct, whereas a *liability system* mandates no specific conduct but allows private parties to recover damages for harm caused by certain conduct. Before the 1970s, pollution control was implemented largely by a liability system along with a hodgepodge of state and local regulations (Goklany 2000). Before the mid-1960s, lawsuits against industry were uncommon, but by the end of the decade, industry began to face a growing threat of significant environmental litigation (Green 1998). Individuals, newly organized public-interest environmental groups, and state attorneys general had begun to bring expensive environmental lawsuits against polluters (Turner 1998). In the face of this rising tide of litigation, regulatory approaches to pollution, particularly uniform federal regulation, became increasingly attractive to industry. A system of regulatory standards administered by a centralized agency began to seem much less expensive to industry than the growing costs of the liability system administered by the courts or the uneven topology of state regulations.

Even though the federal environmental statutes of the 1970s did not preempt the liability system, industry stood to benefit from the new regulatory regime. Because of a psychological phenomenon known as the hindsight bias, polluters are particularly vulnerable to losing environmental lawsuits. The *hindsight bias* refers to the tendency for people to believe that accidents were more predictable than was actually the case. Consequently, when pollution causes harm and results in a lawsuit, defendants have a hard time showing that their decision not to undertake more pollution prevention measures was reasonable. As a result, even defendants who took reasonable precautions against causing harm are apt to be found liable. leaving many polluters strictly liable for any harm they cause. The existence of authoritative regulations governing pollution control, however, creates a defense against the hindsight bias, thereby lowering the costs of these lawsuits to industry.

Regulations reduce not only industry's liability for pollution, but also the social costs of a liability-based approach to pollution. Among the three possible systems to control pollution—pure regulation, pure liability, or a combination of the two—the combined system that emerged from the 1970s is arguably the most efficient of the three. The first part of this chapter discusses the benefits for industry of this system, as a partial explanation for why industry supported it. The chapter then reviews the social costs and benefits of each system.

REGULATION VERSUS LIABILITY FROM INDUSTRY'S PERSPECTIVE

Although regulatory approaches to environmental quality differ in many ways from liability approaches, few of these differences reveal any advantages of one system over the other for industry. Consideration of the hindsight bias, however, demonstrates that industry is better off under a regulatory approach than under a liability system. Furthermore, an analysis of the influence of the bias on the liability system also reveals that the addition of the regulatory system to a liability system would benefit industry. Although other factors might also have accounted for Congress's ability to pass environmental statutes in the 1970s, the impact of the hindsight bias on the liability system provides at least one reason for industry to have supported these statutes.

Regulating Safety versus Allocating Liability in Environmental Law

Determining why industry would prefer either a regulatory or a liability approach to pollution control is difficult because both systems arguably have the same goals. The regulatory approaches commonly taken to control pollution consist of creating a governmental body that either identifies and enforces pollution-control measures (a command-and-control system) or identifies and enforces emissions levels (a performance-based system). A liability approach to pollution control consists of giving individuals the right to obtain compensation from polluters, either for all harm that pollution causes (a strict liability system) or for the harm caused by the polluter's failure to undertake reasonable pollution-control measures (a negligence system). Both systems are designed to create incentives for polluters to undertake pollution-control measures that cost less than the cost of the pollution that the measures prevent, that is, socially efficient pollution-control measures.

The Costs of the Liability System for Industry

Before the passage of the environmental statutes of the 1970s, pollution was governed primarily by a combination of common law liability along with some state and local regulation. The common law provides four basic theories of liability for pollution: negligence, nuisance, trespass, and strict liability. For the most part, each theory incorporates a cost-benefit approach to liability. Polluters are liable for harm that could have been prevented by implementing socially efficient pollution-control measures. Polluters that implement these measures are unlikely to be held liable for any harm caused by their activities. In effect, despite some rhetoric to the contrary, the common law rarely holds polluters strictly liable for the costs of their pollution.

Consider the *negligence* theory. A plaintiff can recover under a negligence theory if he or she can prove that a defendant had a legal duty to him or her, that was breached, thereby causing damage (American Law Institute 1965, § 281; Keeton et al. 1984, § 30). The kind of duty depends on the relationship between the parties, but in most cases of pollution a defendant must avoid imposing an "unreasonable" risk of injury. Courts assess the reasonableness of risks by balancing the costs and the benefits of the defendant's activities. An *unreasonable risk* is one in which the magnitude of an injury discounted for the likelihood of its occurrence exceeds the cost of precautions that would avoid the injury (American Law Institute 1965, § 291). A defendant that takes all reasonable precautions against causing harm to others is not liable. The kind of cost-benefit assessment that is explicit in a negligence case is implicit in the other theories of liability for pollution.

Nuisance actions, the "common law backbone of modern environmental . . . law" (Rodgers 1994), incorporate a similar cost-benefit analysis. A nuisance consists of an "interference with the use and enjoyment of land" (American Law Institute 1965, § 822). The law of nuisance has been called "an impenetrable jungle" (Keeton et al. 1984, § 86: 616), but liability in a nuisance action essentially depends on a comparison of the cost of pollution prevention to its benefits. To be actionable under a nuisance theory, a polluter's interference must be "substantial and unreasonable" (American Law Institute 1965, § 821F). As Landes and Posner (1987, 49) put it, "where the nuisance causes substantial damage that exceeds the cost of eliminating it and where, moreover, the defendant (injurer) can eliminate the nuisance at a lower cost than the plaintiff (victim)," a defendant is liable to the plaintiff. A polluter that takes cost-effective pollution-control measures is unlikely to be liable for any harm caused by the pollution that nevertheless occurs.

For the most part, *trespass* actions in environmental law also include a comparison of the costs and the benefits of pollution prevention measures. Because a trespass action essentially allows for recovery for any physical invasion of property, it looks like polluters are strictly liable for any trespass (American Law Institute 1965, § 158). Historically, however, trespass actions in environmental law have been difficult to establish. Courts traditionally have not considered airborne contaminants, including odors, to constitute physical invasions, and, therefore, these intrusions could not support a trespass action (Keeton et al. 1984, § 13:71). Courts that have considered airborne contaminants to be a trespass have also required proof of substantial harm and incorporated a cost-benefit analysis into the elements of the cause of action.[2]

Finally, the common law holds anyone engaged in an "ultrahazardous" activity *strictly liable* for any harm that the activity causes (American Law Institute 1965, § 520). Courts have considered some activities that create significant pollution to be ultrahazardous, particularly the storage of hazardous wastes (Keeton et al. 1984, § 78:552). To establish that an activity is ultrahazardous, however, a plaintiff must demonstrate that it is an "abnormal" activity that cannot be undertaken safely (Keeton et al. 1984, § 78:551). Ultrahazardous activities, therefore, are undertakings that fail a meta-judgment that their costs always outweigh their benefits, regardless of how they are undertaken.

In sum, under the common law liability system, polluters are liable for any harm that could be prevented with cost-effective measures. If the cost of pollution exceeds the cost of prevention, then a polluter is liable, but not otherwise. This system gives potential defendants the incentive to take precisely the socially optimal level of precautions against harm.[3] Polluters that respond properly to this incentive should take the efficient level of care. If they do, the cost of this system to polluters consists only of the cost of taking all socially efficient precautions. A system of strict liability would likewise create incentives for polluters to take socially efficient precautions (Shavell 1980). Strict liability would be more expensive for polluters, however, because they would have to pay for all harm that their activities cause, regardless of whether they were negligent.

The Costs of the Regulatory Approach for Industry

A pure regulatory system (meaning one that completely supplants a liability system) that adopts the goal of enforcing socially efficient pollution-control technologies or emissions standards, at first glance appears to impose the same costs on industry as a system of liability for negligence. If a regulatory agency balances the costs and the benefits of pollution-control technologies, then industry has the incentive to adopt these precautions and no incentive to do any more than this. Regulatory approaches, however, are criticized for being too expensive: either because they are inflexible or because they require implementing an excess of precautions (Ackerman and Stewart 1985). A regulation that applies in all places at all times is apt to be too stringent in some places and not stringent enough in others (Shavell 1984). Inflexibility, however, is a social problem. So long as regulations do not, on average, require more than a reasonable level of care, then industry as a whole is as well off under a regulatory system as under the common law liability system. Regulations only make industry worse off if they consistently require an excess of precautions.

For the most part, the regulatory system adopted by Congress in the 1970s, does not deliberately aspire to set standards that are inefficiently high. Most of the federal pollution-control statutes require that the Environmental Protection Agency (EPA) incorporate the costs of pollution control into the process of setting pollution-control standards. The Clean Air Act, for example, requires the EPA to consider cost when setting performance standards for stationary sources of the most common air pollutants.[4] Although the Clean Air Act did not originally include cost considerations in the setting of standards for other hazardous air pollutants, the 1990 amendments added cost to the factors that the EPA must consider (Percival et al. 1996). In fact, substantial industry opposition prevented the EPA from promulgating standards successfully under the pre-1990 system (Dwyer 1990). Similarly, the Clean Water Act requires that the EPA consider cost when setting standards for water pollution permits[5]. The one prominent exception is hazardous waste disposal. The federal statute governing hazardous waste disposal, the Resource Conservation and Recovery Act (RCRA), requires the EPA to set disposal standards that protect "health and the environment," without regard to cost.[6] Hazardous waste disposal, however, is also the one type of pollution for which the common law often provides strict liability. Industry therefore would appear to have little reason to prefer a liability system over the regulatory system that Congress adopted.

The Costs of a Combined Regulatory and Liability System

The system that Congress ultimately adopted, however, was not a pure regulatory system. Congress retained the existing system of environmental liability. The Clean Air Act, the Clean Water Act, and RCRA all contain "savings clauses" that preserve common law liability actions.[7] In the case of water pollution, the Supreme Court has explicitly held that although the passage of the Clean Water Act preempted federal common law liability for interstate pollution (*City of Milwaukee v. Illinois* 1981), it preserved state common law liability for such actions (*International Paper Co. v. Ouellette* 1987).

Even in this combined scheme, if all functions well, industry should be able to take the socially optimal level of precautions and incur no further costs. The combined system, however, makes it less likely that all will function well. Regulations effectively set a minimum of pollution control; any facility that fails to comply with this minimum risks significant criminal and civil sanctions. If the regulations are too high, then industry will be forced to pay for the excess cost of unnecessary pollution-control technology. If the regulations are too low, however, industry cannot simply comply with the lesser standards because they also face common law liability. A court could also mistakenly hold liable in a common law action a polluter that complied with regulations mandating socially efficient precautions. In short, the combined system creates two opportunities for an excess of regulation. Even if industry might have been indifferent to a choice between a pure regulatory system and a pure liability system, it seems as if it should have vigorously opposed the combined system that Congress ultimately adopted.

Regulation and liability, however, are not a static combination; they interact. In the common law, the failure to comply with a health-and-safety regulation is per se evidence of negligence (American Law Institute 1965, § 286). Thus, absent an excuse, a polluter that fails to comply with the regulations promulgated pursuant to the environmental statutes will almost certainly be liable for any harm that the resulting pollution causes. Compliance with a health regulation or a safety regulation is also evidence, albeit not conclusive evidence, that a polluter was not negligent (American Law Institute 1965, § 288C). Thus, a polluter that complies with the environmental statutes will have a much greater chance of being found not negligent. Regulatory compliance, therefore, could be of some benefit to industry. Determining how beneficial it is, however, requires a closer analysis of the liability system.

The Hindsight Bias and Environmental Disputes

A properly functioning system of liability for pollution depends on reasonably accurate, unbiased determinations of whether conduct was negligent. The liability system, however, incorporates biases in judgment that cloud these determinations. Once these biases are accounted for, the benefits of the regulatory system for industry become clearer.

The Hindsight Bias

People overestimate the predictability of past events, a phenomenon that cognitive psychologists refer to as the *hindsight bias* (Fischhoff 1975; Hawkins and Hastie 1990; Rachlinski 1998). As one psychologist described the effect: "In hindsight, people consistently exaggerate what could have been anticipated in foresight. They not only tend to view what has happened as having been inevitable but also to view it as having appeared 'relatively inevitable' before it happened. People believe that others should have been able to anticipate events much better than was actually the case" (Fischhoff 1982, 341). In short, hindsight vision is 20/20.

Psychologists have conducted more than one hundred experiments that demonstrate the existence of the hindsight bias (Christensen-Szalanski and Willham 1991). In one of the original studies of the bias, Baruch Fischhoff presented subjects with a brief account of the circumstances leading up to a war between the British and the Nepalese Gurkhas in the early nineteenth century (Fischhoff 1975). The account included a description of the advantages and the disadvantages held by each side. Fischhoff informed the subjects that the war had four possible outcomes: British victory, Gurkha victory, stalemate with no peace treaty, or stalemate with a peace treaty. Four groups of subjects were told that one of the four outcomes had actually occurred. Each subject was then asked to estimate the probability that he or she would have assigned to each outcome had he or she not been told of the actual outcome. A fifth group of subjects was not given any outcome and was asked merely to estimate the probability of each of the four outcomes. The results showed clear evidence of a hindsight bias. Subjects who were told of an outcome rated the outcome as more probable than subjects who were not given an outcome and subjects who were given a different outcome. In a similar version of the experiment, subjects were asked to estimate the response of subjects in the fifth condition who were not given an outcome; these subjects provided similar results.

The hindsight bias has proven remarkably robust. Dozens of studies have replicated the findings in Fischhoff's British-Gurkha study with a different variation on the question used to elicit the probability estimates and with different materials (Rachlinski 1998). Furthermore, psychologists have shown that people even tend to misremember their own predictions of past events. For example, in one study, experimenters asked subjects to estimate the likelihoods of various outcomes in the trial of the four police officers charged in the beating of Rodney King just before the verdict was announced (Gilbertson 1994). Ten days later, the experimenters asked the same subjects to recall their estimates. Many subjects remembered their actual estimates; but subjects that could not reported inflated estimates of the likelihood of the actual outcome. This bias occurred even though the subjects knew that the experimenters had recorded their original responses.

The hindsight bias has proven difficult to avoid. Psychologists studying cognitive biases in judgment usually manage to develop successful debiasing techniques—ways in which a decision maker can avoid the bias. The hindsight bias, however, has proven resistant to all debiasing techniques. This failure has arisen because the bias results not merely from an inability to suppress or to ignore knowledge of the outcome, but from the natural tendency to use outcome knowledge to make further inferences. For example, subjects in the British-Gurkha study who were told that the British had won learned more than just this outcome. They learned things about colonial warfare in general (Wasserman, Lempert, and Hastie 1991). They may have concluded, for example, that the advantages that the British had over the Gurkhas (better weapons and training) are more important in such conflicts than the Gurkha advantages (better knowledge of the terrain and higher motivation). When asked to estimate the probability of a British victory, these subjects may have ignored the outcome, but they relied on their new belief that better weapons and training are more important than knowledge of the terrain and higher motivation. These inferences then induced them to make higher estimates for the probability of the known outcome.

In more general terms, because ignoring known outcomes is unnatural, successful debiasing techniques will be difficult to develop. It is normal for people to integrate new information into their existing store of knowledge and to use it to make future predictions. When assessing the predictability of past events, however, the outcome must be ignored. Perhaps because such judgments are so uncommon and unnatural, people have problems making them accurately.

Hindsight Bias and the Law

A courtroom might be the one place where determining the predictability of past events is common. In all manner of cases, from securities fraud to auto accidents, the law requires judges and juries to determine what people knew or should have known about the likely consequences of their actions. Determining which outcomes were predictable is a fundamental component of assigning legal liability.

Studies of the hindsight bias have demonstrated that it influences judgments of legal liability. For example, one study compared subjects randomly assigned either to decide in foresight whether a defendant should take a precaution against flooding or to judge in hindsight whether a decision not to take the same precaution was negligent (Kamin and Rachlinski 1995). In foresight, the subjects listened to evidence on the costs and the benefits of the precaution. They learned that the precaution had an annual cost of $100,000 but would completely eliminate any likelihood of a flood that would cause $1,000,000 in damage to a nearby bakery. Most of the evidence related to the probability that the flood would occur. Subjects had to estimate this probability to decide whether the precaution should be taken. Subjects judging liability in hindsight were told that the precaution had not been taken and that the $1,000,000 flood had occurred. They then reviewed the same evidence on the probability of the flood that the foresight subjects reviewed and decided whether the precaution should have been taken. In foresight, 76 percent of the subjects concluded that the flood was so unlikely that the precaution was unnecessary. In hindsight, 57 percent of the subjects concluded that the flood was so likely that the failure to take the precaution was negligent.

The influence of the hindsight bias on judgments of liability has been replicated twice. LaBine and LaBine showed that the hindsight bias influences judgments of the liability of psychiatrists for violence committed by their patients (LaBine and LaBine 1996). In foresight, subjects rated such violence as unlikely, but in hindsight, subjects held psychiatrists liable for failing to prevent it. Hastie demonstrated that the bias influences the determination of whether a defendant was reckless for failing to undertake safety precautions (Hastie 1998). In this study, subjects in foresight determined that the failure to close a potentially dangerous set of railroad track was reasonable; in hindsight, subjects found that the failure to close the same track was reckless.

The hindsight bias makes it much more difficult for tort defendants to convince judges and juries that their actions were reasonable. The bias influences a critical component of the negligence calculation: the likelihood that an adverse outcome would result from the defendant's conduct. As Judge Learned Hand described the negligence calculation: "If the probability [of an accident] be called P; the injury, L; and the burden [of taking a precaution that would avoid the accident] B; liability depends on whether B is less than L multiplied by P" (*United States v. Carroll Towing* 1947, 173). The *Restatement (Second) of Torts* tracks Judge Hand's definition of negligence closely (American Law Institute 1965, § 291). Although judges and juries are supposed to ignore the known outcome in determining the probability of an adverse outcome (Keeton et al. 1984, § 31:170, and n. 15), the hindsight bias makes this impossible. Judges and juries will inevitably inflate the likelihood of an adverse outcome in hindsight.

As a consequence of the hindsight bias, the application of a negligence standard results in a kind of strict liability (Rachlinski 1998). Under a negligence rule, defendants are not supposed to be liable for the harm that their actions caused, so long as they took reasonable precautions. Because of the hindsight bias, however, defendants who take all reasonable precautions will nevertheless be found liable. Defendants who take an excess of precautions could still be exonerated, because the hindsight bias only increases the perceived probability of an adverse outcome; it does not automatically cause defendants to be found liable. Defendants who come close to the line dividing negligence from reasonable care, however, are apt to be held liable. In effect, negligence judged in hindsight actually resembles strict liability and is perhaps best described as "quasi-strict liability" (Rachlinski 1998, 597).

Hindsight Bias and Environmental Liability

Industries that create risks of environmental harm can expect to face this quasi-strict liability system. From industry's perspective, the hindsight bias will have two undesirable consequences. First, the bias could convert the negligence system into a strict liability system, leaving industry liable for any harm pollution causes. Second, industry might, depending on the relationships between the cost of precautions, the probability of an accident, and the magnitude of the hindsight bias, take an excess of precautions to avoid liability. Thus, under a negligence system influenced by the hindsight bias, industry will either pay more in damages or undertake more precautions than they would under the application of an unbiased negligence standard.

Table 10.1   Hypothetical Relationship between Precautions and Costs

			Total Cost to Facility			
1 *Level of* *Precautions*	*2* *Cost of* *Precaution*	*3* *Probability* *of an* *Accident*	*4* *Strict* *Liability*	*5* *Negligence* *(no bias)*	*6* *Negligence* *(.20 bias)*	*7* *Negligence* *(.08 bias)*
1	0	.50	50*	50*	50*	50*
2	10	.30	40*	40*	40*	40*
3	20	.15	35*	20	35*	35*
4	30	.10	40*	30	40*	30
5	40	.09	49*	40	40	40

Note: * indicates that the facility will be liable for any damages.

The example described in table 10.1 documents this problem. Table 10.1 depicts the cost structure that the legal system imposes on an imaginary facility that accepts hazardous wastes for permanent impoundment. The facility has a choice of five different levels of precautions that it can take against an accidental release of hazardous waste (including no precautions). Columns 2 and 3 describe the cost of each level of precautions and the likelihood of a release at each level of precaution. A release would be a discrete event that would cause 100 units of damage. Given these circumstances, level 3 is the socially optimal level of care. The marginal cost of moving from level 2 to level 3 is only 10 units, whereas the expected savings is 15 units; therefore, level 2 is suboptimal. Level 4 is excessive, however, as moving from level 3 to level 4 costs 10 units, but it saves only an expected 5 units.

In table 10.1, columns 4 through 7 document the cost to the facility of each level of care under four different circumstances. The total cost to the facility is the sum of the cost of any precautions taken and any amount of compensation that the facility must pay in the event of an accidental release of hazardous wastes. Under a strict liability system, the facility would minimize its operating costs at level 3 and operate at an expected cost of 35 units. Under an unbiased negligence system, the facility would also minimize its costs at level 3 and would operate at an expected cost of 20 units. The difference between the cost of negligence and strict liability for the facility is the expected cost of an accidental release, which the facility would have to pay under a system of strict liability, but not under a negligence system. Both the negligence and the strict liability system gives potential defendants incentives to take the socially optimal level of precautions (Shavell 1980).

The hindsight bias alters the calculations, however. The bias raises the ex post perception of the ex ante probability of an accident at the level of precautions taken, although it does not affect the estimated probability of an accident for an untaken precaution (because such estimates are still made in foresight). As a consequence, the bias increases the perceived marginal value of the next untaken level of precautions. The size of this increase depends on the magnitude of the bias. For example, consider column 6, which describes the effects of a bias that increases the perceived probability of the accident by 20 percent (.20). Under these circumstances, if the facility takes level of precaution 3 and a release occurs, a judge or a jury would act as if the probability of a release was .35, even though it was actually .15. Consequently, the perceived advantage of moving to level 4, where the perceived probability of a release is only .10, would be 25 units. Because this perceived marginal benefit exceeds the marginal cost of increasing the level of precautions (which is only 10 units), the defendant will be found negligent. In fact, with a bias of this magnitude, the defendant is essentially strictly liable.

The situation changes, however, if the bias is somewhat smaller. As column 7 shows, the bias can encourage a potential defendant under a negligence regime to take an excess of precautions. If the bias increases the perceived probability of an accident by only 8 percent, then the defendant will not be liable at level 4. By moving to level 4, the facility will avoid incurring the expected costs of a release. The resulting savings will outweigh the cost of the precautions for the facility. At level 3, the facility has a 15 percent chance of being held liable for the 100-unit accident, and at level 4, the facility has no chance of being held liable. The expected 15-unit savings outweighs the 10-unit cost. As a result, negligence judged in hindsight encourages potential defendants to take an excess of precautions under these circumstances. Beyond this specific example, the hindsight bias generally creates the potential for this problem to occur under any application of a negligence rule (Rachlinski 1998).

In the late 1960s, as the number of environmental lawsuits brought under a negligence standard began to rise, industry faced either a regime of strict liability for environmental harm or incentives to exceed the socially optimal level of precautions against causing environmental harm. Both would have been much more costly to industry than common law liability under an unbiased negligence standard.

Regulatory Compliance and the Hindsight Bias

The law has developed methods for reducing the influence of the hindsight bias on trial outcomes (Rachlinski 1998). Such methods vary with specific circumstances in different areas of law, but there is a commonality: they all avoid requiring a court to assess what a defendant knew or should have known. Instead, courts try to evaluate whether the defendant complied with a specific standard of conduct that was established beforehand, if one is available.

In environmental litigation, the most likely means of avoiding the influence of the hindsight bias would be to compare the polluter's conduct to regulations. Instead of judging whether a defendant took reasonable precautions, if liability turned on whether a defendant complied with regulations, then the hindsight bias would largely be avoided because this assessment does not depend on a determination of the predictability of an accident. To be sure, it is possible that the hindsight bias also makes it difficult for a defendant to prove that he or she complied with the relevant standard or that the standard is even relevant. Nevertheless, the determination of whether a defendant complied with a health-and-safety regulation is probably influenced much less by the hindsight bias than is a determination of whether a defendant's conduct was reasonable.

No court has adopted a "strong" version of the regulatory compliance defense, in which liability depends completely on whether a defendant complied with regulations (Ausness 1996). Instead, the failure to comply with a health-and-safety regulation, absent an excuse, is legally conclusive evidence of negligence and compliance with regulations is evidence that the defendant was not negligent. This system has the potential to greatly reduce the influence of the hindsight bias.

A regulatory compliance defense, however, requires regulations. Before 1970, industry had only a sporadic array of state and local environmental regulations with which to comply and mount a defense. The regulations created by the new environmental statutes enable a widespread and predictable use of the regulatory compliance defense in pollution cases. Assuming (for the moment) that the pollution-control regulations mimic the requirements of due care in negligence, then industry benefited from the passage of the federal environmental statutes. Instead of facing the quasi-strict liability that a negligence standard influenced by the hindsight bias had created, industry faced something closer to a pure negligence regime. The new regulations therefore had the potential to reduce industry's liability for pollution.

Even if the regulatory standards do not precisely match the socially optimal level of pollution prevention, they probably still benefit industry. Low standards provide industry with the ability to take less than the socially optimal level of precautions and avoid liability for negligence. Although a defendant that pursues this strategy might still be found negligent, the regulations give the defendant a much better chance of winning the case. Consequently, low standards might allow polluters to take inadequate precautions and still avoid liability. Even a standard that is too high can benefit industry. The cost of complying with an excessive standard might be lower than the cost of negligence influenced by the hindsight bias. Because negligence judged in hindsight produces either strict liability or incentives to take an excess of precautions, either of these costs might exceed the cost of an excess of precautions required by regulations. So long as the regulatory standards are not too excessive, industry is still better off with a regulatory system superimposed on a liability system than with just a liability system.

Industry need not have understood the intricacies of the hindsight bias, or its influence on liability judgments, in order to recognize the benefits of developing a regulatory compliance defense. Polluters need only have understood that they were losing lawsuits brought under a negligence theory in cases in which they had taken reasonable pollution-control measures. Polluters who repeatedly took reasonable pollution-control measures only to be found liable at trial would realize that the negligence system was biased, in some way, against them. Industry could have viewed the development of a regulatory compliance defense as part of a strategy to start winning these cases, even if it did not fully understand why polluters were losing such cases.

Evidence against the Theory

The content of the environmental legislation of the early 1970s supports the theory that industry benefited from its passage because of the regulatory compliance defense. The principal environmental statutes mostly require the EPA to create some form of pollution standards that are based on health and safety. As such, the standards could serve as the basis for a regulatory compliance defense. Nevertheless, there is some evidence contradicting the theory, and there are other explanations for the existence of the environmental legislation of the 1970s.

Contradictory Evidence

The fact that the environmental legislation does not preempt the common law suggests that industry did not win the environmental battles of the 1970s. Industry would have benefited more from full preemption of the common law than from the mere superimposition of a regulatory regime onto the common law. Preemption would have provided a better defense against liability than regulatory compliance would because it would have eliminated the prospect of any liability under the common law.

Industry's failure to obtain full preemption, however, was not a total loss. The advantages of the regulatory compliance defense do much to counteract the failure to obtain full preemption. The availability of this defense makes it much more difficult for a plaintiff to establish negligence against a defendant that has complied with regulation. Indeed, in the late 1970s, as the EPA began to implement regulations required by these statutes, environmental lawsuits brought under common law theories of liability tailed off and ultimately declined (Green 1998).

Furthermore, although industry could have relied on state regulation to create a regulatory compliance defense, the uniform federal standards promised by the new statutes provided a more secure basis for such a defense. Although some states did have environmental statutes and regulations, many did not, leaving industries in such states vulnerable to liability. Although industries in such states could have lobbied for state or local regulation, it would have been cheaper for industry to consolidate its political resources to lobby for the passage of federal regulations.

Another piece of evidence suggesting that industry opposed environmental legislation is the tendency for industry to fight the establishment of regulations by the EPA. In the first twenty years of the Clean Air Act, for example, because of industry opposition, the EPA was able to establish emissions standards for only eight hazardous air pollutants (Dwyer 1990). If industry needs pollution-control standards to support a regulatory compliance defenses, why would they oppose the creation of such standards? The answer may be that even though industry not only needs these standards to defend against common law liability, it also surely wants to see the standards set as low as possible. The goal of low, inexpensive standards might be worth some delay in the creation of standards.

In the case of standards for hazardous air pollutants, the Clean Air Act initially required the EPA to disregard cost in the adoption of emissions standards. Hence, until Congress amended the Clean Air Act in 1990 to incorporate cost considerations, industry probably would not benefit from the adoption of regulations, because the regulations would have been much more expensive than common law liability, even as influenced by the hindsight bias.

Alternative Explanations

Other factors could also have accounted for Congress's ability to pass environmental legislation in the 1970s (Farber 1992). First, this legislation might be an instance in which the magnitude of the diffuse public interest sufficiently outweighed concentrated interests. Second, concentrated interests favoring environmental legislation might have outfought industry. Third, some other aspect of the new regulatory system might have benefited industry. Fourth, industry might have seen the environmental statutes as benign symbolism designed only to placate public demand for environmental regulation. Although these factors doubtless influenced the legislative outcome, they do not fully explain the pattern of legislation in the early 1970s.

EX ANTE REGULATION VERSUS EX POST LITIGATION AS A SOCIAL MATTER

Even if the availability of the regulatory compliance defense in environmental law benefits industry, it might not be good for society in general. The influence of the hindsight bias on judgments of liability for negligence, however, supports the use of the regulatory compliance defense as a socially beneficial component of environmental law. Environmental liability judgments made under a negligence standard, as influenced by the hindsight bias, have costs that the establishment and enforcement of ex ante norms of reasonable conduct avoid. Although environmental regulations and their use in litigation have potential costs, recognition of the hindsight bias supports the regulatory compliance defense overall and also suggests a beneficial reform to the combined system that is in place today.

Social Benefits of the Regulatory Compliance Defense

At a superficial level, it is hard to see how the regulatory compliance defense has any social advantages or disadvantages. If the relevant health-and-safety regulations are a product of regulatory efforts to require industry to take reasonable precautions, then the conduct required by the regulation is precisely the conduct that constitutes due care in a tort suit. Both the regulation and the prospect of tort liability create incentives to take reasonable care and create no incentives to exceed reasonable care.

The influence of the hindsight bias on the liability system, however, alters the incentive structure. As noted in the example described by table 10.1, negligence judged in hindsight can create incentives for defendants to take an excess of precautions. Depending on the relationship between the size of the bias, the cost of precautions, and the likelihood of an accident, the hindsight bias will either induce defendants to act as if they are strictly liable (and take only reasonable precautions) or induce them to take an excess of precautions to avoid liability. Although strict liability would give industry incentives to be efficient, inducing polluters to take an excess of pollution-prevention measures would be socially undesirable.

A regulatory compliance defense avoids much of this problem. Assuming (for the moment) that regulations track the socially optimal levels of pollution prevention, then if liability turned on compliance with regulations, the incentive to take an excess of precautions would be eliminated. Polluters could comply with the regulations and be reasonably assured that they would not incur liability. This would avoid any possibility that the liability system would create unwanted incentives.

As an alternative to this regulatory cure for the hindsight bias, switching completely to a system of strict liability would also avoid creating unwanted incentives. This solution, however, could have other, undesirable consequences. Changing from a negligence system to a system of strict liability has the potential to alter the level of the underlying activities and the care that plaintiffs take. To paraphrase one of Professor Polinsky's examples, if drivers were strictly liable for all injuries that they cause to pedestrians, negligently or otherwise, there would likely be fewer drivers and more pedestrians than if drivers were responsible only for injuries caused by their negligence (Polinsky 1989). Furthermore, under the strict liability standard, pedestrians would have no incentive to take any precautions of their own, even if such precautions would be a socially cost-effective way to avoid accidents (Polinsky 1989). Negligence rules always entail some version of comparative fault that avoids these problems. The hindsight bias also likely interacts with any system of comparative fault. If there is any evidence that a defendant was also negligent, then both litigants might be affected by the hindsight bias, possibly canceling out the influence of the bias (Rachlinski 1998).

In cases of liability for pollution, the clear trend has been to adopt some form of negligence as some element of liability, rather than to hold polluters strictly liable. The history of common law liability for air pollution illustrates both this trend and the reasons behind it. Historically, air pollution was not considered a trespass, because it was not a visible physical encroachment. The legal fiction that invisible particles were not physically invading property could not survive indefinitely. As the courts began to acknowledge that odors and poisonous gases were physical invasions, they also had to abandon the concept of strict liability for trespass (at least as to airborne pollutants). To do otherwise would make every air polluter liable for any incident of harm of any magnitude done to anyone, anywhere, anytime. Strict liability might even have allowed courts to issue injunctions to arrest all airborne pollutants. In short, strict liability is a disfavored doctrine in the common law of pollution control, and therefore changing to a strict liability system is probably not the best means of addressing the problem of the hindsight bias in the negligence system.

All in all, negligence judged in hindsight with regulatory compliance as a defense gets things about right. It creates incentives to take reasonable care, and no more. It also avoids the problems that strict liability can create in pollution cases.

Downside of Agency Regulation

The creation of a regulatory system also has its costs. There are administrative costs to creating and enforcing regulations that get added to the administrative costs of the common law liability system. The added costs of promulgating regulations, however, might lead to savings in the administrative costs of lawsuits. Litigating whether a polluter complied with an EPA regulation is probably cheaper than a more open-ended inquiry into whether a polluter took reasonable pollution-control precautions. The real costs of regulation are not administrative ones; they lie with the fact that regulations might not correspond to the reasonable level of pollution prevention.

Regulations can fail to map onto the socially optimal level of pollution for several reasons. Sometimes, the underlying statutes might not require that the regulations actually track the socially optimal level of pollution control. Also, even when the EPA is supposed to promulgate regulations mandating socially optimal levels of pollution prevention, the EPA might fail to do so. This chapter describes a bias that afflicts the system of assigning liability, but other biases (and incentives) surely affect regulators (Noll and Krier 1990). As just one example, many scholars have commented that regulators seem to have a myopic tendency to promulgate regulations that eliminate all risk (Breyer 1983). Furthermore, the EPA is a political entity, subject to the influence of interest-group politics, just as surely as Congress is. Depending on whether environmental interests or industrial interests hold more sway over the EPA, it could promulgate regulations that are either too strict or too weak. Although judicial review provides some check on the EPA, the forces identified in this paragraph suggest that regulations will often fail to hit the socially optimal mark.

Finally, like most regulatory systems, environmental regulations are primarily administered by a central bureaucracy that adopts rules of general applicability that are not tailored to individual circumstances (Shavell 1984). Command-and-control regulations that require the installation of particular pollution-control technologies are especially likely to fail to accommodate individual variation in a facility's needs or problems. Even performance-based standards that set a cap on the pollution a facility may emit without mandating any specific control technology fail to take into account local conditions. A small amount of pollution could be more damaging in a pristine area than in an urban center; the opposite could also be true if the area is sufficiently free of pollution that the local ecosystem could easily absorb it. This problem is especially exacerbated in the environmental legislation of the 1970s by the fact that this legislation essentially federalized a uniform system of pollution control (Macey and Butler 2000).

Comparison of the Costs and the Benefits of Regulation

As compared to a pure system of liability, the pure system of regulation might be inferior. The costs of one-size-fits-all regulation implemented by an agency influenced by political motives and other biases might well exceed the costs of a decentralized liability system. The regulatory system did not supplant the liability system, however; it was superimposed onto a liability system that contains a regulatory compliance defense. This fact reduces some of the costs of regulation.

Consider the consequences of regulations that require less pollution control than is socially efficient. In such a case, the regulatory component of the system allow for too much pollution. The liability system ameliorates this problem somewhat because it allows plaintiffs who suffer from the inefficient excess of pollution to recover damages from those polluters who merely complied with the regulation and failed to undertake socially optimal precautions. The polluter, however, can use the regulatory compliance defense as a shield in such cases, even though the regulations are inadequate. The regulatory compliance defense still allows for the possibility that plaintiffs can recover damages; but recovering damages is more difficult for them than it would be without such regulations. Thus, regulations that are too low make it difficult for a plaintiff to recover, undermining the incentive structure of the liability system somewhat.

Regulations that require an excess of precautions are also socially costly. Because pollution regulations are enforceable with extremely large fines and criminal penalties, polluters must comply with the regulations, even if they are excessive. The social costs of complying with excessive regulations are offset somewhat by the beneficial effect that the regulatory compliance defense has on the liability system. Without regulations, assignment of liability is heavily influenced by the hindsight bias. Polluters either are strictly liable or take an excess of precautions. Excessively high regulations cost, but it is not clear that they cost more than negligence assigned under the influence of the hindsight bias.

Standards versus Regulations: A Modest Reform

Some of the unwanted adverse consequences of the regulatory system arise because industry must comply with regulations that exceed the socially efficient level of pollution-prevention measures. These consequences could be avoided by using regulations as standards that guide the liability system, rather than as mandates to industry. For example, instead of mandating that particular polluters adopt specific control technologies, regulations could be used only as a guide to liability determinations under the current common law rules.

This reform would not entirely eliminate the costs of regulations that are too strict, but it would mitigate them. An industry faced with an excessive standard would have to choose between complying with it and refusing to comply and being strictly liable for any harm pollution might cause. This choice closely resembles the choice described in table 10.1, faced by any potential defendant that is judged under a negligence standard influenced by the hindsight bias. There is some chance that a potential defendant would be better off taking the excess of precautions because this saves the cost of being held liable for the harm caused by pollution. But if the cost of compliance with the regulation is high enough, then potential defendants would minimize their costs by acting as if they were strictly liable. Just as the effect of the hindsight bias on negligence has unwanted consequences, so too does this combination of regulation and liability. However, because this combination has the potential to create incentives to take the socially optimal level of precautions, it is superior to the existing system in which regulations are strictly enforced, even if they require industry to take an excess of precautions.

To be sure, there are other reasons to enforce regulations through an administrative regime. As Shavell observed, the liability system does not function properly if defendants lack the resources to compensate victims fully or if injured parties are unlikely to sue. Also, the harm that pollution causes is often so diffuse or so delayed that plaintiffs cannot effectively organize a lawsuit (Shavell 1984). When these two considerations are not a factor, however, then the proposed reform would be an improvement over the current system.

CONCLUSIONS

Certainly the case can be made that an unbiased liability system would be the optimal way to regulate pollution. That system, however, is unavailable. Liability must be assigned by human beings, who make judgments that are clouded by heuristics and biases. Given this problem, it is not clear what constitutes the best second-best system, but negligence liability judged in hindsight with a superimposed regulatory system is a strong candidate. It is, at the very least, the system that environmentalists favor and that industry seems willing to tolerate. Whatever other effects regulation has, regulating in foresight improves judgment in hindsight and, therefore, has the potential to improve the liability system.

NOTES

1. Note that I exclude from consideration here remedial statutes that create liability, such as the Comprehensive Environmental Response, Compensation, and Liability Act, or statutes that regulate some aspect of the environment that had not been regulated by the common law, such as the Endangered Species Act.

2. Keeton et al. (1984, § 13: 71–72). See, for example, *Martin v. Reynolds Aluminum* (1959), cert. denied 362 U.S. 918 (1960).

3. Posner (1972) and Shavell (1980); but see Calfee and Craswell (1984).

4. Clean Air Act, 42 U.S.C. § 7411(a)(1).

5. 33 U.S.C. § 1314(b).

6. Resource Conservation and Recovery Act, 42 U.S.C. § 6924.

7. The Clean Air Act, 42 U.S.C. § 7604(e); the Clean Water Act, 33 U.S.C. §§ 1365(e); and RCRA, 1370; 42 U.S.C. § 6972 (f).

REFERENCES

Ackerman, Bruce A., and Richard B. Stewart. 1985. Reforming Environmental Law. *Stanford Law Review* 37: 1333–65.

American Law Institute. 1965. *Restatement (Second) of Torts.* St. Paul: West.

Ausness, Richard C. 1996. The Case for a "Strong" Regulatory Compliance Defense. *Maryland Law Review* 55: 1210–67.

Breyer, Stephen. 1983. *Breaking the Vicious Circle: Toward Effective Risk Regulation.* Cambridge, MA: Harvard University Press.

Calfee, John E., and Richard Craswell. 1984. Some Effect of Uncertainty on Compliance with Legal Standards. *Virginia Law Review* 70: 965–1003.

Christensen-Szalanski, J. J., and Cynthia Fobian Willham. 1991. The Hindsight Bias: A Meta-Analysis. *Organizational Behavior & Human Decision Processes* 48: 147–68.

Dwyer, John. 1990. The Pathology of Symbolic Legislation. *Ecology Law Quarterly* 17: 233–316.

Farber, Daniel A. 1992. Politics and Procedure in Environmental Law. *Journal of Law, Economics, and Organizations* 8(1): 59–81.

Farber, Daniel A., and Philip P. Frickey. 1991. *Law and Public Choice: A Critical Introduction.* Chicago: University of Chicago Press.

Fischhoff, Baruch. 1975. Hindsight ≠ Foresight: The Effect of Outcome Knowledge on Judgment under Uncertainty. *Journal of Experimental Psychology* 1: 288–99.

————. 1982. For Those Condemned to Study the Past: Heuristics and Biases in Hindsight. In *Judgment under Uncertainty: Heuristics and Biases*, ed. Daniel Kahneman, Paul Slovic, and Amos Tversky. Cambridge, UK: Cambridge University Press, 335–51.

Gilbertson, Lee J. 1994. A Study of Hindsight Bias: The Rodney King Case in Retrospect. *Psychological Reports* 74: 383–86.

Goklany, Indur M. 2000. Empirical Evidence Regarding the Role of Nationalization in Improving U.S. Air Quality, this volume.

Green, H. Marlow. 1998. Can the Common Law Survive in a Statutory World? *Cornell Journal of Law & Public Policy* 8(1): 89–109.

Hastie, Reid. 1998. Juror Judgment in Civil Cases: Hindsight Effects on Liability Judgments. Department of Psychology, University of Colorado, Boulder.

Hawkins, Scott A., and Reid Hastie. 1990. Hindsight: Biased Judgments of Past Events after the Outcomes Are Known. *Psychological Bulletin* 107: 311–27.

Kamin, Kim A., and Jeffrey J. Rachlinski. 1995. Ex Post ≠ Ex Ante: Determining Liability in Hindsight. *Law and Human Behavior* 19: 89–103.

Keeton, W. Page, Dan B. Dobbs, Robert E. Keeton, and David G. Owens, eds. 1984. *Prosser & Keeton on the Law of Torts.* 5th ed. St. Paul: West Publishing Co.

LaBine, Susan J., and Gary LaBine. 1996. Determinations of Negligence and the Hindsight Bias. *Law and Human Behavior* 20: 501–16.

Landes, William A., and Richard A. Posner. 1987. *The Economic Structure of Tort Law.* Cambridge, MA: Harvard University Press.

Macey, Jonathan R., and Henry N. Butler. 2000. Federalism and the Environment, this volume.

Noll, Roger C., and James E. Krier. 1990. Some Implications of Cognitive Psychology for Risk Regulation. *Journal of Legal Studies* 19: 747–79.

Percival, Robert V., Alan S. Miller, Christopher H. Schroeder, and James P. Leape. 1996. *Environmental Regulation: Law, Science, and Policy.* 2d ed. Boston: Little, Brown.

Polinsky, A. Mitchell. 1989. *An Introduction to Law and Economics.* 2d ed. Boston: Little, Brown.

Posner, Richard A. 1972. A Theory of Negligence. *Journal of Legal Studies* 1: 29–96.

Rachlinski, Jeffrey J. 1998. A Positive Psychological Theory of Judging in Hindsight. *University of Chicago Law Review* 65: 571–625.

Rodgers, William H., Jr. 1994. *Environmental Law.* 2d ed. St. Paul: West.

Shavell, Steven. 1980. Strict Liability versus Negligence. *Journal of Legal Studies* 9: 1–25.

————. 1984. Liability for Harm versus Regulation of Safety. *Journal of Legal Studies* 13: 357–74.

Stewart, Richard B. 1993. Environmental Regulation and International Competitiveness. *Yale Law Journal* 102: 2039–106.

Turner, Tom. 1998. The Legal Eagles. *Amicus Journal* (Winter): 25–27.

Wasserman, David, Richard O. Lempert, and Reid Hastie. 1991. Hindsight and Causality. *Personality and Social Psychology Bulletin* 17: 30–35.

CASES CITED

City of Milwaukee v. Illinois, 451 U.S. 304 (1981)

International Paper Co. v. Ouellette, 479 U.S. 481 (1987)

Martin v. Reynolds Aluminum Co., 221 Or. 86, 342 P.2d 790 (1959), cert. denied, 362 U.S. 918 (1960)

United States v. Carroll Towing Co., 159 F.2d 169 (2d Cir. 1947)

Index

About the Political Economy Forum
and the Authors

The Political Economy Research Center (PERC) is a nonprofit research center located in Bozeman, Montana, that focuses on market solutions to environmental problems. For almost two decades, PERC has been a pioneer in recognizing the value of the market, personal initiatives, and the importance of property rights and voluntary activity. This approach is known as the new resource economics or free market environmentalism. PERC associates have applied this approach to a variety of issues, including resource development, water marketing, chemical risk, private provision of environmental amenities, public land management, and endangered species protection.

In 1989, PERC organized the first of an ongoing series called the Political Economy Forum aimed at applying the principles of political economy to important policy issues. The forum brings together scholars in economics, political science, law, history, and other disciplines to discuss and refine academic papers that explore new applications of political economy to policy analysis.

The chapters in this volume emanate from the Political Economy Forum held in October 1998, where nine papers were presented and discussed. The forum was organized and directed by Roger E. Meiners (a PERC senior associate and professor of law and economics at the University of Texas at Arlington) and Andrew P. Morriss (a professor of law and associate professor of economics at Case Western Reserve University and a visiting scholar at PERC in 1999). Biographical information on the paper authors follows. The authors were joined by participants who commented on the papers and discussed numerous issues concerning the effectiveness of alternative legal regimes for environmental protection. These participants were: Terry Anderson (PERC and Hoover Institution); Andy Barnett (Auburn University); David Bernstein (George Mason University); Karol Boudreaux (Foundation for Economic Education); Christine Corcos (Louisiana State University); Michael Greve (Center for Individual Rights); Dean Lueck (Montana State University); Robert Natelson (University of Montana); Paul Rubin (Emory University); Richard Stroup (PERC and Montana State University); Barton Thompson (Stanford University); and Wendy Wagner (Case Western Reserve University). Observers to the proceedings included Candace Allen (University of Southern Colorado), Daniel Benjamin (Clemson University and PERC), and Vernon Smith (University of Arizona and a PERC board member). The chapter by Roger Bate, who was a 1998 PERC Fellow, was added to the volume after the forum.

Roger Bate is an economics graduate from Thames Valley University and holds an M.Sc. in environment and resource economics from University College, London. He is currently completing his Ph.D. at Cambridge University. Bate is the editor of *What Risk?*, a book that critically assesses the way risk is regulated in society. He has also written numerous scholarly papers, and his shorter articles have appeared in many newspapers and magazines, including the *Wall Street Journal Europe* and the *Financial Times*. Bate is a fellow of the Royal Society of Arts. He was founding director of the Environment Unit at the Institute of Economic Affairs in London and remains codirector.

Henry N. Butler is founder and director of the Law and Organizational Economics Center and is the Fred and Mary Koch Distinguished Professor of Law and Economics at the University of Kansas. Butler has been active in the development of law and economics as a field throughout his professional career. He has an M.A. and a Ph.D. in economics from Virginia Tech, where he was a student of Nobel Laureate James Buchanan, and a J.D. from the University of Miami, where he was a John M. Olin Fellow in Law and Economics. After serving on the faculty at Texas A&M University, Butler spent the 1985–86 academic year as a John M. Olin Fellow in Law and Economics at the University of Chicago Law School. Prior to coming to the University of Kansas in 1993, Butler was a professor of law at George Mason University where he served as director of the George Mason Law and Economics Center. Butler is an expert in public policy analysis and has published numerous articles and several books on government regulation.

Indur M. Goklany obtained his Ph.D. in Electrical Engineering from Michigan State University and has more than twenty-five years experience addressing science and policy aspects of environmental and natural resource issues in state and federal government and in the private sector. At the EPA's Chicago regional office, he helped develop particulate matter and sulphur-dioxide control strategies and regulations for the U.S. industrial heartland. He also established the region's first air permitting group. Subsequently, as chief, Technical Assessment Division, National Commission on Air Quality, he investigated national impacts of pollution and its control. After a period as a Washington-based consultant on energy and environmental issues, he helped develop the EPA's first ever new source emission trade (bubble), for which he received an EPA bronze medal. Working with the EPA's Regulatory Reform Staff, he was also responsible for helping the EPA adopt the emissions trading policy statement in the mid-1980s. At the Department of the Interior, Office of Policy Analysis, he served on various national and international panels and groups dealing with global climate change and acid rain before focusing on issues related to population, biodiversity, and natural resources. He has published extensively in various scholarly journals on air pollution, climate change, biodiversity, and the role of technology, economic growth, and trade in creating as well as solving environmental problems.

Jason Scott Johnston is professor of law and coordinator of the Program on Law and the Environment at the University of Pennsylvania. He received his A.B. from Dartmouth College and his J.D. and Ph.D. in economics from the University of Michigan. Johnston's articles have appeared in a number of leading law reviews and economics journals. His research focuses on the economic analysis of environmental and natural resource law and policy. Current research interests include the positive economic theory of the centralization of environmental regulation, the design of efficient property rights regimes, the political economy of the takings doctrine, and environmental contracting.

Jonathan R. Macey is the J. DuPratt White Professor of Law and director of the John M. Olin Program in Law and Economics at Cornell Law School. He earned his B.A. from Harvard and his J.D. from Yale Law School, where he was article and book review editor of the *Yale Law Journal*. Following law school, Macey was law clerk to Judge Henry J. Friendly, U.S. Court of Appeals, Second Circuit. Professor Macey specializes in law and economics (including public choice), corporate finance, market microstructure, corporate and securities law, and banking regulation. He is the author of several books, including the two-volume treatise *Macey on Corporation Laws*, more than one hundred scholarly articles, and numerous editorials in such publications as the *Wall Street Journal*, the *Los Angeles Times*, and the *National Law Journal*. He has taught at major universities around the world and, in 1995, was awarded the Paul M. Bator Prize for Excellence in Teaching, Scholarship, and Public Service.

Roger E. Meiners is professor of law and economics at the University of Texas at Arlington and senior associate of PERC. His economics degrees are from Washington State University, the University of Arizona, and Virginia Tech; his law degree is from the University of Miami, where he was a John M. Olin Fellow. Meiners has also been a faculty member of Texas A&M University, Emory University, and Clemson University and was a regional director for the Federal Trade Commission. His research focuses on common law and market solutions to environmental issues and on the economics of higher education. Meiners serves on the board of the Roe Foundation and Consumer Alert and has published several books, including *Taking the Environment Seriously* (with Bruce Yandle).

Andrew P. Morriss is professor of law and associate professor of economics at Case Western Reserve University in Cleveland, Ohio. He received his law and master's of public affairs degrees from the University of Texas at Austin and his Ph.D. in economics from Massachusetts Institute of Technology. Between law school and graduate school, he clerked for U.S. District Judge Barefoot Sanders in Dallas, Texas, and then practiced with the Texas Rural Legal Aid in Hereford and Plainview. In addition to writing on the history of the U.S. codification movement, Morriss has written articles using empirical methods to analyze the law.

Jeffrey J. Rachlinski earned his bachelor's and master's degrees in psychology from Johns Hopkins University. He also holds a J.D. from Stanford Law School and a Ph.D. in psychology from Stanford University, where he was a National Science Foundation Graduate Fellow. He practiced law briefly at Wilson, Sonsini, Goodrich, and Rosati in Palo Alto before joining the faculty at the Cornell Law School in 1994. He is currently an associate professor of law at Cornell Law School. Professor Rachlinski teaches and writes about the application of cognitive psychology to legal decision making, especially as it applies to environmental law and policy.

David Schmidtz is professor of philosophy and joint professor of economics at the University of Arizona. Schmidtz is the author of *Limits of Government, Rational Choice and Moral Agency*, and, most recently, *Social Welfare and Individual Responsibility*, coauthored with Robert E. Goodin. He is currently editing a text for courses in environmental ethics, stressing perspectives of the social and the natural sciences as well as philosophy.

David Schoenbrod is professor at New York Law School and an adjunct scholar of the Cato Institute. He is author of *Power without Responsibility: How Congress Abuses the People through Delegation* and coauthor of *Remedies: Public and Private*. He also has published articles on remedies, environmental law, and the law and politics of regulation in scholarly journals as well as on the editorial pages of the *Wall Street Journal, Legal Times*, and the *New York Times*. After graduating from Yale College, he attended Oxford University as a Marshall Scholar gaining a graduate degree in economics, and then completed Yale Law School, where he was an editor of the law journal. As an attorney at the Natural Resources Defense Council from 1972 to 1979, Schoenbrod was in charge of the litigation to get the lead out of gasoline.

Stacie Thomas is currently a majority staff economist for the Senate Banking Committee. She holds a master's degree in economics and a bachelor's in Spanish and international trade, both from Clemson University. As a PERC fellow in 1998, Thomas explored institutional arrangements for delivering water quality on U.S. rivers with a focus on the Cuyahoga River.

Bruce Yandle, a PERC senior associate, is Alumni Distinguished Professor of Economics and BB&T Scholar at Clemson University. Yandle received an A.B. from Mercer University and a Ph.D. from Georgia State University. He served as senior economist on the President's Council on Wage and Price Stability and as executive director of the Federal Trade Commission. Yandle is author or editor of many books, including *The Political Limits of Environmental Regulation*; *Common Sense and Common Law for the Environment*; and *Land Rights: The 1990s Property Rights Rebellion*.

Todd J. Zywicki is assistant professor of law at George Mason University School of Law in Arlington, Virginia. Prior to joining the faculty at George Mason, he taught at Mississippi College School of Law from 1996 to 1998. Prior to that, Zywicki clerked for Judge Jerry E. Smith, U.S. Court of Appeals for the Fifth Circuit and practiced law with Alston & Bird in Atlanta, Georgia. He received his J.D. from the University of Virginia, a master's degree in economics from Clemson University, and his undergraduate degree cum laude with distinction in his major from Dartmouth College in 1988. Professor Zywicki has published numerous articles, essays, and book reviews in law reviews and economics journals. He has written widely in the areas of bankruptcy, environmental law, constitutional law, constitutional history, and economic analysis of law.